PHILOSOPHY OF L

"This exceptional text fulfills two essential criteria of a good introductory textbook in the philosophy of language: it covers a broad range of topics well, all of which are the basis of current active research, and does so in an accurate manner accessible to undergraduate students."

Mike Harnish, *University of Arizona*

"I liked the book very much and think it will make an excellent textbook for teaching. The examples throughout are delightful and students will love them."

Edwin Mares, *Victoria University of Wellington*

The philosophy of language has been much in vogue throughout the twentieth century, but only since the 1960s have the issues begun to appear in high resolution. This book is an introduction to those issues and to a variety of linguistic mechanisms. Part I explores several theories of how proper names, descriptions, and other terms bear a referential relation to nonlinguistic things. It is argued that there is a puzzle, nearly a paradox, regarding the reference of proper names. Part II surveys seven theories of meaning more generally: the Ideational Theory, the Proposition Theory, a Wittgensteinian "Use" Theory, the Verification Theory, and two versions of the Truth-Condition Theory and shows their advantages and disadvantages. Part III concerns linguistic pragmatics and Part IV examines four linguistic theories of metaphor.

William G. Lycan is a leading philosopher of language and mind. He is William Rand Kenan, Jr. Professor at the University of North Carolina. His published works include over 100 articles as well as six books, among them *Logical Form in Natural Language* (1984), *Consciousness* (1987), *Judgement and Justification* (1988), *Modality and Meaning* (1994), and *Consciousness and Experience* (1998).

Routledge Contemporary Introductions to Philosophy

Series Editor:
Paul K. Moser,
Loyola University of Chicago

This innovative, well-structured series is for students who have already done an introductory course in philosophy. Each book introduces a core general subject in contemporary philosophy and offers students an accessible but substantial transition from introductory to higher-level college work in that subject. The series is accessible to nonspecialists and each book clearly motivates and expounds the problems and positions introduced. An orientating chapter briefly introduces its topic and reminds readers of any crucial material they need to have retained from a typical introductory course. Considerable attention is given to explaining the central philosophical problems of a subject and the main competing solutions and arguments for those solutions. The primary aim is to educate students in the main problems, positions and arguments of contemporary philosophy rather than to convince students of a single position. The initial eight central books in the series are written by experienced authors and teachers, and treat topics essential to a well-rounded philosophy curriculum.

Epistemology
Robert Audi

Ethics
Harry Gensler

Metaphysics
Michael J. Loux

Philosophy of Art
Noel Carroll

Philosophy of Language
William G. Lycan

Philosophy of Mind
John Heil

Philosophy of Religion
Keith E. Yandell

Philosophy of Science
Alexander Rosenberg

PHILOSOPHY OF LANGUAGE
A contemporary introduction

William G. Lycan

Routledge
Taylor & Francis Group

LONDON AND NEW YORK

First published 2000
by Routledge
11 New Fetter Lane, London EC4P 4EE

Simultaneously published in the USA and Canada
by Routledge
29 West 35th Street, New York, NY 10001

Reprinted 2001, 2002, 2003

Routledge is an imprint of the Taylor & Francis Group

Typeset in Aldus Roman by RefineCatch Limited, Bungay, Suffolk
Printed and bound in Great Britain by
Biddles Ltd, Guildford and King's Lynn

British Library Cataloguing in Publication Data
A catalogue record for this book is available from the British Library

Library of Congress Cataloging in Publication Data
Lycan, William G.
Philosophy of language : a contemporary introduction / William G. Lycan.
p.   cm.—(Routledge contemporary introductions to philosophy)
Includes bibliographical references and index.
1. Language and languages—Philosophy.   I. Title.   II. Series.
P106.L886   2000
401—dc21   99–29547
CIP

ISBN 0–415–17115–6 (hb)
ISBN 0–415–17116–4 (pb)

To Bob and Marge Turnbull,
with gratitude

Contents

Preface

As its title slyly suggests, this book is an introduction to the main issues in contemporary philosophy of language. Philosophy of language has been much in vogue throughout the twentieth century, but only since the 1960s have the issues begun to appear in high resolution.

One crucial development in the past thirty years is the attention of philosophers of language to formal grammar or syntax as articulated by theoretical linguists. I personally believe that such attention is vital to success in philosophizing about language, and in my own work I pay as much of it as I am able. With regret, however, I have not made that a theme of this book. Under severe space limitations, I could not expend as many pages as would be needed to explain the basics of formal syntax, without having to omit presentation of some philosophical issues I consider essential to competence in the field.

Since around 1980, some philosophers of language have taken a turn toward the philosophy of mind, and some have engaged in metaphysical exploration of the relation or lack thereof between language and reality. These adversions have captured many philosophers' interest, and some fine textbooks have focused on one or both (for example, Blackburn (1984) and Devitt and Sterelny (1987)). But I have chosen otherwise. Whatever the merits of those sorts of work, I have not found that either helps us sufficiently to understand specifically linguistic mechanisms or the core issues of philosophy of language itself. This book will concentrate on those mechanisms and issues. (Readers who wish to press on into metaphysics or philosophy of mind should consult, respectively, Michael J. Loux's *Metaphysics* and John Heil's *Philosophy of Mind*, both of the Routledge Contemporary Introductions series.)

Many of my chapters and sections will take the form of presenting data pertinent to a linguistic phenomenon, expounding someone's theory of that phenomenon, and then listing and assessing objections to that theory. I emphasize here, because I will not always have the space to do so in the text, that in each case what I will summarize for the reader will be only the *opening moves* made by the various theorists and their opponents and objectors. In particular, I doubt that any of the objections to any of the theories is fatal; champions of theories are remarkably good at avoiding or refuting objections. The real theorizing begins where this book leaves off.

I have used some notation of formal logic, specifically the predicate calculus, for those who are familiar with it and will find points made clearer by it. But in each case I have also explained the meaning in English.

Many of the writings to be discussed in this book can be found in the following anthologies: T. Olshewsky (ed.) *Problems in the Philosophy of Language* (New York: Holt, Rinehart and Winston, 1969); J. F. Rosenberg and C. Travis (eds) *Readings in the Philosophy of Language* (Englewood Cliffs, NJ: Prentice-Hall, 1971); R. M. Harnish (ed.) *Basic Topics in the Philosophy of Language* (Englewood Cliffs, NJ: Prentice-Hall, 1994); A. Martinich (ed.) *The Philosophy of Language*, 3rd edn (Oxford: Oxford University Press, 1996); P. Ludlow (ed.) *Readings in the Philosophy of Language* (Cambridge, MA: Bradford Books/MIT Press, 1997); A. Nye (ed.) *Philosophy of Language: The Big Questions* (Oxford: Basil Blackwell, 1998); M. Baghramian (ed.) *Modern Philosophy of Language* (Counterpoint, 1999).

Acknowledgements

I thank my editor, Moira Taylor, for her bracing encouragement and (especially) for her patience. The latter was severely tried.

Mike Harnish, Greg McCulloch, and Ed Mares each very kindly read an early draft and supplied me with many thoughtful comments and suggestions. I believe the book is much improved as a result, and I am most grateful.

Peter Alward and Laura Morgan produced much of the early draft by transcribing many hours of lectures from very bad audio recordings. I thank them warmly and I hope that each of them will soon make a full recovery.

Sean McKeever's months of editorial help and advice have been invaluable. (He suffered through some transcribing as well.) Thanks especially to Sean for suggesting some needed cuts, and for organizing the bibliography.

The last few chapters of this book were completed during my tenure as a Fellow of the National Humanities Center, in 1998–99. I thank the Center and its wonderful staff for their generous support. For additional funding I am indebted to the National Endowment for the Humanities (#RA–20169–95).

1
Introduction: meaning and reference

Overview

Meaning and understanding

The Referential Theory

Summary

Questions

Notes

Further reading

Overview

That certain kinds of marks and noises have *meanings*, and that we human beings grasp those meanings without even thinking about it, are very striking facts. A philosophical theory of meaning should explain what it is for a string of marks or noises to be meaningful and, more particularly, what it is in virtue of which the string has the distinctive meaning it does. The theory should also explain how it is possible for human beings to produce and to understand meaningful utterances and to do that so effortlessly.

A widespread idea about meaning is that words and more complex linguistic expressions have their meanings by standing for things in the world. Though commonsensical and at first attractive, this Referential Theory of meaning is fairly easily shown to be inadequate. For one thing, comparatively few words do actually stand for things in the world. For another, if all words were like proper names, serving just to pick out individual things, we would not be able to form grammatical sentences in the first place.

Meaning and understanding

Not many people know that in 1931, Adolf Hitler made a visit to the United States, in the course of which he did some sightseeing, had a brief affair with a lady named Maxine in Keokuk, Iowa, tried peyote (which caused him to hallucinate hordes of frogs and toads wearing little boots and singing the *Horst Wessel Lied*), infiltrated a munitions plant near Detroit, met secretly with Vice-President Curtis regarding sealskin futures, and invented the electric can opener.

There is a good reason why not many people know all that: none of it is true. But the remarkable thing is that just now, as you read through my opening sentence – let us call it sentence (1) – you *understood* it perfectly, whether or not you were ready to accept it, and you did so without the slightest conscious effort.

Remarkable, I said. It probably does not strike you as remarkable or surprising, even now that you have noticed it. You are entirely used to reading words and sentences and understanding them at sight, and you find it nearly as natural as breathing or eating or walking. But, how did you understand sentence (1)? Not by having seen it before; I am certain that never in the history of the universe has anyone ever written or uttered that particular sentence, until I did. Nor did you understand (1) by having seen a very similar sentence, since I doubt that anyone has ever produced a sentence even remotely similar to (1).

You may say that you understood (1) because you speak English and (1) is an English sentence. That is true so far as it goes, but it only pushes the mystery to arm's length. How is it that you are able to "speak English," given that speaking English involves being able to produce and understand, not only elementary expressions like "I'm thirsty," "Shut up," and "More gravy," but novel sentences as complex as (1)? That ability is *truly amazing*, and much harder to explain than how you breathe or how you eat or how you walk, each of which abilities is already well understood by physiologists.

One clue is fairly obvious upon reflection: (1) is a string of words, English words, that you understand individually. So it seems that you understand (1) because you understand the words that occur in (1) and you understand something about how they are strung together. As we shall see, that is an important fact, but for now it is only suggestive.

So far we have been talking about a human ability, to produce and understand speech. But consider linguistic expressions themselves, as objects of study in their own right.

(2) w gfjsdkhj jiobfglglf ud
(3) It's dangerous to splash gasoline around your living room.
(4) Good of off primly the a the the why.

(1)–(4) are all strings of marks (or of noises, if uttered aloud). But they differ dramatically from each other. (1) and (3) are meaningful sentences, while (2) and (4) are gibberish. (4) differs from (2) in containing individually meaningful English words, but the words are not linked together in such a way as to make a sentence, and collectively they do not mean anything at all.

Certain sequences of noises or marks, then, have a feature that is both scarce in nature and urgently in need of explanation: that of *meaning something*. And each of those strings has the more specific property of meaning something in particular. For example, (3) means that it is dangerous to splash gasoline around your living room.

So our philosophical study of language begins with the following data.

- Some strings of marks or noises are *meaningful sentences*.
- Each meaningful sentence has parts that are themselves meaningful.
- Each meaningful sentence means something in particular.
- Competent speakers of a language are able to understand many of that language's sentences, without effort and almost instantaneously; they also produce sentences, in the same way.

And these data all need explaining. In virtue of what is any sequence of marks or noises meaningful? In virtue of what does such a string mean what it distinctively does? And how, again, are human beings able to understand and produce appropriate meaningful speech?

The Referential Theory

There is an attractive and commonsensical explanation of all the foregoing facts – so attractive that most of us think of it by the time we are ten or eleven years old. The idea is that linguistic expressions have the meanings they do because they *stand for things*; what they mean is what they stand for. On this view, words are like labels; they are symbols that represent, designate, name, denote or refer to items in the world: the name "Adolf Hitler" denotes (the person) Hitler; the noun "dog" refers to dogs, as do the French "chien" and the German "Hund." The sentence "The cat sat on the mat" represents some cat's sitting on some mat, presumably in virtue of "The cat" designating that cat, "the mat" designating the mat in question, and "sat on" denoting (if you like) the relation of sitting-on. Sentences thus mirror the states of affairs they describe, and that is how they get to mean those things. For the most part, of course, words are *arbitrarily* associated with the things they refer to; someone simply decided that Hitler was to be called "Adolf," and the inscription or sound "dog" could have been used to mean anything.

This *Referential Theory of Linguistic Meaning* would explain the significance of all expressions in terms of their having been conventionally associated with things or states of affairs in the world, and it would explain a human being's understanding a sentence in terms of that person's knowing what the sentence's component words refer to. It is a natural and appealing view. Indeed it may seem obviously correct, at least so far as it goes. And one would have a hard time denying that reference or naming is our cleanest-cut and most familiar relation between a word and the world. Yet when examined, the Referential Theory very soon runs into serious objections.

Objection 1

Not every word does name or denote any actual object.

First, there are the "names" of nonexistent items like Pegasus or the Easter Bunny. "Pegasus" does not denote anything, because there is in reality no winged horse for it to denote. (We shall discuss such names at some length in Chapter 3.) Or consider pronouns of quantification, as in:

(5) I saw nobody.

It would be a tired joke to take "nobody" as a name and respond, "You must have very good eyesight, then." (Lewis Carroll: "Who did you pass on the road?" . . . "Nobody[.]" . . . ". . . So of course nobody walks slower than you."[1] And e.e. cummings' poem, "Anyone lived in a pretty how town,"[2] makes little sense to the reader until s/he figures out that cummings *is* perversely using expressions like "anyone" and "no one" as names of individual persons.)

Second, consider a simple subject–predicate sentence:

(6) Ralph is fat.

Though "Ralph" may name a person, what does "fat" name or denote? Not an individual. Certainly it does not name Ralph, but describes or characterizes him (fairly or no).

We might suggest that "fat" denotes something abstract; for example, it and other adjectives might be said to refer to *qualities* (or "properties," "attributes," "features," "characteristics," etc.) of things. "Fat" might be said to name fatness in the abstract, or as Plato would have called it, The Fat Itself. Perhaps what (6) says is that Ralph has or exemplifies or is an instance of the quality fatness. But that suggestion leaves the copula "is" untreated. If we try to think of subject–predicate meaning as a matter of concatenating the name of a property with the name of an individual, we would need a second abstract entity for the "is" to stand for, say the relation of "having," as in the individual's having the property. But then we would need a third abstract entity to relate *that* relation to the original individual and property, and so on – and on, and on, forever and ever. (The infinite regress here was pointed out by F. H. Bradley 1930: 17–18.)

Third, there are words that grammatically are nouns but do not, intuitively, name either individual things or kinds of things – not even nonexistent "things" or abstract items such as qualities. Quine (1960) gives the examples of "sake," "behalf," and "dint." One sometimes does something for someone else's sake or on that person's behalf, but not as if a sake or a behalf were a kind of object the beneficiary led around on a leash. Or one achieves something by dint of hard work; but a dint is not a thing or kind of thing. (I have never been sure what a "whit" or a "cahoot" is.) Despite being nouns, words like these surely do not have their meanings by referring to particular kinds of objects. They seem to have meaning only by dint of occurring in longer constructions. By themselves they barely can be said to mean anything at all, though they are words and meaning*ful* words at that.

Fourth, many parts of speech other than nouns do not even seem to refer to things of any sort or in any way at all: "very," "of," "and," "the," "a," "yes," and for that matter "hey" and "alas." Yet of course such words are meaningful and occur in sentences that any competent speaker of English understands.

(Not everyone is convinced that the Referential Theory is so decisively refuted, even in regard to that last group of the most clearly nonreferential words there are. In fact, Richard Montague (1960) set out to construct a very sophisticated, highly technical theory in which even words like those *are* assigned referents of a highly abstract sort, and do have a meaning, at least in part, by referring to what they supposedly refer to. We shall say more of Montague's system in Chapter 10.)

Objection 2

According to the Referential Theory, a sentence is a list of names. But a mere list of names does not say anything.

(7) Fred Martha Irving Phyllis

cannot be used to assert anything, even if Martha or Irving is an abstract entity rather than a physical object. One might suppose that if the name of an individual is concatenated with the name of a quality, as in

(8) Ralph fatness,

the resulting string would have normal subject–predicate meaning, say that Ralph is fat. But in fact, (8) is ungrammatical. For it to take on normal subject–predicate meaning, a verb would have to be inserted:

(9) Ralph {has/exemplifies} fatness,

which would launch Bradley's regress again.

Objection 3

As we shall see and discuss in the next two chapters, there are specific linguistic phenomena that seem to show that there is more to meaning than reference. In particular, coreferring terms are often not synonymous; that is, two terms can share their referent but differ in meaning – "John Paul" and "the Pope," for example.

It looks as though we should conclude that there must be at least one way of being a meaningful expression other than by naming something, possibly even for some expressions that do name things. There are a number of theories of meaning that surpass the Referential Theory, even though each theory faces difficulties of its own. We shall look at some of the theories and their besetting difficulties in Part II. But first, in the next three chapters, we shall look further into the nature of naming, referring, and the like, in part because despite the failings of the Referential Theory of Meaning, reference remains important in its own right, and in part because a discussion of reference will help us introduce some concepts that will be needed in the assessment of theories of meaning.

Summary

- Some strings of marks or noises are *meaningful sentences*.
- It is an amazing fact that any normal person can instantly grasp the meaning of even a very long and novel sentence.
- Each meaningful sentence has parts that are themselves meaningful.
- Though initially attractive, the Referential Theory of Meaning faces several compelling objections.

Questions

1 Can you think of any further objections to the Referential Theory as stated here?
2 Are Objections 1 and 2 entirely fair, or are there plausible replies that the referential theorist might make?

Notes

1 *Alice's Adventures in Wonderland and Through The Looking Glass* (London: Methuen, 1978), p. 180.
2 *Complete Poems, 1913–1962* (New York: Harcourt, Brace, Jovanovich, 1972).

Further reading

Probably the most persistent critic of the Referential Theory is Wittgenstein (1953: Part I). A more systematic Wittgensteinian attack is found in Waismann (1965a: Chapter VIII). Arguments of the sort lying behind Objection 3 are found in Frege (1892/1956).

Bradley's regress is further discussed by Wolterstorff (1970: Chapter 4) and by Loux (1998: Chapter 1).

PART I
Reference and referring

2
Definite descriptions

Overview

Singular terms

Russell's Theory of Descriptions

Objections to Russell's theory

Donnellan's distinction

Anaphora

Summary

Questions

Notes

Further reading

Overview

Even if the Referential Theory of Meaning does not hold for all words, one might think it would apply at least to singular terms (terms that purport to refer to single individuals, such as proper names, pronouns, and definite descriptions). But Bertrand Russell argued powerfully that definite descriptions, at least, do not mean what they mean in virtue of denoting what they denote. Rather, he contended, a sentence containing a definite description, such as "The woman who lives there is a biochemist," has subject–predicate form only superficially, and is really – logically – a trio of generalizations: it is equivalent to "At least one woman lives there, and at most one woman lives there, and whoever lives there is a biochemist."

Russell argues for this analysis both directly and by showing that it affords solutions to each of four vexing logical puzzles: the Problems of Apparent Reference to Nonexistents and Negative Existentials, Frege's Puzzle about Identity, and Substitutivity.

A variety of objections have been raised against Russell's Theory of Descriptions. P. F. Strawson pointed out that it is at odds with our usual linguistic habits: though a sentence having "the present King of France" as its subject presupposes that there is at least one King of France, it is not *false* for lack of a King; rather, it cannot be used to make a proper statement at all, and so it has no truth-value. And Russell's theory ignores the fact that most descriptions are context-bound, and denote uniquely only within a circumscribed local setting ("Bring me the book on the table"). Strawson argues more generally that Russell treats sentences and their logical properties in too abstract and disembodied a fashion, forgetting how they are actually used by flesh-and-blood people in concrete conversational practice.

Keith Donnellan notes that even if Russell is right about some uses of descriptions, he has ignored a common sort of case in which a description *is* used "referentially," merely to indicate a particular person or thing, regardless of that referent's attributes.

Finally, there are further uses of descriptions, called "anaphoric" uses, which may defy Russellian treatment.

Singular terms

In English or any other natural language, the paradigmatic referring devices are *singular terms*, expressions which purport to denote or designate particular individual people, places, or other objects (as opposed to *general terms* such as "dog" or "brown" that can apply to more than one thing). Singular terms include proper names ("Jane," "Winston Churchill," "Djakarta," "3:17 p.m.," "3"), definite descriptions ("the Queen of England," "the cat on the mat," "the last department meeting but one"), singular personal pronouns ("you," "she"), demonstrative pronouns ("this," "that"), and a few others.

Even if the Referential Theory of Meaning is not true across the board, one might reasonably expect it to be true of singular terms. But in a famous series of works, Bertrand Russell (1905/1956, 1918/1956, 1919/1971) showed that it is not true of definite descriptions, and raised serious doubts as to whether it is true of other ordinary singular terms either.

Drawing on the work of Gottlob Frege (1892/1952b), Russell set forth four puzzles about singular terms, posed initially in terms of definite descriptions. (He was interested in the logic of the word "the": "It may be thought excessive to devote two chapters [of his *Introduction to Mathematical Philosophy*] to one word, but to the philosophical mathematician it is a word of very great importance: like Browning's grammarian with the enclitic δε, I would give the doctrine of this word if I were 'dead from the waist down' and not merely in a prison"[1] (1919/1971: 167).)

The Problem of Apparent Reference to Nonexistents

Consider:

(1) The present King of France is bald.

The following set of statements is inconsistent (that is, on pain of logical contradiction, the statements cannot all be true):

K1 (1) is meaningful (significant, not meaningless).
K2 (1) is a subject–predicate sentence.
K3 A meaningful subject–predicate sentence is meaningful (only) in virtue of its picking out some individual thing and ascribing some property to that thing.
K4 (1)'s subject term fails to pick out or denote anything that exists.
K5 If (1) is meaningful only in virtue of picking out a thing and

ascribing a property to that thing (K1, K2, K3), and if (1)'s subject term fails to pick out anything that exists (K4), then either (1) is not meaningful after all (contrary to K1) or (1) picks out a thing that does *not* exist. *But*:

K6 There is no such thing as a "nonexistent thing."

The Problem of Negative Existentials

This is a special case of the foregoing puzzle, but as we shall see, an aggravated one. Consider:

(2) The present King of France does not exist.

(2) seems to be true and seems to be about the present King of France. But if (2) is true, (2) cannot be about the present King of France, for there is no such King for it to be about. Likewise, if (2) *is* about the present King of France, then it is false, for the King must then in some sense exist.

It is worth noting a couple of solutions to the Problems of Apparent Reference to Nonexistents and Negative Existentials, that had previously been defended but were rejected by Russell. K1 is uncontroversial; K2 seems obvious; K4 is just a fact; and K5 is trivially true. So Frege had rejected K3, by positing abstract entities that he called "senses" and arguing that a singular term is meaningful in virtue of having one of those over and above its referent – or in the case of a nonreferring singular term, instead of a referent. (We shall consider a descendant of Frege's view in Chapter 10.) Alexius Meinong (1904/1960) boldly leapt to deny K6, insisting *à la* St Anselm that any possible object of thought – even a self-contradictory one – has being of a sort even though only a few such things are so lucky as to exist in reality as well. That idea gave Russell fits.

Frege's Puzzle about Identity

An *identity-statement* such as

(3) Elizabeth Windsor = the present Queen of England

contains two singular terms, both of which (if the statement is true) pick out or denote the same person or thing. It seems, then, that what the statement says is simply that that person is identical with that person, that that person is identical with herself. If so, then the statement is *trivial*. Yet (3) seems nontrivial, in each of two ways: first, (3) is informative, in that someone might learn something new upon reading (3) (either something about Windsor or something about who rules England); second, (3) is *contingent*, as philosophers say – the fact (3) states is one that could have been otherwise. So it seems that ~~at least one of the singular terms figuring in (3) must have and contribute some kind of meaning over and above its referent~~.

Frege himself held that the two singular terms have different "senses," and that is why (3) is informative. It is not clear how Frege's hypothesis would explain (3)'s contingency.

The Problem of Substitutivity

Eric Blair = the author of 1984. synonymous

The function of a singular term is to pick out an individual thing and introduce that thing into discourse. Even if one stops short of the entire Referential Theory of Meaning, one might think it is in virtue of that denoting role that singular terms are meaningful at all. Therefore, we would expect that any two singular terms that denote one and the same thing would be semantically equivalent: we could take any sentence containing one of the terms and substitute the other of the two for the first term, without changing the meaning or at least without changing the truth-value of the sentence. But consider the sentence:

ex: the author of 1984 is an intelligent man.

(4) Albert believes that the author of *Nothing and Beingness* is a profound thinker.

Wouldn't we really substitute different titles? why not his name. that's co-referent.

and suppose (4) is true. Now, Albert is unaware that the author of *Nothing and Beingness* moonlights by writing cheap, disgusting pornography. We cannot substitute the term "the author of *Sizzling Veterinarians*" for "the author of *Nothing and Beingness*" in (4) without changing (4)'s truth-value: the result is a false sentence, since Albert believes that the author of *Sizzling Veterinarians* is a drooling moron. (I am afraid this reveals that Albert has read *Sizzling Veterinarians*.) In W. V. Quine's (1960) terminology, the sentential position occupied by the definite description in (4) is referentially *opaque* ("opaque" for short), as opposed to referentially *transparent*. What causes the opacity is the "believes that" construction, since the sentence "The author of *Nothing and Beingness* is a profound thinker," standing alone, is transparent.

∴ NOT really synonomous

Not too surprisingly, Russell argued on the basis of these puzzles[2] that definite descriptions do have and contribute meanings that go beyond their referents alone. His Theory of Descriptions, as it has since been called and capitalized, takes the form of a *contextual definition* of the word "the" as it occurs in typical definite descriptions. That is, rather than defining the word explicitly (how would you go about completing the formula, "*The* = _{def} . . ."?), Russell offers a recipe for paraphrasing standard types of whole sentence containing "the," in such a way as to exhibit the role of "the" indirectly, and to reveal what he called the sentences' "logical forms." (He does not here treat plural uses of "the," or the generic use as in "The whale is a mammal." Notice that definite descriptions can be formed without use of "the," for example by way of possessives, as in "my brother" or "Doris' egg salad sandwich," though perhaps we might paraphrase those along the lines of "the brother of me.")

Russell's Theory of Descriptions

this is his answer to the above problems
ex: non-synonomous descriptions.

Here is Russell's contextual definition of "the." Let us take a paradigmatic sentence, of the form "The F is G."

(5) The author of *Waverley* was Scotch.[3]

(5) *appears* to be a simple subject–predicate sentence, referring to an individual (Sir Walter Scott) and predicating something (Scottishness) of him. But appearances are deceiving, Russell says. Notice that the ostensible singular term, "The author of *Waverley*," consists of our troublesome word "the" pasted onto the front of a *predicative* expression, and notice too that the meaning of that expression figures crucially in our ability to recognize or pick out the expression's referent; to find the referent we have to look for someone who did write *Waverley*. Russell suggests that "the" abbreviates a more complex construction involving what logicians and linguists call *quantifiers*, words that quantify general terms ("*all* teenagers," "*some* bananas," "*six* geese a-laying," "*most* police officers," "*no* light bulbs," and the like). Indeed, he thinks that (5) as a whole abbreviates a conjunction of three quantified general statements, none of which makes reference to Scott in particular:

(a) At least one person authored *Waverley*, and
(b) at most one person authored *Waverley*, and
(c) whoever authored *Waverley* was Scotch.

Each of (a)–(c) is intuitively necessary for the truth of (5). If the author of *Waverley* was Scotch, then there was such an author; if there were more than one author, "the" should not have been used; and if the author was Scotch it follows trivially that whoever did the authoring was. And (a)–(c) taken together certainly seem sufficient for the truth of (5). So we seem to have a set of individually necessary and jointly sufficient conditions for (5); that in itself is a powerful argument for Russell's analysis.

In standard logical notation: Let "W" represent the predicate ". . . authored *Waverley*" and "S" represent ". . . was Scotch." Then Russell's three conditions are:

(a) $(\exists x)Wx$. *atleast 1 person authored waverly.*
(b) $(x)(Wx \rightarrow (y)(Wy \rightarrow y = x))$. *At most 1 person authored waverly.*
(c) $(x)(Wx \rightarrow Sx)$. *whoever authored waverly was scotch.*

(a)–(c) are conjointly equivalent to

(d) $(\exists x)(Wx \ \& \ ((y)(Wy \rightarrow y = x) \ \& \ Sx))$.

Russell's position is that (d) correctly expresses the *logical form* of (5), as distinct from (5)'s superficial grammatical form. We have already *Denies* encountered an example of this distinction, in Chapter 1, illustrated by the *K2 here.* sentence "I saw nobody." Superficially, that sentence has the same form as *Not trying to* "I saw Martha" – Subject + Transitive Verb + Object. Yet the two differ *pick out a* sharply in their logical properties. "I saw Martha" entails that I saw some- *thing.* one, while "I saw nobody" entails precisely the opposite; it is equivalent to "It's not the case that I saw anyone" and to "There is no one that I saw." Though someone just beginning to learn English might take it as one, "nobody" is *not really a singular term*, but a quantifier. In logical notation, letting "A" represent ". . . saw . . ." and "i" represent "I," "I saw nobody" is expressed as "$\sim(\exists x)Aix$" or, equivalently, "$(x)\sim Aix$," and the explicit inference rules governing this formal notation explain the logical behavior of the English sentence thus translated into it.

So too, Russell maintained, the apparent singular term in (5), "The author of *Waverley*," is not really (that is, at the level of logical form) a singular term at all, but a convenient (if misleading) abbreviation of the more complicated quantificational structure displayed in (a)–(c). As he puts it, the apparent singular term "disappears on analysis." Our puzzles have arisen in fact from applying principles about singular reference to expressions that are not *really* singular terms at all but only masquerade as such.

Let us now go through the four puzzles and exhibit Russell's solutions one by one.

Apparent Reference to Nonexistents

Let us paraphrase (1) according to Russell's method:

> At least one person is presently King of France [more
> perspicuously: ". . . presently kings France"], and
>
> at most one person is presently King of France, and
>
> whoever is presently King of France is bald.

No problem. The first of the foregoing three conjuncts is simply false, since no one kings France at present; so (1) itself comes out false on Russell's analysis. When we first stated the puzzle, it looked as though one had to reject either K3 or (outrageously) K6, since K2 seemed as obvious as the other undeniable K-statements; but now Russell ingeniously denies statement K2, since he denies that "The present King of France" is "really" a singular term (notice again that our three conjuncts are all general statements and that none mentions any specific individual corresponding to the alleged King). Alternatively and less dramatically, we could keep K2, understanding it as alluding to superficial grammatical form, and reject K3 on the grounds that a *superficially* subject–predicate sentence can be meaningful without picking out any particular individual because it abbreviates a trio of purely general statements.

Negative Existentials

Let us apply Russell's analysis to (2) ("The present King of France does not exist"). Now, there is a Russellian paraphrase of (2) that leaves (2) just as anomalous as it seems to the naive hearer. That is the paraphrase that takes "exist" to be an ordinary predicate like "was Scotch" or "is bald," and takes "not" to modify or apply to that predicate:

> At least one person is presently King of France, and
>
> at most one person is presently King of France, and
>
> whoever is presently King of France does not exist.

The anomaly is that the first conjunct asserts the existence of a present King, while the third conjunct denies it. No wonder (2) sounds peculiar to us. To make sense of (2), we must understand "not", not as modifying the verb "exist", but as applying to the rest of (2) as a whole, thus:

Not: (The present King of France exists). [That is, it is false that:
the present King of France exists],

which is obviously what would be meant by someone who tokened (2)
seriously. Then we apply Russell's pattern of analysis *inside* the "not," as
follows.

Not: (At least one person is presently King of France, and at most
one person is presently King of France, and whoever is presently
King of France exists).

In symbols:

$$\sim(\exists x)(Kx \ \& \ ((y)(Ky \rightarrow y = x) \ \& \ Ex)),$$

where "E" represents "exists." (Actually, "exists" is itself treated as a
quantifier in logical theory, and so the conjunct "Ex" ought properly to be
replaced by "$(\exists z)(z = x)$," which is redundant.) The intuitive content of (2)
is just, "No one is uniquely King of France," or "No one uniquely kings
France," and Russell's paraphrase has the virtue of being precisely equivalent to that. Nowhere in Russell's analysis do we pick out an individual
and say of that individual that *he* does not exist, so the Problem of
Negative Existentials vanishes, at least for the case of definite descriptions.

In this preferred understanding of (2), the description occurs in what
Russell called "secondary" position; that is, we have construed its underlying quantifiers "at least," "at most," and "whoever" as falling inside the
"not." The previous, dispreferred paraphrase gave the description "primary" position, placing it first in the logical order with the "not" inside
and governed by it. A meaning distinction of this kind is called a *scope*
distinction: in more contemporary terminology, the secondary reading is
that on which the quantifiers take "narrow" scope, falling inside the scope
of "not"; on the primary reading the quantifiers are outside the scope of
"not," and "not" is in their scope.

Frege's Puzzle

The right-hand term of (3) is a definite description, so let us paraphrase it
away in Russell's manner:

At least one person is presently Queen of England, and

at most one person is presently Queen of England, and

Russell's paraphrase.

whoever is presently Queen of England is one and the same as Elizabeth Windsor.

In symbols:

$$(\exists x)(Qx \ \& \ ((y)(Qy \rightarrow y = x) \ \& \ x = e)).$$

Now we see easily why our original identity-statement is nontrivial. *Of course we learn something when we hear Russell's paraphrase, something substantive about Elizabeth and the present Queen both*. And of course the identity-statement is contingent, since someone else might have been Queen (there might even have been no Queen at all), Elizabeth might have run away from home and formed a rock band rather than be crowned, or whatever. The Theory of Descriptions seems to give a correct account of the identity-statement's intuitive content. Note that on Russell's view the statement is only superficially an *identity*-statement; really it is a predication and attributes a complex relational property to Elizabeth. That leaves us with the problem of how a *real* identity-statement could manage to be both true and informative, more of which in Chapter 3.

Substitutivity

Let us return to the troublesome (4) ("Albert believes that the author of *Nothing and Beingness* is a profound thinker"). Here the definite description occurs as part of what Albert believes, so we shall start our paraphrase with "Albert believes" and then apply Russell's pattern of analysis, giving the description secondary occurrence or narrow scope:

> Albert believes the following: (At least one person authored *Nothing and Beingness*, and at most one person authored *Nothing and Beingness*, and whoever authored *Nothing and Beingness* is a profound thinker).

This is a pretty good account of what Albert believes.[4] And now it is obvious why we may not substitute "the author of *Sizzling Veterinarians*" into (4), for the corresponding analysis of the resulting sentence would come out:

> Albert believes the following: At least one person authored *Sizzling Veterinarians*, and at most one person authored *Sizzling Veterinarians*, and whoever authored *Sizzling Veterinarians* is a profound thinker.

Since this attributes an entirely different belief to Albert, there is no wonder that it is false even though (4) is true. (Of course, at the level of logical form we have not made a substitution at all, for the singular terms have "disappeared on analysis" and are no longer there to be substituted.)

The four puzzles made it clear that definite descriptions do not hook onto the world by directly naming and nothing else. But we needed a positive theory of how they do hook onto it. Russell has provided one very well motivated theory. Notice that even though definite descriptions are not assigned referents in the way that names are, and even though they are not "really" singular terms at all, they still purport to have single individuals that answer to them; when a description does in fact have the corresponding individual that it purports to have – that is, when there does exist a unique so-and-so – I shall speak of the description's *semantic denotatum* or *semantic referent*. But the "hook" between a definite description and its semantic referent is (on Russell's view) far less direct than is the hook between a simple name and its bearer.

Objections to Russell's theory

Impressive as Russell's achievement is, a number of objections have been brought against the Theory of Descriptions, chiefly by Strawson (1950). *use theorist.* Before we take these up, I note an important criticism that might be made at just this point, though Russell quickly moved to forestall it.

When I set out the four puzzles with which we began, I called them puzzles "about singular terms." I expounded each of them by using examples featuring definite descriptions, and wielded Russell's Theory of Descriptions against them. But they are indeed puzzles about singular terms across the board, not just descriptions. We can use proper names or even pronouns to make apparent reference to nonexistents ("Pegasus," "you" [said by Scrooge to Marley's ghost]); Frege's Puzzle arises for proper names ("Samuel Langhorne Clemens = Mark Twain"); names do not substitute in belief contexts (Albert may have beliefs about Mark Twain that he does not have about Clemens and vice versa); and Pegasus is neither bald nor nonbald. These seem to be exactly the same problems as those which I happened to state in terms of descriptions. It looks as though Russell has simply missed the boat, because he has given a theory which by its nature applies only to one very special subclass of singular terms, while any adequate solution to the puzzles ought to generalize.

Russell's solution to this problem was if anything even more ingenious than the Theory of Descriptions itself. In brief, it was to invoke another

Not false – but Not a statement ex: the present king of France.

People use sentences. Sentences themselves don't make sense.

distinction between surface appearance and underlying logical reality, and claim that what we ordinarily call proper names are not really proper names at all, but rather they are abbreviations for definite descriptions. I shall postpone examination of this thesis until the next chapter.

Strawson's critique was radical and searching. Indeed, Russell and Strawson were respectively figureheads for two very different approaches to the study of language (and to a lesser degree for two great rival systems of twentieth-century philosophy), though we shall not go into that until Chapter 6. To set the stage for Strawson's objections, I shall merely note that while Russell thought in terms of sentences taken in the abstract as objects in themselves, and their logical properties in particular, Strawson emphasized how the sentences are used and reacted to by human beings in concrete conversational situations. Russell's most famous article (1905/ 1956) was called "On Denoting," and in it denoting was taken to be a relation between an expression, considered in abstraction, and the thing that is the expression's referent or denotatum. Strawson's title was "On Referring," which he meant ironically, because he thought of referring not as an abstract relation between an expression and a thing but as an *act* done by a person at a time on an occasion. This way of looking at things gave Strawson quite a new slant on the four problems.

Strawson holds that *expressions* do not refer at all; people refer, using expressions for that purpose. This is reminiscent of the (US) National Rifle Association's slogan, "Guns don't kill people, people kill people." Certainly there is an obvious sense in which Strawson is right. To use an example of his, if I write down, "This is a fine red one," "This" does not refer to anything – and no determinate statement has been made – until I do something to make it refer. An expression will come to refer only if I use it in a suitably well-engineered context, so that it does refer to a particular thing or person. But that is a matter of the expression being used, and when I do use it, it is I that am doing the work, not the expression.

Objection 1

According to Russell, sentence (1) ("The present King of France is bald") is *false* owing to the lack of any such King. Strawson points out that that verdict is implausible. Suppose someone comes out and asserts (1). Would that person's hearers react by saying "That's false" or "I disagree"? Surely not. Rather, Strawson maintains, the speaker has produced an only ostensibly referring expression that has misfired; the speaker has simply failed to refer to anything and so has failed to make a complete statement. The speaker's utterance is certainly defective, but not in the same way that "The present Queen of England has no children" is defective. It is not incorrect but abortive; it does not even get a chance to be false. Since no proper statement has been made in the first place, it follows that nothing either true *or* false has been said. A hearer would either just not comprehend or would say "Back up" and question the utterance's presupposition ("I'm not following you; France doesn't have a king"). Strawson therefore solves the Problem of Apparent Reference to Nonexistents by denying K3: (1) is meaningful, in that it has a legitimate use in the language and *could* be used to say true or false things if the world (or the French) were more cooperative, but not because it succeeds in picking out any individual thing.

Russell thought of a meaningful sentence as a sentence that has a meaning, or as he put it, a sentence that expresses a proposition. A sentence's logical form, on his view, is really that of the proposition the sentence expresses. But propositions by their nature are either true or false. Strawson eschews talk of "propositions," and denies that *sentences* are the kind of things that can be true or false at all. What bears the properties truth and falsity are rather the statements made when speakers succeed in saying something, and not every act of uttering does succeed in that way, for not every meaningful sentence is always used to make a statement.

[handwritten margin note: T/F this seems to be the basis of Russell's argument.]

Russellians have a standard reply to Objection 1, but it depends on some notions that I shall not develop until Chapter 13, so I shall postpone it until then.

Objection 2

Strawson further criticizes the claim, which he attributes to Russell, that "part of what [a speaker] would be asserting [in uttering (1)] would be that there at present existed one and only one king of France" (1950: 330). That claim too is implausible, for although the speaker presupposes that there is one and only one king, that is certainly not part of what the speaker asserts.

But that is a misunderstanding: Russell had made no such claim. He said nothing at all about acts of *asserting*. Perhaps Strawson is assuming on Russell's behalf that whatever is logically implied by a sentence is necessarily asserted by a speaker who utters that sentence. But the latter principle is false: if I say "Fat Tommy can't run or climb a tree," I do not *assert* that Tommy is fat, even though my sentence logically implies that he is; if I say "Tommy is five feet seven inches tall," I do not assert that Tommy is less than eighteen miles tall.

Objection 3

Strawson points out that many descriptions are context-bound. He offers the example of:

(6) The table is covered with books.

Presumably the subject term is a definite description, used in a standard way rather than in any different or unusual way. But if we apply Russell's analysis, we get "At least one thing is a table and at most one thing is a table and any thing that is a table is covered with books" – which by way of its second conjunct entails that there is at most one table, in the entire universe. *That* cannot be shrugged off. However unwillingly, Russell is going to have to take some notice of the context of utterance.

He has several options. After all, Strawson has no monopoly on the fact that when someone says "The table," we hearers generally know which table is meant, because something in the context has made it salient. It may be the only table in sight, or the only one in the room, or the one we have just been talking about. Russell may say that there is ellipsis here, that in the context, "The table" is *short for* a more elaborate description that is uniquely satisfied. (As we shall see in the next chapter, Russell was no enemy of ellipsis hypotheses.)

The ellipsis view has some disturbing implications. Russell thinks of logical form as objectively real – that sentences really do have the logical forms he posits. So if "The table" is elliptical, there has got to be a determinate answer to the question, "What material is ellipsized?" And the answer will matter, because depending upon which candidate you pick, (6) will turn out to say something completely different. If we say that "The table" means the table in this room, then we have introduced the concept "room," and construed (6) as being literally about a room, indeed as having the predicate "room" hidden in its underlying logical structure.

Perhaps a better approach would be an appeal to *restricted quantification* (as in Lycan 1984 and Neale 1990). Often we say things like "Everyone likes her," meaning, not every person in the universe, but everyone in a certain contextually indicated social circle. Or, "Nobody goes to that restaurant any more," which is unlikely to mean that no human being at all goes there; it would more commonly mean, no one of our sort (whatever sort that is).[5] What logicians call the *domains* over which quantifiers range need not be universal, but are often particular classes roughly presupposed in the context. In fact (you can check this for yourself), practically all quantification that occurs in English is restricted quantification: "I'll eat anything on pizza," "There's no beer," and even "I wouldn't trade this car for anything in the world."

Of course the usual Russellian analysis starts with a quantifier: "At least one thing is a table. . . ." Let us simply regard that quantifier as restricted in the appropriate way. The same restriction will apply to the "at most one thing," and so we lose the unwanted implication that there is at most one table in the universe; (6) will now imply only that there is at most one table of the contextually indicated sort, which is fine.

The appeal to restricted quantification differs from the ellipsis hypothesis, in that it does not require that explicit conceptual material be clandestinely mentioned in (6). The quantifier restriction is more like a silent demonstrative pronoun: "At most one table of *that* sort," where the context fixes the reference of "that." So we seem to have solved the table problem on Russell's behalf. (For a neat objection, however, see Reimer 1992.)

There is still a general problem of how quantifiers get restricted in context, what determines the exact restricted domains (which are almost always vague to boot), and how on earth hearers identify the right domains as quickly and as effortlessly as they do. But we have that general problem anyway; it poses no special objection to Russell's Theory of Descriptions.

I pause to offer a partial rebuttal of Strawson's notion that people rather than expressions refer. Recall the National Rifle Association's slogan, "Guns don't kill people, people kill people." An appropriate response is, "Yes, but they kill them much more easily and efficiently using guns," and there is a perfectly good sense in which the gun did kill the victim. So too there is at least a secondary sense in which expressions do refer. There is nothing at all wrong with saying that in a particular context, the expression "The table" refers to the salient piece of furniture. Moreover, we have already introduced the notion of the "semantic referent" of a description: in context, remember, a description's semantic referent is whatever object (if any) in fact uniquely satisfies the description.

Notice that Russell too has an objection to talking about the referent of a description. He wants to insist that descriptions are not really referring expressions at all; a sentence containing one abbreviates a mass of quantificational material that is entirely general and not about anyone in particular. But my notion of a semantic referent applies equally against Russell on this point. There is at least that secondary sense in which a description can have a referent. And it is perfectly harmless for a Russellian to grant that definite descriptions do refer, so long as s/he remembers that they do not do it directly, in the way we may have thought proper names do.

I turn to an objection made by Keith Donnellan (1966).

Objection 4

Donnellan noticed cases in which we do seem to use definite descriptions as if they are just tags or names, solely to refer to individuals. And in such cases the Russellian analysis does not capture what seems to be said when the relevant sentences are uttered.

Though Donnellan intended his article modestly as an adjudication of the Russell–Strawson dispute, his insight has wider application, and I shall expound it in its own terms.

Donnellan's distinction

Donnellan called attention to what he called the "referential use," as opposed to the "attributive use," of a definite description. The most obvious type of referential use is when a description has grown capital letters and is really used as a title. A classic example is "The Holy Roman Empire," whose referent, as Voltaire observed, was neither holy, nor Roman, nor an empire. Or "The Grateful Dead," which is the name of a rock band; sentences containing that title do not mean that at least one thing is grateful and dead and. . . .

Russell might fairly retort that, as the capital letters show, those titles are not being used as descriptions at all, but (of course) as fused *titles*. "The Swan" is the name of a piece of instrumental music by Saint-Saëns, and sentences containing that title are about music, not about water fowl. But Donnellan shows that there are less formal cases in which we use descriptions solely to focus on a particular individual regardless of that person or thing's attributes.

For contrast, here is a standard Russellian example. We come across the hideously murdered body of Smith, and I assert

(7) Smith's murderer is insane,

meaning that whoever committed this terrible crime is insane. Donnellan has no quarrel with Russell here; this is what he calls the attributive use of the description.

But suppose instead that we have not seen the body and have no other direct knowledge of the matter; Jones has been arrested and charged with the crime and we are attending his trial. The prosecution's case is excellent, and we are privately presuming that Jones is guilty; also, he is rolling his eyes and drooling in a homicidal manner. Here too I say to you (7), "Smith's murderer is insane." In the context I am only using the description "Smith's murderer" to refer to the person we are looking at, the defendant, regardless of what attributes he has. Moreover, what I said is true if and only if the defendant is insane, regardless of his having committed the murder. This is what Donnellan calls the referential use.

Donnellan's objection to the Theory of Descriptions is just that the theory overlooks the referential use; Russell writes as if all descriptions were used attributively. But against Strawson, Donnellan complains that equally he did not see the attributive use, that Strawson writes as if all descriptions were used referentially, in a context to draw somebody's attention to a particular person, place or thing. Thus both Strawson and Russell were mistaken in thinking that definite descriptions always work in one way, because there is an ambiguity acknowledged by neither. Donnellan does not take a position as to what kind of ambiguity it is; in particular he does not try to decide whether the sentence (7) itself has two different meanings explaining the description's evidently distinct "uses."

Here is the single best literary example I know of Donnellan's distinction, from Kingsley Amis' *Girl, 20:*[6] Sir Roy Vandervane is explaining to the novel's narrator, Douglas Yandell, what he sees in Sylvia, his horrible teenage mistress.

> ". . . Another point about her is that she isn't my wife."
> "True. Very few people are Kitty."
> "It isn't Kitty she isn't, you bloody fool. What she isn't is my wife. Not the same thing at all. . . ."

Donnellan gives several informal characterizations of the new referential use: "A speaker who uses a definite description referentially in an assertion . . . uses the description to enable his audience to pick out whom or what he is talking about . . ." (p. 285). The description does not "occur essentially," but is "merely one tool for doing a certain job – calling attention to a person or thing – and in general any other device for doing the same job, another description or a name, would do as well" (p. 285). "[W]e expect and intend our audience to realize whom we have in mind . . . and, most importantly, to know that it is this person about whom we are going to say something" (pp. 285–6). This all sounds straightforwardly correct, for the "Smith's murderer" case.[7]

However, Donnellan goes on to add a further characterization: in the attributive use of "The ø is Y," "if nothing is the ø then nothing has been said to be Y," while in the referential case "the fact that nothing is the ø does not have this consequence" (p. 287). He takes this point from Linsky (1963), who offers the example of someone (perhaps at a party) who observes a woman and her male companion and says, "Her husband is kind to her." Donnellan and Linsky agree that even if the woman is in fact unmarried, it is the companion that is referred to, and that what is said is that that person is kind to her regardless of his not actually being her husband. On this view, the real referent differs from what I have been calling the semantic referent, there being no semantic referent in Linsky's example.

Or suppose that in the Smith case, against all the evidence, Jones is innocent; Smith committed suicide and there is no murderer. (Or perhaps Smith is not even dead, but has been languishing in a state of deep suspended animation.) Intuitively, Donnellan maintains, that does not change what I said. And what I said is true if and only if Jones is insane, regardless of there being no murderer. Donnellan gives the further example of a party guest seeing an interesting-looking person sipping from a martini glass; the guest asks, "Who is the man drinking a martini?" In fact the glass holds only water, but, Donnellan maintains, the guest's question is about the interesting-looking man, and not about (say) Dino, off in the billiard room, who is in fact the one and only man at the party drinking a martini.

Examples like these, sometimes called "near-miss" cases, are disputed. Following Grice (1957) and flouting Strawson, Kripke (1979a) distinguishes between what a linguistic expression itself means or refers to and what a speaker means or refers to in using the expression. For example, taken literally, the sentence "Albert's an elegant fellow" means that Albert is an elegant fellow, but a speaker might use it sarcastically to point out that Albert is a revolting slob. (We shall say much more of disparities between speaker-meaning and literal expression meaning in Chapters 7 and 13.) So too, I may say "Smith's murderer," which phrase taken literally means whoever murdered Smith, and (myself) honestly mean Jones on the stand and accurately be taken to mean Jones. Linsky's speaker himself means the lady's companion, but the expression "Her husband" according to the rules of English means whoever (if anyone) is married to her; Donnellan's party guest obviously means the interesting-looking man, though the phrase "the man drinking a martini" literally means whatever man is in fact drinking a martini. Speakers in "near-miss" cases do mean what Donnellan says they mean, and mean true things, but (as with "Albert's an elegant fellow") they do those things *by* uttering sentences that are in fact false.

Let us define *speaker-reference* a little more formally, to contrast with semantic reference. The speaker- or utterer's referent of a description on an occasion of its use is the object, if any, to which the speaker who used the description intended to call to the attention of her/his audience. (The speaker-referent is the object that the utterer means to be talking about.)

Fortunately, *communication* goes by speaker-meaning and speaker-reference: if I (speaker-)mean Jones when I say "Smith's murderer" and you take me to mean Jones and understand me to have said that Jones is insane, then you have understood me correctly and communication has succeeded; it does not matter that the sentence I uttered was according to its literal meaning untrue, any more than it matters that "Albert's an elegant fellow" is literally false.

Thus, according to Kripke, Donnellan has failed to show that a sentence containing a definite description can be true even if nothing (or something extraneous) is the description's semantic referent.

Even if Kripke is right about the near-miss examples, it is important to hold on to some version of Donnellan's distinction. The distinction is amply illustrated by the original "Smith's murderer" example and others, even if Donnellan is wrong about the meanings and truth-values of the near-miss sentences. Donnellan's paper raises the question of specifying the circumstances under which one succeeds in referring, by using a description, to the person or thing one intends to refer to, and he has shown that this does not always go by semantic referent. Further, the distinction unmistakably matters to the truth-value of sentences that embed descriptions within clauses of certain kinds. Suppose I were to say:

(8) I know that's right because I heard it from the town doctor.

You might have to ask me, "You mean because she's a doctor and this is a medical matter, or do you mean because you heard it from *her* and she's also an authority on true crime?" (8)'s truth-value may depend on whether "the town doctor" is used attributively or referentially. Or consider:

(9) I wish that her husband weren't her husband.

The most natural reading of (9) is to take the first occurrence of the description referentially but the second attributively; what the speaker wishes is that the man in question were not married to the woman in question. But (9) has several other readings, depending on which way the descriptions are taken, even though they are fairly silly. (And recall the Amis passage quoted above.)

In light of Kripke's distinction between speaker- or utterer's referent and semantic referent, one might be tempted simply to write off Donnellan's issue as verbal, and maintain that the Theory of Descriptions is still correct as an account of the truth-values of sentences taken literally, while Donnellan is often right about speaker-referent and speaker-meaning. But the ambiguity of sentences like (8) and (9) still seems to elude Russell's analysis.[8]

Also, even if one is persuaded by Kripke and has discounted the near-miss examples, it remains controversial whether, for the referential case, the *actual* referent is always the speaker-referent. Notice that this question presupposes a third notion, that of "actual" referent, that is conceptually distinct from the other two. What is meant seems to be that the actual referent is the object *about* which the speaker actually succeeded in making a statement (asking a question, issuing a command, etc.), it being left open whether this tracks the literal semantic interpretation of the sentence uttered. (Of course, if the Theory of Descriptions is correct, either the actual referent is always the semantic referent or, since according to Russell definite descriptions do not really refer at all, there is no actual referent.)

MacKay (1968) argues that in some cases, even if one misspeaks, one's actual referent may be the semantic referent rather than the speaker-referent. Suppose there are a rock and a book on the table, and, wanting you to bring me the book, I fumblemouth and say, "Bring me the rock on the table," using "the rock" referentially and speaker-referring to the book, I have still asked you to bring me the rock, and you would not be complying if you brought me the book instead.

Or suppose I say to you, "I bet you $5 that the glorious winner [of a big auto race] is over forty years of age." I am using "the glorious winner" referentially, thinking of Dale Earnhart, completely confident that he has the race won, and I have him very much in mind, clear mental image and all. But although he crossed the finish line first, Earnhart does not in fact win; by a little-known technicality he comes in second to Fat Freddy Phreak, who has got loose again and entered the race at the last minute. Fat Freddy is only twenty-two. I owe you $5.

MacKay makes the general point that a speaker's intentions may be arbitrarily crazy. Suppose I have formed the insane belief that Keith Donnellan is the illegitimate son of Santa Claus and Margaret Thatcher. Using the description referentially, I say "Mrs Thatcher's Christmas bastard wrote a classic article on descriptions." If you know enough about my weird beliefs, you will pick out the right individual and understand what I meant, but no one could correctly describe me as having *said that* Keith Donnellan wrote the classic paper.

It should be questioned whether there is any rightfully separate notion of an "actual referent." The concept of a semantic referent is clear, and the theory of communication requires that of a speaker-referent, but perhaps the idea of an "actual referent" is just a confusion of the two based on our failure to see the difference between literal sentence-semantics and the theory of communication. Then we would have to explain away the fact of our having intuitions about "actual referents" in cases like some of the foregoing. Kripke takes roughly that line, making use of an idea of Grice's that we shall discuss in Chapter 13.

Anaphora

One final objection to the Theory of Descriptions must be mentioned. As we have noted, Russell deals only with what he considers the central use of "the," and exempts the theory from having to explain plural uses or the generic use. One may think that a theory of definite descriptions ought not to be pampered thus forever. But in any case Russell does not mention anaphoric uses, and it has certainly been wondered why the theory should not be required to cover those, since unlike plural and generic uses, anaphoric descriptions are ostensibly singular referring expressions.

In general, an *anaphoric* expression inherits its meaning from another expression, its *antecedent*, usually though not always occurring earlier in the sentence or in a previous sentence. For example, in

(10) The man who lived around the corner was eccentric. He used to snack on turtle heads,

"he" refers back to the man who lived around the corner. Geach (1962) called such a term a "pronoun of laziness" and suggested that it merely abbreviates a boilerplate repetition of the antecedent phrase, so that (10)'s second clause is precisely equivalent to "The man who lived around the corner used to snack on turtle heads." Geach's suggestion is only one among several theories of anaphoric pronouns, but the general idea is that the pronoun has the referent that it does only in virtue of its relation to the antecedent phrase.

If Geach is right, then (10) poses no problem for the Theory of Descriptions; its second clause would be analyzed in the usual manner and that analysis seems at least as correct as other central Russellian paraphrases. But as Evans (1977) points out, a parallel treatment fails when the antecedent is a quantifier phrase or an indefinite description:

(11) Just one turtle came down the street. It was running as if it were being pursued by a maniac.
(12) A rabbit appeared in our yard after dinner. It seemed unconcerned.

(11)'s second clause is not equivalent to "Just one turtle was running as if it were being pursued . . . ," because the latter might be false even when (11) is true (our own pet turtle, in the dining room with us, may have been running as well). (12)'s second clause is not equivalent to "A rabbit seemed unconcerned," for that paraphrase misses the fact that the original "It" referred to the particular rabbit that appeared in the yard.

Russell may fairly rejoin that what he offered was a theory of definite descriptions, and neither (11) nor (12) contains a definite description. But if the "It"s in (11) and (12) are not pronouns of laziness, why should we think that "He" in (10) is one? Also, definite descriptions can themselves be anaphors:

(13) Just one turtle came down the street. The turtle was running as if it were being pursued by a maniac.
(14) A rabbit appeared in our yard after dinner. The rabbit seemed unconcerned.

It is plausible enough to take "The turtle" in (13) as abbreviating "The turtle *that came down the street*," in which case (13) does not threaten Russell's analysis. But the same will not do for (14): if we try to suppose that "The rabbit" abbreviates "The rabbit that appeared in our yard after dinner," then by the usual uniqueness clause, (14) would entail that at most one rabbit appeared in the yard, and – notice – (14) itself does not entail that, but (since its opening phrase is only "*A* rabbit") is logically consistent with more than one rabbit's having appeared in the yard. True, a speaker who utters (14) does somehow suggest that there was just one. But notice that it would not be contradictory to utter (14) and then add, "In fact, there were several rabbits, and none of them looked very worried."

Neale (1990) has tried to accommodate anaphora within a conservative Russellian theory; Heim (1990), Kamp and Reyle (1993) and others have argued that a broader semantic format is required. But I shall leave the topic at this point.

Summary

- Russell argued that sentences containing definite descriptions should be analyzed as triples of general statements.
- Russell defended this Theory of Descriptions both directly and by appeal to its affording solutions to the four logical puzzles.
- Strawson argues that Russell views sentences and their logical properties too abstractly and ignores their standard conversational uses by real people in real life.
- In particular, Russell misses the fact that sentences containing non-denoting descriptions are not regarded as false, but lack truth-value altogether due to presupposition failure. Also, Russell ignores context-bound descriptions.

- Donnellan calls attention to the referential use of descriptions, also ignored by Russell, and tries not altogether successfully to distinguish it from the attributive use.
- It is not obvious that Russell's theory can accommodate all the anaphoric uses of descriptions.

Questions

1   Given (for the sake of argument) that the Theory of Descriptions is otherwise plausible, are you convinced by Russell's solutions to the four puzzles?
2   Is Strawson's critique more persuasive than I have granted? Develop it a bit further against Russell.
3   To what extent does the theory correctly predict and explain the entire use of "the" in English?
4   What do you make of Donnellan's distinction? Can it be rendered more precise? Try to refine the intuitive contrast with which Donnellan begins.
5   Dispute or defend any of Donnellan's interesting intuitive judgements about "actual referents" in particular hypothetical speech situations. Then comment on the significance, for Donnellan's program, of your own position on such a case.
6   Donnellan regards his article as a contribution to the Russell–Strawson dispute. But he does not say much in the article about the four puzzles with which that whole issue began. Does his theory, as you construe it, solve any or all of the four puzzles?
7   Can you help Russell extend his theory to cover our examples of anaphora? Are there other anaphoric examples that create further problems for him?

Notes

1   No, sorry, you will have to get that story from Russell's biographies.
2   There was a fifth puzzle as well, which we may call the Problem of Excluded Middle: Neither (1), "The present King of France is bald," nor its apparent negation, "The present King of France is not bald," is true. Yet a law of logic says that, of a sentence and its negation, one must be true. (Russell added that since it seems the King is neither bald nor not bald, "Hegelians, who love a synthesis, will probably conclude that he wears a wig" (1905/1956: 48).) I leave it to you as an exercise to solve this fifth puzzle, after we have seen how Russell solves the other four.

3 He meant "Scottish". (In later twentieth-century usage, Scotch is a type of whisky, indeed the only type which is allowed to be spelled "whisky" as opposed to "whiskey".) But since the example is a famous one of Russell's I shall stick with it as it is.

4 As you should expect, there is a second way of applying the analysis to (4), just as there were two ways of applying it to (2) due to our having a choice as to where to put the "not." The other way is to give the description primary occurrence, or wide scope with respect to "Albert believes that." The Russellian paraphrase would then be: "At least one person authored *Nothing and Beingness*, and at most one person authored *Nothing and Beingness*, and whoever authored *Nothing and Beingness* is believed by Albert to be a profound thinker." On this reading, (4) asserts a relation of belief holding between Albert and our moonlighting author – the person himself, regardless of how he is described – but this reading is exceptionally hard to hear, especially since coreferring descriptions do substitute into it without changing truth-value. The "secondary" understanding of (4) is much more common and natural.

5 G. K. Chesterton bases one of his Father Brown mystery stories, "The Invisible Man," entirely on this phenomenon.

6 Harcourt Brace Jovanovich, 1971, p. 73.

7 Actually Donnellan's characterizations do not perfectly line up with each other. For example, even in the referential case as he intends it we do not always "expect and intend our audience to realize whom we have in mind, and most importantly, to know that it is this person about whom we are going to say something," for I may breathe "Smith's murderer is insane" solely to myself, without expecting or intending anyone to realize anything. "Donnellan's distinction" seems to be a family of related but distinct distinctions; commentators have gone on to try to sort this out (for example, Searle (1979b), Bertolet (1980) and Devitt (1981b)).

8 A determined Russellian might try to explicate the ambiguities along the lines of that of (2) and (4), as depending on whether we apply Russell's analysis inside or outside "because" and "wish" respectively. Try it.

Further reading

Kaplan (1972) is an excellent detailed exposition of the Theory of Descriptions. See also Cartwright (1987) and Neale (1990).

Russell (1957) replied to Strawson's critique.

Linsky (1967) surveys the Russell–Strawson dispute well.

Despite Russell's contempt for it, Meinong's view has been stoutly defended by Routley et al. (1980) and by Parsons (1980).

Donnellan (1968) replied to MacKay. And Donnellan (1979) is a more extended treatment and also takes up questions of anaphora.

Taylor (1998: Chapter II) offers a fuller but still accessible survey of anaphoric phenomena.

Ostertag (1998) contains many important papers on definite descriptions.

3
Proper names: the Description Theory

Overview

Russell's Name Claim

Opening objections

Searle's "Cluster Theory"

Kripke's critique

Summary

Questions

Notes

Further reading

Overview

Russell seems to have refuted the Referential Theory of Meaning for definite descriptions, by showing that descriptions are not genuinely singular terms. Perhaps that is not so surprising, since descriptions are complex expressions in that they have independently meaningful parts. But one might naturally continue to think that ordinary proper names are genuinely singular terms. What is more surprising is that the four puzzles – about nonexistents, negative existentials, and the rest – arise just as insistently for proper names as they did for descriptions.

Russell solved this problem by arguing, fairly persuasively, that ordinary proper names are really disguised definite descriptions. This hypothesis allowed him to solve the four puzzles for proper names by extending his Theory of Descriptions to them.

Yet Russell's claim that proper names are semantically equivalent to descriptions faces serious objections: for example, that it is hard to find a specific description to which a given name is equivalent, and that people for whom the same name expresses different descriptions would be talking past each other when they tried to discuss the same person or thing. John Searle proposed a looser, "cluster" description theory of proper names that avoids the initial objections to Russell's view. But Saul Kripke and others have amassed further objections that apply as much to Searle's looser theory as to Russell's.

Russell's Name Claim

We may have agreed with Russell that the Referential Theory of Meaning is false of descriptions because descriptions are not really (logically) singular terms, but we may continue to hold the Referential Theory for proper names themselves. Surely *names* are just names; they have their meanings simply by designating the particular things they designate, and introducing those designata into discourse. (Let us call such an expression a *Millian* name, since John Stuart Mill (1843) seemed to defend the view that proper names are merely labels for individual persons or objects and contribute no more than those individuals themselves to the meanings of sentences in which they occur.)

But recall our initial objection to Russell's Theory of Descriptions: that although it was motivated entirely by the four puzzles, the puzzles are not at all specific to definite descriptions, because they arise just as insistently for proper names as well. As follows.

Apparent Reference to Nonexistents:

(1) James Moriarty is bald[1]

generates just the same inconsistent set of statements K1–K6 as did "The present King of France is bald."

Negative Existentials:

(2) Pegasus does not exist.

As before, (2) seems to be true and seems to be about Pegasus, but if (2) is true, (2) cannot be about Pegasus. . . . Notice that there is a worse complication here than is raised by the Problem of Apparent Reference to Nonexistents alone: while (1) is meaningful despite the nonexistence of James Moriarty, (2) is not only meaningful despite Pegasus' nonexistence but actually and importantly true.[2]

Frege's Puzzle:

(3) Samuel Langhorne Clemens = Mark Twain

contains two proper names, both of which pick out or denote the same person or thing, and so – if the names are Millian – should be trivially true. Yet (3) seems both informative and contingent. (A fictional example is

"Clark Kent = Superman"; according to Mr Jerry Siegel's comic-book saga, dilettante millionaires spent time and money trying to discover Superman's secret identity.)

Substitutivity:

(4) Albert believes that Samuel Langhorne Clemens had a pretty funny middle name.

But substituting "Mark Twain" for "Samuel Langhorne Clemens" in (4) produces a falsehood; as in the previous chapter, the singular-term position governed by "believes that" is referentially opaque. If the names were Millian, and contributed nothing to meaning besides the introduction of their referents into discourse, the substitution should make no difference at all and the position would be transparent.

So the Theory of Descriptions seems to have bought us very little; its solutions are parochial to just one highly distinctive subclass of singular terms.

Russell's response is both brilliant and strongly defended. He turns around and offers a new thesis, which I will call the "Name Claim." The claim is that everyday proper names *are not really names*, at least not genuine Millian names. They look like names and they sound like names when we say them out loud, but they are not names at the level of logical form, where expressions' logical properties are laid bare. But in fact, Russell maintains, they are equivalent to definite descriptions. Indeed he says they "abbreviate" descriptions, and he seems to mean that fairly literally.

Thus Russell introduces a second semantic appearance–reality distinction; just as definite descriptions are singular terms only in the sense of surface grammar, the same – more surprisingly – is true of ordinary proper names themselves. Here, of course, the difference is more dramatic. If you look at a definite description without Referentialist bias, you can see that it has got some conceptual structure to it, in the form of independently meaningful words occurring in it that seem to contribute to its own overall meaning. So it is not too big a surprise to be told that underlying the misleadingly simple appearance of the word "the," there is quantificational material. But now we are told the same about a kind of expression that looks conceptually simple.

If the Name Claim is true, then Russell's solution to the four puzzles does generalize after all – because we just replace the names by the definite descriptions they express and then proceed as in Chapter 2; the Russellian solutions apply just as before (whether or not we think they are good ones in the first place). Thus names have what Frege thought of as "senses," that can differ despite sameness of referent, but Russell gives an analysis of these rather than taking them as primitive items of some abstract sort.

It is important to see that the Name Claim is entirely independent of the Theory of Descriptions itself. (People often use the phrase "Russell's theory of descriptions" as lumping together a number of different things Russell believed, including the Name Claim.) But one might accept either doctrine while rejecting the other: some theorists hold the Theory of Descriptions as a theory of definite descriptions themselves, while rejecting the Name Claim entirely; less commonly, one could embrace the Name Claim but hold a theory of descriptions different from Russell's.

In support of the Theory of Descriptions, Russell gave a direct argument; then he touted the theory's power in solving puzzles. He makes a similar explanatory case for the Name Claim, in that the claim lends his theory of proper names the same power to solve puzzles – puzzles that looked considerably nastier for names than they did for descriptions. But he also gives at least one direct argument, and a second is easily extracted from his writings.

First, just as Russell argued in the case of definite descriptions, his theory captures the intuitive logic of sentences containing definite descriptions; that is, such a sentence does intuitively entail each of the three clauses that make up his analysis of it and the three clauses jointly entail the sentence. He argues that the same is true of proper names.

Take one of the toughest cases of all, a negative existential. (2) ("Pegasus does not exist") is actually true. What, then, could it mean? It does not pick out an existing thing and assert falsely that the thing is nonexistent; rather, it assures us that in fact there was no such winged horse. Similarly, "Sherlock Holmes never existed" means that there never actually was a legendary English detective who lived at 221B Baker Street and so on. This is surely plausible.

The second direct argument (never given explicitly so far as I know) calls attention to a kind of clarificatory question. Suppose you hear someone using a name, say "Lili Boulanger," and you do not know who the speaker is talking about. You ask who that is. The speaker replies, "Oh, the first woman ever to have won the Prix de Rome, in 1913, with her cantata *Faust et Hélène*"; and that is a proper answer. You asked because, so to speak, you did not understand the name you heard. In order to come to understand it, you had to ask a "who" question, and the answer had to be a description. (Merely giving a second proper name of Boulanger would not have done the trick, unless you had previously associated *that* name with a description.)

Or we could use "who" questions as a kind of testing, which might be called the spot-check test. Suppose you used the name "Wilfrid Sellars," and I whip around and say "Who's that?" All you can reply, all that comes out, is "Um, the famous philosopher at Pittsburgh who wrote those really dense books" or the like. In general, when asked "Who [or what] do you mean?" after one has just used a name, one immediately and instinctively comes up with a description, as an explanation of what one meant.

John Searle (1957) made a similar appeal to learning and teaching: how do you teach a new proper name to a child, and how do you learn the referent of a particular name from someone else? In the first case, you produce one or more descriptions; in the latter, you elicit them.

These are very robust phenomena; so the Name Claim is not just a desperate lunge made in order to solve the proper-name versions of the four puzzles.

Russell speaks aggressively of names' "abbreviating" descriptions, as if they were merely *short for* the descriptions as "the USA" is short for "the United States of America." That seems too strong. All Russell actually needs for his analytical purposes is the weaker contention that names are somehow equivalent in meaning to descriptions (let us call that weaker thesis the "Description Theory" of proper names). Yet even the less ambitious Description Theory has since come in for severe criticism.

Opening objections

Objection 1

Searle (1957) complained that if proper names are equivalent to descriptions, then for each name, there must be some particular description that it is equivalent to. For example, if I unreflectively muse,

(5) Wilfrid Sellars was an honest man,

what am I saying, given that I know a fair number of individuating facts about Sellars? Searle tries out a couple of candidate description types, and finds them wanting. We might suppose that "Wilfrid Sellars" is for me equivalent to "The one and only thing x such that x is F and x is G and . . .," where "F," "G," and the rest are *all* the predicates which I would apply (or believe truly applicable) to the man in question. But this would have the nasty consequence that (5) in my speech *entails*

(6) There is at least one philosopher with whom I had a fairly violent argument in George Pappas' living room in 1979.

– and (5) surely does not entail (6).

Now, the Spot-Check Test ought to supply a more local answer for each use of a name, and as we have seen, it is plausible to think that a speaker can normally cough up a fairly specific description when prodded. But it is unclear that this is always because the description was one the speaker already had determinately in mind. If you ask me, "Who is Sellars?," I might make any of a number of answers that come to mind, depending on what sort of information I think you may want about him. It hardly follows that the answer I do produce is the precise description that my use of "Sellars" antecedently expressed.

Notice: the complaint is not merely that it would be hard to *find out* which description a speaker "had in mind" in uttering some name. It is the stronger thesis that at least in many cases *there is no single determinate description that the speaker "has in mind,"* either consciously or subconsciously. I see little reason (independent of the semantical puzzles) for thinking that there is a fact of the matter as to whether "Wilfrid Sellars" is used as equivalent to "The author of *Philosophy and the Scientific Image of Man*," or "Pittsburgh's most famous philosopher," or "The inventor of the 'Theory' theory of mental terms," or "The man on whose paper I had to comment at the Tenth Chapel Hill Colloquium in 1976," not forgetting "The visiting philosopher with whom I had a fairly violent argument in George Pappas' living room in 1979." I need have had none of these in particular in mind when I unreflectively uttered (5).

Objection 2

Undeniably, different people know different things about other people. In some cases X's knowledge about Z and Y's knowledge about Z may not even overlap. It follows from the Name Claim that the same name will have (many) different senses for different people; every name is multiply and unfathomably ambiguous. For if names are equivalent to definite descriptions, they are equivalent to different definite descriptions in different people's mouths, and for that matter to different descriptions in the same person's mouth at different times, both because one's knowledge keeps fluctuating and because what is psychologically prominent about one person for another keeps fluctuating too.

And things get worse. Suppose that I am thinking of Wilfrid Sellars as "the author of *Philosophy and the Scientific Image of Man*," and suppose you are thinking of Sellars as "Pittsburgh's most famous philosopher." Then we would be curiously unable to disagree about Sellars. If I were to say, "Sellars used to tie his shoes with one hand," and you said "That's ridiculous, Sellars did no such thing," we would (on Russell's view) not be contradicting one another. For the sentence I had uttered would be a generalization:

(7) One and only one person wrote *Philosophy and the Scientific Image of Man*, and whoever wrote *Philosophy and the Scientific Image of Man* used to tie his shoes with one hand,

while yours would be just a different generalization:

(8) One and only one person was a philosopher more famous than any other in Pittsburgh, and whoever was a philosopher more famous than any other in Pittsburgh did no such thing as tie his shoes with one hand.

And the two statements would be entirely compatible from a logical point of view. What looked like a spirited dispute, verging on fistfight, is no real dispute at all; we are merely talking past each another. But that seems quite wrong.

Searle's "Cluster Theory"

In light of these three objections (and several others) to Russell's version of the Description Theory, John Searle offered a looser and more sophisticated variant. He suggested that a name is associated, not with any particular description, but with a vague cluster of descriptions. As he puts it, the force of "This is N," where "N" is replaced by a proper name, is to assert that a sufficient but so far unspecified number of "standard identifying statements" associated with the name are true of the object demonstrated by "this"; that is, the name refers to whatever object satisfies a sufficient but vague and unspecified number (SBVAUN) of the descriptions generally associated with it. (Searle adds the metaphysical claim that *to be* the person N is to have a SBVAUN of the relevant properties.)

The vagueness is important; Searle says it is precisely what distinguishes names from descriptions, and in fact is why we have and use names as opposed to descriptions. Notice that if the Name Claim were correct, then proper names' only function would be to save breath or ink; they would be just shorthand. Searle insists that, rather than being equivalent to a single description, a name functions as a "peg . . . on which to hang descriptions" (p. 172), and that is what enables us to get a linguistic handle on the world in the first place.

We would need to make some refinements. For example, if one is a

Searlean it seems natural to require that a "sufficient number" be at least *over half* – otherwise two obviously distinct individuals could both be the name's referent. Also, we would surely want to say that some of a person's identifying properties are more important than others in determining his or her identity; some way of *weighting* the identifying descriptions is involved.

This Cluster Theory allows Searle to avoid the three objections we have raised for Russell's view. Objection 1 is mooted because Searle has abandoned the commitment that for each name, there must be some one particular description that it expresses. The name is tied semantically just to a loose cluster of descriptions. Objection 2 is blunted (Searle believes) by the fact that different people can have different subclusters of descriptive material in mind, yet each have a SBVAUN of identifying descriptions and thereby succeed in referring to the same individual.[3]

Thus Searle tried to mitigate the opening objections to Russell's theory by offering his looser cluster version of the description approach. This version seems to qualify as a sensible middle way between Russell's view and the Millian conception of names apparently discredited by the four puzzles. But, building on some important ideas of Ruth Barcan Marcus (1960, 1961), Saul Kripke (1972/1980) went on to subject Russell's Name Claim and Searle's Cluster Theory together to a more sustained critique. He argued that Searle had not backed far enough away from Russell, for Searle's view inherits problems of much the same kinds; rather, the whole Descriptivist picture of proper names is misguided. The theory of reference has never been the same.

Kripke's critique

Objection 3

Suppose that "Richard Nixon" is equivalent to "the winner of the 1968 US Presidential election." And now consider a question about possibility. (Questions about possibility and necessity are called *modal* questions; more about these in the next chapter.) Could Richard Nixon have lost the 1968 election? The answer seems *unequivocally* to be "Yes," assuming that "could" here expresses merely theoretical, logical, or metaphysical possibility rather than something about the state of our knowledge. But according to the Description Theory, our question means the same as

(9) Is it possible that: one and only one person won the 1968 election and whoever won the 1968 election lost the 1968 election?

the answer to which is clearly "No."

Searle's Cluster Theory may seem to offer an improvement, because it *is* possible that a person who satisfies a SBVAUN of the description cluster associated with "Richard Nixon" nonetheless does not satisfy the particular description "winner of the 1968 election." But, Kripke points out, human possibility extends further than that: Nixon the individual person might not have done *any* of the things generally associated with him. He might have apprenticed himself at age twelve to a sandal-maker and gone on to make sandals all his life, never going anywhere near politics or public life at all and never once getting his name in any newspaper. Yet, obviously, it is not possible that a person who satisfies a SBVAUN of the description cluster associated with "Richard Nixon" nonetheless does not satisfy any at all of the descriptions in that cluster. On Searle's view, the character who went into sandal-making would not have been the referent of "Richard Nixon" and for that matter would not have been Richard Nixon. And that seems wrong.

Michael Dummett (1973) has protested that Objection 3 is simply invalid as it stands; at least, it rests on a hidden assumption which is false. We may infer that our modal question is synonymous with (9) only by assuming that if "Richard Nixon" is equivalent to a description at all, it is equivalent to one that has narrow scope, in the terminology of Chapter 2 that is, a "secondary" occurrence with respect to "It is possible that." What if the relevant description has wide scope? Then our original question is synonymous, not with (9), but with

(10) One and only one person won the 1968 election, and,
       concerning whoever won the 1968 election, is it possible that
       that person lost?

(10) is clumsy; also, there are other, irrelevant disambiguations of our question due to the fact that the interrogative operator itself has scope, so let me make the point more simply using just the indicative versions of the two readings. The sentence

(11) It is possible for Richard Nixon to have lost the 1968 election,

presuming that "Richard Nixon" is equivalent to "the winner of the 1968 election," is ambiguous as between the narrow-scope reading

Possible: $(\exists x)(Wx \ \& \ (y)(Wy \rightarrow y = x) \ \& \ (z)(Wz \rightarrow {\sim}Wz))$,

which corresponds to (11) and is false (I have represented "lost" as "did not win"), and the wide-scope reading

$$(\exists x)(Wx \ \& \ (y)(Wy \rightarrow y = x) \ \& \ (z)(Wz \rightarrow \text{Possible: } {\sim}Wz))$$

which presumably is true. Colloquially, (11) means that one and only one person won the election and whoever won it is such that s/he could have lost.

Objection 4

Kripke (1972/1980: 83–7) offers an (utterly fictional) example regarding Gödel's Incompleteness Theorem, a famous metamathematical result. In Kripke's fiction, the theorem was proved in the 1920s by a man named Schmidt, who died mysteriously without publishing it. Kurt Gödel came along, appropriated the manuscript, and scurrilously published it under his own name.[4] Now, most people know Gödel, if at all, as the man who proved the Incompleteness Theorem. Yet it seems clear that when even those who know nothing else about Gödel utter the name "Gödel," they do refer to Gödel rather than to the entirely unknown Schmidt. For example, when they say "Gödel proved the Incompleteness Theorem," they are speaking falsely, however well justified they may be in their belief.

This objection too goes against Searle's Cluster Theory as well as against the classical Russellian view. Suppose no one in fact proved the Incompleteness Theorem; Schmidt's alleged proof was irreparably flawed, or perhaps there was not even any Schmidt, but "the proof simply materialized by a random scattering of atoms on a piece of paper" (p. 86). Here it is even more obviously true that most people's uses of "Gödel" refer to Gödel rather than to anyone else at all; yet those uses are not even backed by any Searlean cluster.

Objection 5

Consider the sentence

(12) Some people are unaware that Cicero is Tully.

(12) is ostensibly true, but if the Name Claim is correct, (12) is hard to interpret, for "there is no single proposition denoted by the 'that' clause, that the community of normal English speakers expresses by 'Cicero is Tully'" (Kripke 1981: 245). Since "Cicero" and "Tully" are equivalent to different descriptions for different people, there is no single fact of which (12) says some people are unaware. Now, if *I* assert (12), presumably its complement clause expresses what "Cicero is Tully" means in *my* speech.

But since I know that Cicero is Tully, I associate the same set of descriptions (whatever they might be) with both names. Suppose that, like most philosophers, I associate both "Cicero" and "Tully" with "the famous Roman orator who denounced Catiline and who figures in some famous examples of Quine's." Then (12) is equivalent to:

(13) Some people are unaware that one and only one person was a famous Roman . . . [etc.] and one and only one person was a famous Roman . . . [etc.] and whoever was a famous Roman . . . [etc.] was a famous Roman . . . [etc.].

That massively redundant sentence is equivalent to:

(14) Some people are unaware that one and only one person was a famous Roman orator who denounced Catiline and who figures in some famous examples of Quine's.

No doubt (14) is true, but surely it does not express what (12) *means*, even when (12) is uttered by me.

It is far from obvious how Searle might handle Objection 5, either.

Objection 6

If the Name Claim is true, then every name is "backed" by a description which applies *uniquely* to the name's referent. But most people associate "Cicero" only with "a famous Roman orator" or some other indefinite description, and, say, "Richard Feynman" only with "a leading [then] contemporary theoretical physicist"; yet these people succeed not only in using those names correctly but also in referring to Cicero and to Feynman respectively when they do so. Moreover, two names of the same person, such as "Cicero" and "Tully," may well have the same indefinite description as backing, and when they do, no Russellian theory can explain their continuing failure to substitute in belief contexts (Kripke 1972/1980: 80ff.; Kripke 1979b: 246–7).

More generally, it does not take much to succeed in referring to a person. Keith Donnellan (1970) offers an example in which a child who has gone to bed and to sleep is awakened briefly by his parents. They have with them Tom, an old friend of the family who is visiting and wanted just to see the child. The parents say, "This is our friend Tom." Tom says, "Hello, youngster," and the episode is over; the child has only barely woken. In the morning, the child wakes with a vague memory that Tom is a nice man. But the child has no descriptive material at all associated with the name "Tom"; he may not even remember that Tom was the person that he was semi-awake to meet during the night. Yet, Donnellan argues, that does not prevent him from succeeding in referring to Tom; there is a person who is being said to be a nice man, and it is Tom.

Objection 7

Russell emphatically wanted his theory to apply to *fictional* names such as "Hamlet" and "Sherlock Holmes" and "the free lunch." If the Name Claim is correct, then, any sentence containing a fictional name in a "primary" or wide-scope position will come out false. For example,

(15) Sherlock Holmes lived at 221B Baker Street

will come out false because it is supposed to be equivalent to

(16) One and only one person was [that is, *there exists* exactly one person who was] a famous detective who . . . [etc.] and whoever was a famous detective who . . . [etc.] lived at 221B Baker Street,

and (16) is false (there having existed, in fact, no such person). But some fictional sentences, such as (15) itself and "Hamlet was a Dane," are *true* sentences, or at any rate not false ones.

Russell would not have been much swayed by this argument, since he had no inclination to call it *true*, as opposed to merely "make-believe-true" or "true-in-fiction," that Holmes lives at Baker Street or whatever. (NB: if it were true that Holmes lived in Baker Street, then it would be true of Baker Street, a real place to this day, that it had Holmes living in it. Also, if such sentences were true just in virtue of someone's having written them in popular books or stories, then it would be equally true that Holmes *existed*, Hamlet existed, and so on, since people say those things in books and stories too; this point is strangely overlooked.) Yet some people want to insist that fictional sentences are literally truth-valueless rather than *false*; if you are sympathetic to this, you will want to hold a Kripkean theory of fictional names rather than Russell's (Kripke 1972/1980: 156–8). (Donnellan (1974) defends such a theory in more detail.)

Kripke has a further and in a way more fundamental objection to the Description Theory, but it requires a bit of technical apparatus. That apparatus is one we will be needing again anyway. I shall develop it in the next chapter.

Summary

- The four logical puzzles about reference arise just as insistently for ordinary proper names as they did for definite descriptions.
- In response, Russell extended his Theory of Descriptions by defending the Name Claim.
- But the Name Claim faces at least two powerful objections.
- Searle offers a looser, "cluster" version of the Description Theory of names, which avoids the initial objections.
- But Kripke marshalls a host of further objections that apply to Searle's view as trenchantly as they do to Russell's stricter theory.

Questions

1 Suppose you reject Russell's Name Claim. How might you then solve the four puzzles, in regard to names?

2 Respond on Russell's behalf to one or more of the two opening objections; or come up with a further objection.

3 Does Searle's Cluster Theory really avoid Objections 1 and 2, in ways that Russell's stricter version of Descriptivism did not?

4 Can you think of an objection to Searle's theory that does *not* apply to Russell's original theory?

5 Can Russell rebut any of Kripke's objections 3–7? Even if Russell cannot, can Searle?

Notes

1 Professor James Moriarty is Sherlock Holmes's arch-enemy, described most fully in Conan Doyle's story "The Final Problem" (*The Adventures of Sherlock Holmes*, Vol. I, ed. E. W. Smith, New York: Heritage Press, 1950). A curious fact about Moriarty is that he has a brother, an army colonel, who is also named James. (If you are a Holmes buff and you did not already know that, you will enjoy verifying it yourself.)

2 Meinong (as mentioned in Chapter 2) would have insisted that there is a winged horse, named "Pegasus," and what sentence (2) does is predicate nonexistence of that particular horse. On this view, (2) is just like "Pegasus does not eat alfalfa"; existing is something that you and I do because we got lucky, but that Pegasus does not manage to do, whether or not any of us has any choice in the matter.

   Russell cannot accept that view (even though he had once taken it seriously); surely, (2) means rather just that the myth was only a myth, that there was no such winged horse that was ridden by Bellerophon.

3 This point needs further investigation, to say the least, since on Searle's view, even though two such speakers may succeed in picking out the same individual, the sentences they use will still have different meanings, and for all that has been shown, we may still get the nondisagreement problem.

4 In introducing this example in lecture form at Princeton University in 1970, Kripke interpolated, "I hope Professor Gödel is not present" (p. 83).

Further reading

Russell's Name Claim is defended most accessibly in "The Philosophy of Logical Atomism" (1918/1956).

For some criticisms of the Name Claim similar to Kripke's, see Keith Donnellan (1970).

Searle addresses the matter of fictional names in Chapter 3 of Searle (1979a). He replies to some of Kripke's objections in Chapter 9 of Searle (1983).

Burge (1973), Loar (1976), and others have defended Description theories against Kripke. Burge's view in particular avoids some of the objections.

4
Proper names: Direct Reference and the Causal–Historical Theory

Overview

In a further argument against description theories of proper names, Kripke appealed to the notion of a "possible world" or universe alternative to our own. A definite description of Russell's sort changes its referent from world to world; although "the world's fastest woman in 1998" actually refers to Marion Jones, it designates different individuals in other worlds, since Jones might have been slower (or not even have existed) and other women might have been better runners. But typically, a proper name such as "Marion Jones" refers to the very same individual in every world in which that individual exists.

Some theorists claim that names are "directly" referential, in that a name has no meaning but its bearer or referent, and contributes nothing else to the meaning of a sentence in which it occurs. In light of Kripke's arguments against description theories, this view is highly plausible. But the four puzzles return to haunt it. So we are left with something of a paradox.

A separate question is, in virtue of what does a proper name designate its bearer? Kripke offered a causal–historical picture of referring, according to which a given use of "Marion Jones" refers to Marion Jones in virtue of a causal chain that grounds that utterance-event in the ceremony in which Jones was first given the name. But in light of some examples that clearly do not fit that model, considerable refinement is needed to work up that picture into an adequate theory of referring.

Kripke and Hilary Putnam extended the causal–historical view to cover natural-kind terms, like "water," "gold," and "tiger," as well as proper names. If we assume the basic correctness of that move, it has an unexpected consequence: Putnam's famous "Twin Earth" examples seem to show that the meaning of such a term is not determined solely by what is in the heads of speakers and hearers; the state of the external world makes a contribution as well. Thus, two speakers could be molecule-for-molecule duplicates and yet mean different things by their words.

Possible worlds

I shall now set up the apparatus needed to state Kripke's fundamental criticism of description theories. I begin with the notion of a "possible world." (It goes back at least to Leibniz, though it has been incorporated into philosophical logic only in the twentieth century.) Consider the world we live in – not just the planet Earth, but the whole universe. Our talk about things in our universe is talk about what actually exists, what things there really are: Bill Clinton the US President, my left elbow, Bolivia, etc., but not Hamlet, the Easter Bunny or the free lunch. And what is true in this universe is of course actually true. But there are things that are in fact false, yet might have been true. Things might have gone otherwise; the world could have been different from the way it is. Someone else might have been elected President, I might have married a different person (which would have been a mistake), and I know I could have finished writing this book sooner if I had had a private secretary and a retinue of servants including a personal chef and a couple of hired killers.

Thus there are a number of ways the world might have been. To put it slightly more fancifully, there are *alternative worlds*. Different worlds, worlds which could have been ours, but that are only possible and not actual. Think of an array of possible universes, corresponding to the infinitely many ways in which things, very broadly speaking, might have gone. All these possible worlds represent nonactual global possibilities.

Now (obviously) a sentence's truth – even when we hold the sentence's meaning fixed – depends on which world we are considering. "Clinton is President" is true in the actual world, but since Clinton need not have been President, there are countless worlds in which "Clinton is President" is false: in those worlds, he lost the election or never ran for President or never even existed. And in some other worlds, someone else is President – Bob Dole, W. V. Quine, me, Madonna, or Daffy Duck. In still others, there is no US presidency, or not even a United States at all; and so on and so forth. So a given sentence or proposition varies its truth-value from world to world.

(For now, let us take all this talk of "alternate worlds" intuitively, as a metaphor or picture, a heuristic for seeing what Kripke is getting at. Considered as serious metaphysics, it raises many controversial issues,[1] but we may hope that those issues will not much affect Kripke's use of the possible-worlds picture for his purposes in the philosophy of language.)

Just as sentences change their truth-values from world to world, a given singular term may vary its referent from world to world: in our actual world in 1999, "The present US President" designates Bill Clinton. But as before, Clinton might not have been elected, or even run in the first place, or even existed at all. So in some other worlds the same description, meaning what it does here in our world, designates someone else (Dole, Quine, . . .), or no one at all – since in some other possible worlds, Dole was elected, and in some no one was, etc. This is why the description's referent changes from world to world.

Let us call such a singular term, one that designates different things in different worlds, a *flaccid* designator. It contrasts specifically with what Kripke calls a *rigid* designator: a term that is not flaccid, that does not change its referent from world to world, but denotes the very same item in every world (at least in every world in which that item exists.[2])

Rigidity and proper names

Now we are able to state Kripke's further objection to description theories of proper names (1972/1980: 74ff.): a definite description of the sort Russell had in mind is flaccid, as has just been illustrated. Yet proper names, Kripke says, do not (usually) vary their reference across worlds or hypothetical situations in that way. If we imagine a world in which Aristotle does such-and-such, it is one in which *Aristotle* does that thing and has some different properties from those he has here in the real world. Our name "Aristotle" denotes *him* there, not someone else. Names are (normally) in that sense rigid designators, keeping the same referent from world to world, while Russellian descriptions are flaccid. Thus, names are not equivalent to Russellian descriptions. (Of course, if a description is used referentially in Donnellan's sense, it may go rigid.)

The foregoing parenthesized qualifications ("usually," "normally") are important. Kripke does not hold any strict universal thesis about proper names. He is generalizing about normal uses of ordinary proper names and saying only that for the most part, such names are used rigidly. So he is not to be refuted by coming up with unusual flaccid names, which certainly exist: occasionally, a description is offered as conventionally fixing the meaning and not just identifying the referent of an apparent proper name. "Jack the Ripper" is an example. And in popular writings about Scotland Yard or British detective culture of the 1950s, for example, the name "Chummy" was used as a mere synonym for "the culprit"; it meant, attributively or flaccidly, just "whoever committed the crime." For that matter, probably any proper name has occasional flaccid uses. Frege (1892/1952a) offers a famous example: "Trieste is no Vienna," where "Vienna" functions not as the name of a city, but as abbreviating a loose cluster of exciting cultural properties that Vienna has. In the same tone, on an occasion well remembered by American voters, 1988 Vice-Presidential candidate Lloyd Bentsen told his rival Dan Quayle, "Senator, you're no Jack Kennedy." But those are hardly standard uses of the names "Vienna" and "Jack Kennedy."[3]

Kripke offers a further little intuitive test for telling whether a term is rigid: try the term in the sentence frame, "N might not have been N." If we plug in, for "N," a description like "the President of the US in 1970," we obtain "The President of the US in 1970 might not have been the President of the US in 1970"; and the latter sentence is clearly true, at least on its most natural reading: the person who was President in 1970 might not have been President then (or at any other time). The truth of that sentence shows the description to refer to different people in different worlds, hence to be flaccid.

But if we put in the proper name "Nixon," we get "Nixon might not have been Nixon," at best a very strange sentence. It might mean that Nixon might not have existed at all, which is perhaps the most obvious way in which Nixon could have failed to be Nixon. But given that Nixon existed, how could he have failed to be Nixon? He could have failed to be *named* "Nixon," but that is not to have failed to *be Nixon*, himself (because, of course, Nixon need not have been named "Nixon"). He could have failed to have the properties stereotypically associated with Nixon, hence failed to "be Nixon" in the sense that Trieste fails to "be Vienna," but as we saw in the previous chapter such flaccid uses of names are unusual.

Kripke argues that when one uses the name "Nixon" to refer a person in this world and then starts describing hypothetical scenarios or alternative possible worlds, continuing to use the name, one is talking about the same person. So if you ask, "Might Nixon have joined the Black Panthers rather than becoming President?," the answer may be yes or may be no, but the scenario you are considering is one in which Nixon, that very person, is a Black Panther – not one in which whoever or whatever was US President was a Panther. You are not imagining a world in which a Black Panther is President of the US.

But what of Russell's Spot-Check argument? In response to "Whom do you mean by 'Lili Boulanger'/'Wilfrid Sellars'?" you promptly cough up a description or cluster of descriptions. Likewise Searle's appeal to teaching and learning: they also proceed by equating the name in question with a description or cluster. These facts seem undeniable and insuperable.

In response, Kripke introduced an important distinction. Russell and Searle had both assumed that if a name has a description or cluster associated with it in the ways they have respectively pointed out, then the name must share the meaning of that descriptive material (from now on I shall say just "description" for short). But this assumption is unwarranted, because there is a weaker relation that the description might bear to the name and still explain the Spot-Check and pedagogical data: even though the description does not give the linguistic meaning of the name, it is what is used to determine the name's reference on an occasion. Although the name "Lili Boulanger" is not synonymous with "the first woman ever to win the Prix de Rome," the latter description can be used to indicate the person one is referring to when one uses "Lili Boulanger." And it can be used as part of an explanation to a pupil, to identify the individual to which the name is attached.

Thus, even if a name in someone's mouth at a time has a firm psychological association with a particular description in that person's mind, it does not follow that the name is equivalent to the description in meaning. For all that has been shown, when the person obligingly coughs up the description in response to a spot check, the person is merely identifying the name's referent. Similarly, if I tell a small child who "Bill Clinton" is, identifying that name's referent by saying "Bill Clinton is the President of the United States," it does not follow that the name "Bill Clinton" simply means "the President of the United States." (Of course, this is not an argument against the Name Claim itself; it only undermines Russell's use of the Spot-Check Test as an argument for the Name Claim.)

Direct Reference

Russell used the four puzzles and (implicitly) his Spot-Check argument to attack the view that ordinary proper names are Millian names, in favor of the Description Theory. In turn, Kripke attacked the Description Theory in favor of the claim that ordinary proper names are rigid designators. But the latter claim does not quite amount to Millianism, for not all rigid designators are Millian names.

A Millian name, remember, is one that has no meaning but its bearer or referent. Its sole function is to introduce that individual into discourse; it contributes nothing else to the meaning of a sentence in which it occurs. If we say "Jason is fat," and "Jason" is a standard proper name, then the meaning of that sentence consists simply of the person Jason himself concatenated with the property of being fat.

Being Millian certainly implies being rigid. But the reverse does not hold. Although Kripke cites Mill and argues that names are rigid, rigidity does not imply being Millian. For definite descriptions can be rigid. Suppose we fall in with the prevalent view that *arithmetical* truths are all necessary truths. Then there are arithmetical descriptions, such as "the positive square root of nine," that are rigid, because they designate the same number in every possible world, but are certainly not Millian because in order to secure their reference they exploit their conceptual content. Indeed, they seem to Russellize: "The positive square root of nine" seems to mean whatever positive number yields nine when multiplied by itself. So that description is not Millian even though it is rigid, because it does not simply introduce its bearer (the number three) into the discourse; it also characterizes three as being something which when multiplied by itself yields nine. Thus, in defending the rigidity of names, Kripke did not thereby establish the stronger claim. (Nor did he intend to; he does not believe that names are Millian.)[4]

However, other philosophers have championed the Millian conception, which has come to be called the "Direct Reference" theory of names. The first of these in our century was Ruth Marcus (1960, 1961), cited by Kripke as having directly inspired his work. Subsequent Direct Reference (DR) theories of names have been built on Marcus' and Kripke's work (for example, Kaplan (1975) and Salmon (1986)).

The latter theorists have extended DR to cover some other singular terms, notably personal and demonstrative pronouns such as "I," "you," "she," "this," "that," as well as names. (An obvious problem about extending DR to pronouns is that any normal speaker of English knows what they mean, whether or not the speaker knows whom they are being used to designate on a given occasion; if you find "I am ill and will not hold class today" written on the blackboard in an empty classroom, you understand the sentence even if you do not know who wrote it or on what day. This problem will be addressed in Chapter 11.)

Of course, DR must confront the four puzzles, which are generated just as surely by names as they are by descriptions. And, obviously, the DR theorist cannot subscribe to Russell's solution or anything very like it, for according to DR, names do nothing semantically but stand for their bearers.

Let us reconsider the Substitutivity puzzle first. Recall our sentence:

(1) Albert believes that Samuel Langhorne Clemens has a pretty
    funny middle name.

(1) goes false when "Mark Twain" is substituted for "Samuel Langhorne Clemens." How can DR explain or even tolerate that fact?

DR theorists employ a two-pronged strategy. There is a positive thesis and there is a negative thesis (though these are not often explicitly distinguished). The positive DR thesis is that the names in question really do substitute without altering the containing sentence's truth-value. On this view,

(2) Albert believes that Mark Twain has a pretty funny middle name

is true, not false. At the very least, belief sentences have transparent readings or understandings, on which readings the names that fall within the scope of "believes" really do just refer to what they refer to.

We naturally think otherwise; (2) does not seem true to us. That is because when we see a belief sentence, we usually take its complement clause to reproduce the ways in which its subject would speak or think. If I assert (2), I thereby somehow imply that Albert would accept the *sentence* "Mark Twain has a pretty funny middle name" or something fairly close to it. If I say, "Albert doesn't believe that Mark Twain has a pretty funny middle name," I am suggesting that if faced with the sentence "Mark Twain has a pretty funny middle name," Albert would say either "No" or "I wouldn't know."

But the DR theorists point out that such suggestions are not always true, perhaps not ever true. Consider:

(3) Columbus reckoned that Castro's island was only a few miles from India.

We all know what one would mean in asserting (3); the speaker would mean that when Columbus sighted Cuba he thought that he was already in the East Indies and was approaching India proper. Of course, being 450 years early, Columbus did not know anything about Fidel Castro; yet we can assert (3) with no presumption that its complement clause represents things in the way that Columbus himself represented them. *The speaker* makes this reference to Cuba without at all assuming that Columbus would have referred to Cuba in that way or in any parallel or analogous way. Or suppose you and I are among the few people who know that our acquaintance Jacques is in fact the notorious jewel thief who has been terrorizing Paris' wealthy set, called "Le Chat" in the popular press and by the gendarmes. We read in the newspaper after a particularly daring but flawed robbery that police believe "Le Chat dropped the fistful of anchovies as he or she ran." We say to each other, "The police think Jacques dropped the anchovies as he ran."

So it seems undeniable that there are transparent positions inside belief sentences, in which the referring expression does just refer to its bearer, without any further suggestion about the way in which the subject of the belief sentence would have represented the bearer. Singular terms can be and are often understood transparently. We might even say:

(4) Some people doubt that Tully is Tully,

meaning that some people have doubted of the man Cicero that he was also Tully. That would perhaps be a minority interpretation of (4), but we *can* at least hear (4) as asserting that the people doubt of Cicero that he was Tully.[5]

Virtually all the DR literature has been devoted to establishing the positive thesis, that names do have Millian readings even in belief contexts. But the positive thesis is far from all that the DR theorist needs. For although we may be persuaded that every belief sentence does have a transparent reading, most of us also remain convinced that every belief sentence also has an opaque reading, that on which some substitutions turn truths into falsehoods: *in one sense* Columbus believed that Castro's island was just a few miles east of India, but in another, he believed no such thing, for the obvious reason that he had never heard (and would never hear) of Castro. Similarly, in one sense the police believe that Jacques dropped the anchovies, but in another they do not, and likewise for people doubting "that Tully is Tully." Yet it seems DR cannot allow *so much as* a sense in which belief contexts are opaque. That is DR's negative thesis: that names do not have non-Millian readings, even in belief contexts.

The problem gets worse: it is hard to deny that the opaque readings are more readily heard than the transparent readings. Indeed, that is implicitly conceded by the DR theorists, in that they know they have had to work to make us hear the transparent readings. The DR theorists must try to explain the fact away as a particularly dramatic illusion. That is, they must hold that in fact, sentences like (1)–(4) cannot literally mean what we can and usually would take them to mean; there is some extraneous reason why we are seduced into hearing such sentences opaquely. A few such putative explanations have been sketched, using materials we shall encounter in Chapter 13 (Salmon 1986, Soames 1987, Wettstein 1991, and see Marcus 1981). But here, in my opinion, the DR theorists have come up short; at least, none of the sketches produced to date has struck me as either plausible or promising.

As is implied by example (4), Frege's Puzzle is even worse for the Millian. According to DR, a sentence like "Samuel Langhorne Clemens = Mark Twain" can mean only that the common referent, however designated, is himself. Yet such a sentence is virtually never understood as meaning that. And anyone might doubt that Clemens is Twain, seemingly without doubting anyone's self-identity. Here again, the DR theorist bears a massive burden, of explaining away our intuitive judgements as illusory.

The Problems of Apparent Reference to Nonexistents and Negative Existentials are if anything worse yet. If a name's meaning is simply to refer to its bearer, then what about all those perfectly meaningful names that have no bearers?

We have come to a deep dilemma, nearly a paradox. On the one hand, in Chapter 3 we saw compelling Kripkean reasons why names cannot be thought to abbreviate flaccid descriptions, or otherwise to have substantive senses or connotations. Intuitively, names are Millian. Yet because the original puzzles are still bristling as insistently as ever, it also seems that DR is pretty well refuted. This is a dilemma, or rather trilemma, because it has further seemed that we are stuck with one of those three possibilities: either the names are Millian, or they abbreviate descriptions outright, or in some looser way such as Searle's they have some substantive "sense" or content. But none of these views is acceptable.

A few theorists have claimed to find ways between the three horns. Plantinga (1978) and Ackerman (1979) have appealed to rigidified descriptions (see note 3). Devitt (1989, 1996) has offered a radical revision of Frege's notion of sense. I myself (Lycan 1994) have offered a much subtler, more beautiful and more effective weakened version of DR, but it would be immodest of me to tout it here.[6]

We must now make a crucial distinction. So far in this chapter we have been talking about the *semantics of proper names*, that is, about theories of what names contribute to the meanings of sentences in which they occur. DR in particular takes for granted the idea of a name's referent or bearer. But then a separate question is, in virtue of what *is* a thing the referent or bearer of a particular name? Semantics leaves that question to philosophical analysis. A *philosophical theory of referring* is a hypothesis as to what relation it is exactly that ties a name to its referent – more specifically, an answer to the question of what it takes for there to be a referential link between one's utterance of a name and the individual that gets referred to by that utterance.

Semantical theories of names and philosophical accounts of referring vary independently of each other. The difference was blurred by Russell and by Searle,[7] because each gave a very similar answer to both questions. Russell said that a name gets its meaning, and contributes to overall sentence meaning, by abbreviating a description; *also*, what makes a thing the bearer of the name is that the thing uniquely satisfies the description. Likewise for Searle and his clusters. But now notice that if one is a DR theorist, that alone tells us nothing about what attaches a name to its referent. The same goes for Kripke's weaker rigidity thesis; up till now, he has been talking semantics only, and we have seen nothing of his theory of referring. To that we now turn.

The Causal–Historical Theory

As you can verify for yourself, most of Kripke's objections to the Name Claim and to description semantics generally will also translate into objections to the Description Theory of referring; the Description Theory will predict the wrong referent (think of the Gödel/Schmidt example in Objection 5, Chapter 3) or no referent at all (as when there is no particular description the speaker has in mind (Objection 1) or in indefinite cases, as in Objection 6).

Kripke sketches a better idea. He begins memorably (1972/1980: 91): "Someone, let's say, a baby, is born. . . ." (I think we should grant Kripke's assumption that the neonate is a baby. There is such a thing as being too picky.) He continues:

> [The baby's] parents call him by a certain name. They talk about him to their friends. Other people meet him. Through various sorts of talk the name is spread from link to link as if by a chain. A speaker who is on the far end of this chain, who has heard about, say Richard Feynman, in the market place or elsewhere, may be referring to Richard Feynman even though he can't remember from whom he first heard of Feynman or from whom he ever heard of Feynman. He knows that Feynman was a famous physicist. A certain passage of communication reaching ultimately to the man himself does reach the speaker. He then is referring to Feynman even though he can't identify him uniquely.

The idea, then, is that my utterance of "Feynman" is the most recent link in a causal–historical chain of reference-borrowings, whose first link is the event of the infant Feynman's being given that name. I got the name from somebody who got it from somebody else who got it from somebody else who got it from somebody else . . ., all the way back to the naming ceremony. I do not have to be in any particular cognitive state of Russell's or Searle's sort. Nor need I have any interesting true belief about Feynman, or as to how I acquired the name. All that is required is that a chain of communication in fact has been established by virtue of my membership in a speech community that has passed the name on from person to person, which chain goes back to Feynman himself.

Of course, when a new user first learns a name from a predecessor in the historical chain, it can only be by the newbie's and the predecessor's sharing a psychologically salient backing of identifying descriptions. But as before, there is no reason to assume that that particular backing of descriptions fixes the name's sense. It is needed only to fix reference. So long as the newbie has a correct identificatory fix on the predecessor's referent, the newbie can then freely use the name to refer to that person.

Taken at face value, this causal–historical view makes the right predictions about examples such as Donnellan's Tom. In each example, referring succeeds because the speaker is causally connected to the referent in an appropriate historical way.

Kripke (1972/1980: 66–7) offers the further case of the biblical character Jonah. It is similar to the "Nixon" example (Objection 3 in Chapter 3). Kripke points out that we should distinguish between stories that are complete legends and stories that are, rather, substantially false accounts of real people. Suppose historical scholars discover that in fact no prophet was ever swallowed by a big fish, or did anything else attributed by the Bible to Jonah. The question remains of whether the Jonah character was simply made up in the first place, or whether the story is grounded ultimately in a real person. Actually there are subcases: someone could have made up and spread a host of false stories about Jonah immediately after his death; or because Jonah was an exciting individual, all sorts of rumors and stories began to circulate about him, and the rumors got out of hand; or there might have been a very gradual loss of correct information and accretion of false attributions over the centuries. But in either of these cases, it seems that today the Bible is saying false things about the real person, Jonah.[8]

It might be thought that *ambiguous* names – names borne by more than one person – pose a problem for the causal–historical view. ("John Brown" is ambiguous as between the former Scots ghillie who befriended Queen Victoria after Albert's death, the monomaniacal failed farmer who invaded Harper's Ferry in 1859, and doubtless thousands of other males of the English-speaking world. Until 1994, even the highly distinctive name "William Lycan" applied to more than one person. I suppose the vast majority of names are ambiguous; a name is unambiguous only by historical accident.) This is no problem at all for description theories, because according to description theories, ambiguous names simply abbreviate different descriptions. (If anything, description theories make proper names *too richly* ambiguous.) But what if you endorse DR, and you deny that names have senses or descriptive connotations in any sense at all?

I asked that last question only to see if you had been paying attention earlier. It flagrantly ignores the important distinction between the semantics of names and the theory of referring. The Causal–Historical Theory of referring has a straightforward answer to the question of ambiguous names: if a name is ambiguous, that is because more than one person has been given it. What *dis*ambiguates a particular use of such a name on a given occasion is – what else? – that use's causal–historical grounding, specifically the particular bearer whose naming ceremony initiated its etiology.

Kripke emphasizes that he has only sketched a picture; he does not have a worked-out theory. The trick will be to see how one can take that picture and make it into a real theory that resists serious objections. The only way to make a picture into a theory is to take it overliterally, to treat it as if it were a theory and see how it needs to be refined. Kripke does just that, though he leaves the refinement to others.

Problems for the
Causal–Historical Theory

The causal–historical view's key notion is that of the passing on of reference from one person to another. But not just any such transfer will do. First, we must rule out the "naming after" phenomenon. My boyhood friend John Lewis acquired a sheepdog, and named it "Napoleon" after the emperor; he had the historical Napoleon explicitly in mind and wanted to name his dog after that famous person. "Naming after" is a link in a causal–historical chain: it is only because the emperor was named "Napoleon" that John Lewis named his dog that. But it is the wrong kind of link. To rule it out, Kripke requires that "[w]hen the name is 'passed from link to link', the receiver of the name must . . . intend when he learns it to use it with the same reference as the man from whom he heard it" (p. 96). This requirement was clearly not met by John Lewis, who was deliberately changing the referent from the emperor to the dog and meant his friends to be well aware of that.

Second, Kripke adduces the example of "Santa Claus." There may be a causal chain tracing our use of that name back to a certain historical saint, probably a real person who lived in eastern Europe centuries ago, but no one would say that when children use it they unwittingly refer to that saint; clearly they refer to the fictional Christmas character. But then, how does "Santa Claus" differ from "Jonah"? Why should we not say that there was a real Santa Claus, but that all the mythology about him is garishly false? Instead, of course, we say that there is no Santa Claus (apologies to anyone who did not know that). We use the name "Santa Claus" as though it abbreviates a description. A similar example would be that of "Dracula." It is well known that the contemporary use of that name goes back to a real Transylvanian nobleman called "Vlad" (commonly, "Vlad the Impaler," in virtue of his customary treatment of people who had annoyed him). But of course when we now say "Dracula" we mean the vampire created by Bram Stoker and portrayed by Bela Lugosi in the famous movie.

Having merely raised the problem, Kripke does not try to patch his account in response, but moves on. Probably the most obvious feature to note is that "Santa Claus" and "Dracula" as we use those names are associated with very powerful stereotypes, indeed cultural icons in the United States. Their social roles are so prominent they they really have ossified into fictional descriptions, in a way that "Jonah" has not even among religious people. In a way, Jonah's iconic properties are side by side with his historical properties in the Old Testament, but as we might say, "Santa Claus" and "Dracula" are pure icons. And for the average American, the myth utterly dwarfs the historical source.

As Kripke says, much work is needed. Devitt (1981a) offers a fairly well developed view that does qualify as a theory rather than only a picture.

However, here are a few objections that would apply to any version of the Causal–Historical Theory as described above.

Objection 1

We have been offered the notion of a causal–historical chain leading back in time from our present uses of the name to a ceremony in which an actual individual is named. But how, then, can the Causal–Historical Theorist accommodate empty names, names that have no actual bearers?

Perhaps the best bet here is to exploit the fact that even empty names are introduced to the linguistic community at particular points in time, either through deliberate fiction or through error of one kind or another. From such an introduction, as Devitt (1981a) and Donnellan (1974) point out, causal–historical chains begin spreading into the future just as if the name had been bestowed on an actual individual. So reference or "reference" to nonexistents is by causal–historical chain, but the chain's first link is the naming event itself rather than any putative doings of the nonexistent bearer.[9]

Objection 2

Evans (1973) points out that names can change their reference unbeknownst, through mishap or error, but the Causal–Historical Theory as presented so far cannot allow for that. According to Evans,[10] the name "Madagascar" originally named, not the great African island, but a portion of the mainland; the change was ultimately due to a misunderstanding of Marco Polo's. Or:

> Two babies are born, and their mothers bestow names upon them. A nurse inadvertently switches them and the error is never discovered. It will henceforth undeniably be the case that the man universally known as "Jack" is so called because a woman dubbed some other baby with the name. (p. 196)

We do not want to be forced to say that our use of "Madagascar" still designates part of the mainland, or that "Jack" continues to refer to the other former baby rather than to the man everyone calls "Jack."

In reply, Devitt (1981a: 150) suggests a move to *multiple grounding*. A naming ceremony, he says, is only one kind of occasion that can ground an appropriate historical chain; other perceptual encounters can serve also. Instead of there being just the single linear causal chain that goes back from one's utterance to the original naming ceremony, the structure is mangrove-like: the utterance proceeds also out of further historical chains that are grounded in later stages of the bearer itself. Once our use of "Madagascar" has a large preponderance of its groundings in the island rather than the mainland region, it thereby comes to designate the island; once our use of "Jack" is heavily grounded in many people's perceptual encounters with the man called that, those groundings will overmaster the chain that began with the naming ceremony. This is vague, of course, perhaps objectionably so.

Objection 3

We can misidentify the object of a naming ceremony. Suppose I am seeking a new pet from the Animal Shelter. I have visited the Shelter several times and noticed an appealing grey tabby; I decide to adopt her. On my next visit I prepare to name her. The attendant brings out a tabby of similar appearance and I believe her to be the same one I intend to adopt. I say, "Here we are again, then, puddy-tat; your name is now 'Liz', after the composer Elizabeth Poston, and I'll see you again after you've had all your shots" (tactfully I do not mention the mandatory neutering). The attendant takes the cat away again. But unbeknownst to me it was the wrong cat, not my intended pet. The attendant notices the mistake, without telling me, recovers the right cat, and gives her her shots (etc.). I pick her up and take her home, naturally calling her "Liz" ever thereafter.

The problem is of course that my cat was not given that name in any ceremony. The imposter was given it, even if I had no right to name her. Yet surely my own cat is the bearer of "Liz," not just after subsequent multiple groundings have been established, but even just after the naming ceremony I did perform. (It would be different if I had taken the imposter home and continued to call *her* "Liz.") The multiple-grounding strategy does not seem to help here. Rather, what matters is which cat I *had in mind* and believed I was naming in the ceremony. (Devitt (1981a: section 5.1) speaks of "abilities to designate," construing these as mental states of a certain sophisticated type.) If so, then repair of the Causal–Historical Theory on this point will require a significant foray into the philosophy of mind.

Objection 4

People can be *categorially* mistaken in their beliefs about referents. Evans cites E. K. Chambers' *Arthur of Britain*[11] as asserting that King Arthur had a son Anir "whom legend has perhaps confused with his burial place." A speaker in the grip of the latter confusion might say "Anir must be a green and lovely spot"; the Causal–Historical Theory would interpret that sentence as saying that a human being (Arthur's son) was a green and lovely spot. Less dramatically, one might mistake a person for an institution or vice versa. (A former colleague of mine used to use the name of Emerson Hall – the building that houses the Harvard philosophy department – as a way of referring to the department, as in "Emerson Hall isn't going to like this." A casual hearer might easily have gotten the idea that "Emerson Hall" names a person.) Or one might mistake a shadow for a live human being and give it a name. In none of these cases is it plausible to say that subsequent uses of the name in question really refer to the categorially erroneous item.

Devitt and Sterelny (1987) call this the "*qua*-problem." They concede that the celebrant at a naming ceremony, or other person responsible for any of a name's groundings, must not be categorially mistaken and must indeed intend to refer to something of the appropriate category. This is a mild concession to Descriptivism.

There are more objections (some of them further ones of Evans'). The majority position seems to be that Kripke initially overreacted to the Descriptivist picture. He was right to insist that causal–historical chains of some kind are required for referring and that descriptions do not do nearly as much work as Russell or even Searle thought they did; but (as critics, including Kripke himself, maintain) there still are some descriptive conditions as well. The trick is to move back in the direction of Descriptivism without going so far as even Searle's weak Descriptivist doctrine. But that does not leave much room in which to maneuver.

Natural-kind terms and "Twin Earth"

Kripke and Hilary Putnam (1975) went on to extend both the semantic theory of rigid designation and the Causal–Historical Theory of referring from singular terms to some predicates or general terms, chiefly *natural-kind terms*, common nouns of the sort that refer to natural substances or organisms, like "gold," "water," "molybdenum," "tiger," and "aardvark." Such expressions are not singular terms, since they do not purport to apply to just one thing. But Kripke and Putnam argued that they are more like names than they are like adjectives. Semantically they are rigid; each refers to the same natural kind every world in which that kind has membership. And some version of the Causal–Historical Theory characterizes their referring use.

This view sharply opposed a long-held Descriptivist theory of natural-kind terms, which associated each such term with a descriptive stereotype. For example, "water" would have been analyzed as meaning something like "a clear, odorless, tasteless potable liquid that falls from the sky as rain and fills lakes and streams," and "tiger" as something like "a ferocious, carnivorous jungle feline, tawny with distinctive black stripes." Kripke and Putnam urged modal arguments against such analyses, similar to Objection 3 from the previous chapter and to the rigidity argument that began this one. For example, there could have been water even if there had never been rain, lakes or streams, and under different circumstances water might have had an odor or a taste. Tigers might have been born tame, and we might even find out that no tiger has ever in fact had stripes (a worldwide Wonderland-style conspiracy might have had all the stripes painted on).

What does make something a tiger, then, or a sample of water, if not the commonsense stereotype? Kripke and Putnam adverted to the scientific natures of natural kinds. What makes water water is its chemical composition, that it is H_2O; what makes tigers tigers is their distinctive genetic code. In every possible world, water is H_2O, but in some worlds H_2O has an odor or a taste.

It may be objected that the chemical composition of water and the genetic characteristics of tigers were highly substantive empirical discoveries; so surely it was possible that water not be H_2O, and so there are worlds at which water is not H_2O. But Kripke and Putnam rejoined that the alleged "possibility" here is only a matter of scientific ignorance, not a genuine metaphysical possibility; once one does discover the scientific essence of a natural kind, one has discovered the true metaphysical nature of that kind, and the kind has that nature in every possible world in which it is manifested. What change from world to world are the elements of the commonsense stereotype.

If this view is correct,[12] it has a somewhat startling implication about the relation between linguistic meaning and the mind: as Putnam puts it, that meaning "ain't in the head." Putnam imagines that somewhere in another galaxy there is a planet, called "Twin Earth," which is a nearly exact duplicate of our Earth, running along exactly in parallel with our own history. It contains a Twin Putnam, a Twin Brooklyn Bridge, a Twin Lycan and a Twin you, all molecular duplicates of their counterparts here. If one were able to watch both planets simulaneously, it would be like watching the same television program on two different screens. (But it is important to note that Twin Earth is not a different possible world; it is only another planet, within the same world as Earth. Though exactly like Putnam to look at and embedded in an almost exactly similar planetary context, Twin Putnam is a numerically different person.)

I said that Twin Earth is a *nearly* exact duplicate of Earth. There is one difference: what looks and behaves like water on Twin Earth is not water – that is, H_2O – but a different substance that Putnam calls XYZ. XYZ is odorless and tasteless and has the other superficial properties that water does, but it is only "fool's water" (as in "fool's gold"). Of course, the Twin-English-speaking Twin-Earthlings call the XYZ "water," since they are otherwise just like us,[13] but that is an equivocation; "water" in Twin-English means XYZ, not water, just as (I am told) the kind term "chicory" in British English means a different plant from the one meant by the same word in American English.

Now, consider a pair of transworld twins, say Tony Blair and Twin Tony. After a natural disaster, Blair emphasizes the urgency of getting food and water to the victims. Naturally, at the same time Twin Tony emphasizes the urgency of getting food and "water" to the victims. But the word-for-word-identical sentences they utter mean different things. Blair's means that the victims must be provided with food and H_2O, while Twin Tony's means that the victims must be provided with food and XYZ.

Yet Blair and Twin Tony are physical duplicates. Given Putnam's background assumptions, this shows that the meanings of Blair's and Twin Tony's utterances are not determined by the total states of their brains, or even by the total states of their bodies. For their brain states and bodily states are identical, yet their utterance meanings differ.

That is perhaps no big surprise. After all, language is public property; any given language is used by a community, for communication between different people, not often for the mere articulation of someone's private thoughts. But in fact (again given the background assumptions), Putnam's example shows more: that the linguistic meanings of sentences are not determined even by the *totality* of speakers' brain states and bodily states, indeed even by the entire community's pattern of usage. For English speakers and Twin-English speakers are all exactly alike in their physical composition and in the public deployment of words that sound just the same; yet the sentences of their otherwise identical languages mean different things. We shall return to this point in Chapter 6.

Now it is time to branch out and take up the whole matter of meaning and theories of meaning.

Summary

- Kripke argued that proper names normally function as rigid designators, that a name denotes the same individual in every possible world in which that individual exists.
- Taking a more ambitious line, the DR theorists defend the Millian view that a name's sole contribution to the meaning of a sentence in which it occurs is to introduce its bearer into the discourse.
- But our four logical puzzles about reference still arise just as insistently as before, and seem to make DR untenable. We are left with something of a paradox.
- Turning to the theory of referring, Kripke offered his causal–historical picture as a replacement for Description Theories. Michael Devitt and others have refined and ramified the causal–historical view in response to initial objections.
- Kripke and Putnam extended the Causal–Historical Theory to cover natural-kind terms.
- If the Causal–Historical Theory is correct, then Putnam's "Twin Earth" examples seem to show that the meanings of a speech community's words are not entirely determined by the contents of speakers' and hearers' heads; the external world makes a contribution also.

Questions

1   Some philosophers are uneasy about Kripke's notion of a "rigid desig-
    nator" and his ancillary distinction between "fixing sense." If you too
    are uneasy about "rigidity," can you articulate the problem?
2   Do fictional names pose a special problem for Kripke's rigidity thesis?
    How might he treat fictional names?
3   Now that Kripke has rejected the Name Claim, how might he address
    one or more of the four puzzles?
4   Can you help DR address one or more of the four puzzles (a harder
    task)?
5   Can you respond more fully on behalf of the Causal–Historical Theory
    to Objections 1–4?
6   Offer your own criticisms of the causal–historical picture.
7   Assess the Kripke–Putnam view that natural-kind terms rigidly
    designate scientifically characterized kinds.
8   Are you persuaded by Putnam's "Twin Earth" examples that
    meanings "ain't in the head"?

Notes

1   See Lewis (1986) and Lycan (1994).
2   This is an important qualification. If a term designated the same item in every possible
    world there is, that would mean that the item existed in every possible world, and that
    in turn would mean that the item could not but have existed. No ordinary thing or
    person has that kind of inevitability. Though you and I and the Brooklyn Bridge do
    really exist, we might not have, and so there are worlds in which we do not exist. What
    sort of item exists in every possible world? God, perhaps. Kripke is inclined to think that
    the numbers – at least the natural numbers starting 0, 1, 2, . . . – exist in every possible
    world. If so, then the numerals that refer to them presumably do designate the same
    things in every possible world, period. But that is hardly the normal case.
3   For further examples of names used flaccidly, see Boër (1978).
4   In Kripke (1979b) he comes back and he uses a variation on the Substitutivity puzzle
    about referring expressions to refute the Millian view. His argument there also *seems*
    to embarrass his own rigidity thesis, but he does not offer any alternate positive
    view.
        Kaplan (1975) fashions a made-up word "dthat" (pronounced "that"), which takes an
    ordinary description like "the man in the corner" and makes it denote its satisfier
    rigidly rather than flaccidly or attributively. Thus, "dthat man in the corner" refers to a
    given possible world, not to whatever man is in the corner in that world, but to the same
    man who is in the corner in this world. If I use "dthat man in the corner," you should
    understand it as talking simply about that person, and my having put in the conceptual
    content, alluding to manhood and in-the-cornerness, is just a way of calling your atten-
    tion to that man, as if I were fixing the reference of my own description without fixing

its sense. So "dthat" functions as a rigidifier. Plantinga (1978) and Ackerman (1979) enlist Kaplan's idea in defending positive theories according to which proper names are rigid but not Millian.

5 Of course, if "Tully" is also a Millian name, that would amount to doubting that the person referred to is that very person. But this too is a possible understanding of (3).

Incidentally, the point about transparent readings can also be made regarding pronouns. Addressing Jacques himself, we could say "The police think you dropped the anchovies as you ran" (Sosa 1970; Schiffer 1979).

6 Even the paperback edition of Lycan (1994) is expensive, I am afraid, but well worth every penny.

7 And insufficiently emphasized by Kripke. It was first really prosecuted by Devitt (1989).

8 Kripke cites H. L. Ginsberg, *The Five Megilloth and Jonah* (Jewish Publication Society of America, 1969), as seriously defending this view. Notice as well that Jonah's name could not have been "Jonah"; there is no "j" sound in Hebrew.

David Kaplan once maintained (in a 1971 lecture) that there is at least one real-world example of this type that favors the Causal–Historical Theory over Searle's account of referring: the name "Robin Hood." It seems historians had discovered that there really was a person who (causally) gave rise to the Robin Hood legend. It turns out, though, that that person was not poor, he lived nowhere near Sherwood Forest, he was not an outlaw (in fact, he and the Sheriff of Nottingham were fairly close), and his name was not even "Robin Hood." On the causal–historical account, this makes perfect sense.

9 This move would also help with two similar problems: the names of future individuals ("Let's try to have a baby, and if we succeed its name will be 'Kim'"); and the names of abstract objects, such as individual numbers, which have no causal powers.

10 He cites Isaac Taylor's 1898 book, *Names and Their History: A Handbook of Historical Geography and Topographical Nomenclature* (Detroit, MI: Gale Research Co., 1969).

11 London: Sidgwick & Jackson, 1927.

12 It is contested by Searle (1983) and questioned by Rosenberg (1994).

13 The alert reader will have noticed an infelicity in Putnam's example: since a very high proportion of the human body is constituted by water, the Twin-Earthlings can hardly be molecular duplicates of us. Ignore this, or if it really bothers you change the example to a natural kind that is unrepresented in the human body.

Further reading

Further representative papers on Direct Reference may be found in Almog, Perry and Wettstein (1989); a survey and critique is offered in Devitt (1989). See also Recanati (1993). For a recent DR attempt to meet the problems of Apparent Reference to Nonexistents and Negative Existentials, see Salmon (1998).

Kvart (1993) also elaborates a version of the Causal–Historical Theory of referring.

Evans (1973) offers further objections to Kripke's picture, and an interesting revision of it. Evans (1982) makes concessions to Kripke but insists that the idea of a "name-using (social) practice" must be introduced as a further element. McKinsey (1976, 1978) has moved further back toward the *ancien régime*. Further objections are made by Erwin, Kleiman and Zemach (1976) and Linsky (1977).

Salmon (1981) surveys semantic views of kind terms. Schwartz (1977) contains relevant papers. Criticisms of the Kripke–Putnam line are offered by Fine (1975), Dupré (1981), Unger (1983), and others. Boër (1985) responds to some of those criticisms.

The impact of "Twin Earth" examples on the theory of meaning generally is explored in Harman (1982) and Lycan (1984: Chapter 10).

PART II
Theories of meaning

5
Traditional theories of meaning

Overview

If the Referential Theory of Meaning is false, what theory is true? Any theory of meaning must account for the relevant facts, which we may call "the meaning facts": that some physical objects are meaningful (at all); that distinct expressions can have the same meaning; that a single expression can have more than one meaning; that the meaning of one expression can be contained in that of another; and more. We tend to talk of "meanings" as individual *things*.

Meanings have been thought to be particular ideas in people's minds. But several objections show that this cannot mean actual thoughts in the minds of particular people at particular times. At best, meanings would have to be more abstract: *types* of idea that might (or might not) occur in the mind of some being somewhere.

Accordingly, meanings have also been taken to be abstract things in themselves, alternately called "propositions." The sentence "Snow is white" means that snow is white; equally, we may say it "expresses the proposition that" snow is white. Other sentences, even in other languages such as "La neige est blanche" and "Der Schnee ist weiss" express that same proposition, and are therefore synonymous. This Proposition Theory fits the various "meaning facts" well, since "proposition" is essentially another word for "meaning." But critics have questioned whether it *explains* the meaning facts satisfactorily, or indeed at all.

When this book began, the topics of reference and meaning were not separate, because the most common naive idea people have about meaning is that meaning *is* reference. In Chapter 1 we disparaged the commonsensical but untenable Referential Theory of Meaning. So we must now confront meaning directly, and look at some more sophisticated theories of meaning.

Like any theory, a theory of meaning has to have a proprietary set of data. What are the primary data for a theory of meaning? I will refer to them corporately as "the meaning facts."

First, as we emphasized in Chapter 1, there is meaningfulness itself. Some strings of marks or noises in the air are just strings of marks or noises in the air, whereas others – particularly whole sentences – are meaningful. What is the difference? Perhaps that is the basic question for the theory of meaning.

Second, we sometimes say that two distinct expressions are synonymous. Third, we sometimes say of a single expression that it is ambiguous, that is that it has more than one meaning. (So expressions and meanings are not correlated one to one.) Fourth, we sometimes say that one expression's meaning is contained in that of another, as *female* and *deer* are contained in the meaning of "doe." An important special case here is that of one sentence's entailing another: "Harold is fat and Ben is stupid" entails "Ben is stupid." (There is joint entailment too: "Grannie is either in the holding cell or in court already" and "Grannie is not in the holding cell" together entail "Grannie is in court already," even though neither sentence alone entails that.)

There are more exotic meaning facts as well. For example, some disputes or alleged disputes are *merely verbal* or "only semantic," unlike substantive disagreements over fact. X and Y do not disagree about what actually happened; they dispute only over whether what happened counts as a "so-and-so." Onlookers say, "Oh, they're just talking past each other." (That happens a lot in philosophy.)

In stating the foregoing meaning facts, I have at least half-heartedly tried to avoid "reification" of things called meanings, that is, talking about "meanings" as if they were individual things like shoes or socks. I have talked of sentences having features like being mean*ful*, being synonymous, being ambiguous, though I did eventually slip into alluding to "meanings." I could have reified throughout, and said "has a meaning" instead of "is meaningful," "have the same meaning" instead of "are synonymous," and so on, or perhaps even used explicit quantifier expressions, as in "There is a meaning that the sentence has" and "There exists a meaning that is common to each of these sentences." Philosophers have made an issue of this.

Let us use the term "entity theory" to mean a theory that officially takes meanings to be individual things. And there is some considerable support for entity theories in the way we ordinarily talk. We not only seem to refer to things called meanings using the word as a common noun, but we seem to use quantifier expressions in that connection. We sometimes even seem to count them: "This word has four different meanings." So it is not unnatural to turn first to entity theories.

There are at least two different kinds of entities that meanings might be taken to be. First, one could take the entities to be mental. Theories of that kind are sometimes called *ideational* theories.

Ideational theories

The whipping boy here is usually John Locke (1690), since Locke seems to have held that the meanings of linguistic expressions are ideas in the mind. On this sort of view, what it is for a string of marks or noises to be meaningful is for the string to *express*, or somehow significantly correspond to, a content-bearing mental state that the speaker is in, an idea, an image, or perhaps a thought or a belief.

Likewise, one might say that for two expressions to be synonymous is for them to express the same thought. For an expression to be ambiguous is for there to be more than one thought that it could express, and so on. And regarding the phenomenon of merely verbal disagreement, the ideational theorist may say: it is not that one party has one thought and the other has a different, conflicting thought; they both have the same thought, but are confusingly putting it in different words that sound incompatible.

So an ideational theory seems to give us an intuitive way of expressing our meaning facts more precisely. Nonetheless ideational theories have not been popular in this century (though we shall see in Chapter 7 that Paul Grice defends something that could be construed as one). Here are several of the reasons for their disrepute.

Objection 1

If an ideational theory is to be precise enough to test, it must (eventually) specify what sort of mental entity an "idea" is. And then it will run into trouble. Mental *images* will not do at all, as a matter of fact, for images are more detailed than meanings. (An image of a dog is not just, generically, of a dog, but of a dog of a particular breed and size; an image of a triangle is of some particular type of triangle, equilateral or right or whatever.) A better candidate would be a more abstract mental "concept," but that suggestion would be circular until someone managed to tell us what a "concept" is, independently of the notion of meaning. Also, a concept such as that of dog or triangle is not true or false on its own, and so cannot serve as the meaning of a complete sentence.

Objection 2

As with the Referential Theory, there are just too many words that have no particular mental images or contents associated with them: "is," "and," "of." Indeed, if *images* are what are on offer, there are certainly words that psychologically *could not* have images associated with them, for example "chiliagon" or "nonentity," and even when a word does have an associated image, as "red" does, we do not always call that image to mind in the everyday course of understanding the word as it goes by; we may virtually never call it to mind.

Objection 3

Meaning is a public, intersubjective, social phenomenon. An English word has the meaning it does for the entire community of English speakers, even if some members of that community happen not to understand that word. But ideas, images, and feelings in the mind are not intersubjective in that way; they are subjective, held only in the minds of individual persons, and they *differ* from person to person depending on one's total mental state and background. Therefore, meanings are not ideas in the mind. (One might reply by appealing to what is *common* to all English speakers' ideas of "dog," say, but what is common to all "dog"-ideas is not itself an idea but a *type* of idea, a universal or an abstract "quality" in the sense of Chapter 1.)

Objection 4

There are meaningful sentences that do not express any actual idea or thought or mental state. For as we saw in Chapter 1, there are quite long and complicated sentences of English that have never been uttered, and some of those will never be uttered. (Of course, as soon as I gave you an example of one, it was no longer an example of one, because as soon as I had written it down, it became a sentence that had been uttered. But we can extrapolate; there are more where my fanciful Hitler sentence came from.) So there are sentences that are or would be perfectly meaningful but whose contents have never been thought by anyone or even occurred to anyone. Thus, there are meaningful sentences that do not correspond to any actual mental entities.

Much more commonly in this century, the entities invoked by entity theories of meaning have been abstract rather than mental. The meanings of sentences in particular have been called "propositions" (as by Russell, we saw in Chapter 2).

The Proposition Theory

Like ideas, these abstract items are "language-independent" in that they are not tied to any particular natural language. But unlike ideas, they are also people-independent. Mental entities depend upon the minds in which they inhere; a mental state has to be somebody's mental state, a state of some particular person's mind at a particular time. Propositions are entirely general and, if you like, eternal. (Russell himself had little further to say about their nature; his colleague G. E. Moore was clearer and more forthcoming, or at least more forthright.[1] Frege had previously constructed quite an elegant Proposition Theory, but seems to have held that there is nothing to understanding what a proposition is but understanding the role played by "propositions" in the theory.)

Consider a possible reply to Objection 4 above: someone might try to save the ideational theory by suggesting that we need not restrict ourselves to *actual* ideas; we can appeal to merely possible ideas – ideas that someone might have or might have had. But that would be to posit abstract contents that are possible contents of thought but are not related to anyone's actual thoughts. Enter the proposition theorist: "Right, let's call such thinkables 'propositions'." And so (if the ideational theorist does make the move under discussion), the ideational view simply collapses into the Propositional Theory.

The Propositional Theory offers a graphic picture. Suppose we have one string of words, S, that is meaningful, alongside another string, g, that is only gibberish. What is the difference? According to Russell and Moore, it is that there is an abstract content or proposition, call it P, to which S stands in a certain special relation. S is a sentence of a particular language. Poor g does not bear that relation to any such item. The relation is often called *expression*; philosophers commonly talk of sentences expressing propositions. (Though here the term is more bloodless than in ideational theories. Ideational theorists think of sentences almost as being pushed out from inside us by the pressure of our thoughts, but propositions are abstract and changeless and do not push or pull.) So S is meaningful in virtue of expressing the particular proposition P; g's failing is that it expresses no proposition at all.

The other meaning facts are neatly depicted from the present point of view. For sentences S_1 and S_2 to be synonymous is just for S_1 and S_2 to express the same proposition. They are distinct linguistic expressions – they could be different expressions in one and the same natural language or they could be corresponding expressions from different languages. What they have in common is solely that they bear the expressing relation to the same proposition.

So too for ambiguity. A sentence S is ambiguous just in case there are at least two distinct propositions P_1 and P_2, and the single expression S bears the expressing relation to each of P_1 and P_2. In the case of merely verbal disputes, we can say that the parties do not disagree over any proposition; they are merely using different forms of words to express the same proposition, and the particular forms of words look as though they are in conflict even though they are not.

We know some positive things about what propositions are supposed to be, besides their being expressed by sentences. They are identifiable in terms of "that"-clauses: we speak of the proposition that snow is white, and dedicate ourselves to the proposition that all men [sic] are created equal. "Snow is white," "La neige est blanche" and "Der Schnee ist weiss" are synonymous because each of them expresses the proposition that snow is white. Although what follows the "that"-clause is just another sentence of one particular natural language, the one we happen to be speaking, the function of the "that" – creating indirect discourse – is to free the reference to the proposition in question from its particular expression.

Propositions are also objects of mental states. People all over the world may believe that Asian markets are collapsing, doubt that Asian markets are collapsing, hope or fear that Asian markets are collapsing. Here too, the "that" serves to remove the implication that they all thought that thought in English. They could have thought it in any language; it would still be true that they believed, doubted or whatever that Asian markets are collapsing.

Further, propositions are the fundamental bearers of truth and falsity. When a sentence is true/false, it is so only because the proposition it expresses is true/false. One argument for this claim is that sentences change their truth-values from time to time and from context to context.

(1) The present queen of England is bald.

We believe (1) to be false, assuming that Elizabeth Windsor is not following Russell's advice and wearing a wig. But what about the other queens, past or future, that may have been or may be bald? If (1) had been uttered during the reign of a previous queen who was bald, it would have been true, and if it should be uttered decades from now during the reign of a subsequent queen, it might be true or false depending. So whether (1) is false or true depends on when it is uttered. What makes a particular utterance of a sentence true or false is the proposition it expresses on that occasion. The reason (1) changes its truth-value is that it expresses different propositions on different utterance occasions. Sentences derive their truth-values from propositions; propositions' truth-values are permanent.

Most Proposition Theorists hold that propositions have internal structure; they are composed of abstract conceptual parts. The word "snow" is a meaningful expression, but it is not meaningful in virtue of expressing a proposition; just by itself it does not express a full proposition. Only a sentence expresses a proposition or, as they used to say in grammar school, a complete thought. "Snow" does not express a complete thought, but it expresses something that is part of many thoughts – a concept, or a type, or an "idea" in the abstract rather than the mental sense. "Concept" is the usual term used to mean an equally abstract constituent of a larger abstract proposition.[2]

There are "meaning facts" about the parts or constituents of sentences as well, and they can be treated analogously. Words that are synonymous with "snow" can be said to express the same concept; if "snow" is ambiguous, as it is, it is ambiguous in virtue of expressing different concepts: sometimes it means the chilly white stuff that falls from the sky and at other times it means a certain controlled substance.

The Proposition Theory avoids all four of our objections to ideational theories, though one more narrowly than the others. We have already seen that it eludes Objection 4. It avoids 1 because propositions and concepts are not mental entities, and it avoids 3 because, unlike mental entities, propositions and concepts are intersubjective, independent of particular people, languages, and even whole cultures.

It only barely evades Objection 2. The Proposition theorist can insist that words like "is," "and," "of," "chiliagon," and "nonentity" express concepts ("chiliagon" especially, which is a well-defined geometric term). But as I said in response to Objection 1, if this is not to sound empty and perhaps even circular, the proposition theorist will have to give us some further characterization of the relevant concepts, one that does not quietly presuppose some notion of linguistic meaning. (We shall see in Chapter 10 that a sophisticated version of the Proposition Theory can do this.)

The Proposition view is the leading entity theory of meaning. Like any theory of meaning it aims at explaining the meaning facts. It attempts to do that by positing a certain range of entities; that is how we often explain things, especially in science. We posit subatomic particles, unobservable entities of a certain range and kind, to explain the behavior of observable chemical substances and the ratios in which they combine.

A first problem for the theory as stated so far is created by a sort of meaning fact that I have not mentioned up till now. Some philosophers consider this sort even more important than all the ones listed above: we *understand* a sentence S, in an immediate way, while we do not understand a gibberish string of words. Some strings of words are intelligible and other strings are not. This brings another term into the relation. Till now, the Proposition Theory has focused just on linguistic expressions and on propositions, with the expressing relation defined on them. Now it must let in human beings.

What is it for a person to understand a sentence, S? The classic Moorean answer is, for that person to bear a certain relation to a proposition and to know that S expresses that proposition. This relation Moore called "grasping" (or sometimes "apprehending"). To understand S is to grasp some proposition P and to know that S expresses P.

The Proposition Theory too is congenial to common sense. It is easy to agree that certain sentences of various different languages all have something (their meanings) in common, a language-independent content, and it is easy and natural to call that content "the proposition expressed by" the various different sentences. Moreover, the Proposition Theory is a handy tool for describing and discussing the other sorts of "meaning phenomena" we have mentioned, to say nothing of entailment or meaning inclusion, antonymy, redundancy, and more. Finally, as we shall see in Chapters 10 and 11, the Proposition Theory lends itself to elegant mathematical elaboration, in the hands of "possible worlds" semanticists and intensional logicians. But, as always, there are problems.

Objection 1

We have said that "propositions" are abstract entities, even though sentences are now being said to "express" them rather than to *name* them as in the Referential Theory. Considered as entities, these abstract items are somewhat weird. They are not located anywhere in space, and, since they could not be created or destroyed, they are also temporally eternal or at least everlasting. They existed long before any living being did, even though their *contents* have to do with highly specific states of human affairs, such as Fred's having downed four quick Malaga Coolers at He's

Not Here during the early evening of Tuesday 19 September 1995. The propositions will exist long after the last sentient creature is dead. And (necessarily, since they are not in spacetime) they have no causal properties; they do not make anything happen.

A reply

It is right and proper to be wary of positing weird entities. But perhaps this direct appeal to "Occam's Razor" is premature. The medieval philosopher William of Occam told us not to multiply posited entities *beyond explanatory necessity*. But we could know that propositions were unnecessary for explanation only if we had an alternative theory of meaning that explained the meaning phenomena just as well but without dragging in propositions. And (so far) we have no such competitor.

Objection 2

"Propositions" are in a sense unfamiliar and alien to our experience. I hear or see words and I understand them, but this is hardly, or seems hardly, a case of my doing something called "grasping" that puts me in touch with a supra-empirical nonspatial, indestructible, eternal, etc. object. (Bring up spooky mood music.)

Moore's reply

> It is quite plain, I think, that when we understand the meaning of a sentence, something else does happen in our minds *besides* the mere hearing of the words of which the sentence is composed. You can easily satisfy yourselves of this by contrasting what happens when you hear a sentence, which you *do* understand, from what happens when you hear a sentence which you *do not* understand. . . . Certainly in the first case, there occurs, beside the mere hearing of the words, another act of consciousness – an apprehension of their meaning, which is absent in the second case. And it is no less plain that the apprehension of the meaning of one sentence with one meaning, differs in some respect from the apprehension of another sentence with a different meaning. . . . There certainly *are* such things as the two different meanings apprehended. And each of these two meanings is what I call a proposition.
>
> (1953/1962: 73–4)

And, he might add, if you say you do not know what he is talking about, you are a liar. Grasping is something you have directly experienced.

A different reply

Granting the premise instead of challenging it, one might point out that it is common not only in philosophy but in science to explain very familiar phenomena in terms of very unfamiliar, perhaps quite arcane phenomena. That is nothing new or unusual.

Objection 3

Due to Gilbert Harman (1967–8). The Proposition Theory does not in fact explain anything; it merely repeats the data in a fancier jargon. ("Why do 'Snow is white' and 'La neige est blanche' have the same meaning?" – "Because they express the same proposition." – "Oh.") It sounds as though the phrase "expresses a proposition" is just a fancier way of saying "is meaningful"? At least until we are shown some independent way of understanding proposition talk, the suspicion will remain that it is only a pretentious way of re-expressing the meaning facts. Compare Molière's physician on opium and "dormitive virtue."[3]

Reply

We need not be too daunted by this objection either. For when a Proposition Theory is elaborated and refined, complete with a notion of a person's "grasping" a proposition as well as that of a sentence's expressing one, the apparatus has at least a bit of predictive power and so (to that extent) at least a bit of explanatory power. Whether the resulting story is *plausible* is a different question. But perhaps Harman was really getting at the next objection.

Objection 4

Whatever meaning is, it plays a dynamic role in human society. Some of your behavior is causally the result of my saying certain words *that mean what they do*, and some of my behavior results from your saying meaningful words likewise. Legal decisions in capital cases sometimes turn on the meanings of words, and so on. Thus meaning, whatever it is, must have some causal power (some push and pull, some punch, some biff). But *propositions*, as entirely abstract entities, precisely *do not* have causal powers. They sit quiescently and uselessly outside spacetime, and do nothing. So it is hard to see how propositions could figure in the explanation of human linguistic behavior or could in any other way help to account for the dynamic social role of meaning. And therefore they seem to be unnecessary posits after all.

Reply

Even if propositions do not help in the explanation of human behavior, human behavior is not the only thing that needs explaining. The "meaning facts" themselves are our primary data, and *pace* Harman, propositions still help to explain those.

The "ordinary language" philosophers of the 1950s drew a moral from early versions of Objections 1 and 4: that what we need is a theory that explains meaning phenomena in terms that do connect up to human behavior. (Remember that human behavior involves actual physical motion; meaning must somehow contribute to *literal* push and pull.) More specifically, we need to understand meaning in terms of language *use*. Ever since, philosophers have spoken of "use" theories of meaning. But we are little the wiser, for there are many different kinds of modes of "use," some of which are obviously irrelevant to meaning in the characteristically linguistic sense. Different specifically linguistic conceptions of "use" lead to different and competing theories of meaning.

Summary

- A theory of meaning must explain the "meaning facts."
- "Meanings" have often been taken to be entities or individual things.
- Ideational theorists contend that meanings are particular ideas in people's minds.
- But several objections show that, at best, meanings would have to be more abstract: *types* of idea, not actual thoughts in the minds of particular people.
- Proposition theorists take meanings to be abstract things in themselves.
- But critics have questioned whether the Proposition Theory explains the meaning facts satisfactorily (or at all).

Questions

1   Is there more to be said in favor of the Ideational Theory? And/or can you defend it against one or more of our objections?
2   Does the Proposition Theory really explain the meaning facts? Why or why not?
3   Defend the Proposition Theory more thoroughly against our objections. Or raise a new objection of your own.

Notes

1   "The fact is that absolutely all the contents of the Universe, absolutely everything that *is* at all, may be divided into two classes – namely into *propositions*, on the one hand, and into things which are not propositions on the other hand" (1953/1962: 71). Moore reported in an autobiographical note that he had once had a nightmare in which he dreamed that propositions were tables.
2   Though like "idea," "concept" has also been used to mean a kind of particular mental entity. This equivocation has caused some confusion in contemporary cognitive psychology.
3   "Why does opium put people to sleep?" – "Because it has a dormitive virtue." That may sound profound until one realizes that the phrase is just transliterated Latin for "power of producing sleep." The physician (Argan in *Le Malade imaginaire*) might as well have spoken in Pig Latin: "It puts people to sleep because itay utspay eoplepay otay eepslay." That is hardly an explanation.

Further reading

Locke's Ideational Theory is discussed in Bennett (1971).

Frege (1918/1956) criticized ideational theories in favor of the Proposition Theory. Wittgenstein (1953) criticized them from a very different perspective (see Chapter 6), as did Waismann (1965a).

A classic Proposition Theory was offered by Russell (1919/1956).

For some discussion of propositions and their relations to sentences and to utterances, see Cartwright (1962) and Lemmon (1966).

Quinean criticism of the Proposition Theory is best summed up by Gilbert Harman (1967–8), particularly pp. 124–7 (141–7 are also relevant). Lycan (1974) is a rejoinder on the theory's behalf. See also Loux (1998: Chapter 4).

6
"Use" theories

Overview

The Proposition Theory treats sentences and other linguistic items as inert abstract entities whose structure can be studied as if under a microscope. But Ludwig Wittgenstein argued that words and sentences are more like game pieces or tokens, used to make moves in rule-governed conventional social practices. A "meaning" is not an abstract object; meaning is a matter of the role an expression plays in human social behavior. To know the expression's meaning is just to know how to deploy the expression appropriately in conversational settings.

Wilfrid Sellars' version of this idea makes the act of *inferring* central; it is the complexity of patterns of inference that allows the "use" theorist to accommodate long, novel sentences. On this view, one sentence entails another, not because the two "express" "propositions" one of which is somehow "contained in" the other, but because it is socially expected that one's neighbor would perform the act of inferring the second sentence from the first.

"Use" theories of this kind face two main obstacles: explaining how language use differs from ordinary conventional rule-governed activities, such as chess games, that generate no meaning; and explaining how, in particular, a sentence can mean *that* so-and-so (as the French "La neige est blanche" means that snow is white). Robert Brandom has recently offered a "Use Theory" that claims to perform these feats.

As we saw in Chapter 2, Russell's habit was to write a sentence on the blackboard and examine (as he contended) the proposition expressed by the sentence, treating it as an object of interest in itself and trying to discern its structure. Ludwig Wittgenstein and J. L. Austin argued that this picture of how language works and how it should be studied is completely wrong. Languages and linguistic entities are not bloodless abstract objects which can be studied like specimens under a microscope. Rather, language takes the form of behavior, activity – specifically, social practice. Sentences do not have lives of their own. The things we write on blackboards, and the alleged "propositions" they express, are fairly violent abstractions from the utterings performed by human beings in real-world contexts on particular occasions.[1] And for a person to utter something is first and foremost for that person to do something. It is a bit of behavior that by convention has gotten swept up into a rule-governed social practice.

We have already encountered a version of this idea in Chapter 2, for it is from the same perspective that Strawson wielded his several objections against Russell's initially attractive Theory of Descriptions. And whether or not we are ultimately convinced by the objections, they were fresh and striking and, to many people, still intuitively compelling. That is a good letter of recommendation for the perspective itself.

"Use" in a roughly Wittgensteinian sense

Wittgenstein and Austin developed this social-behavioral idea in different ways. Here I shall concentrate on a Wittgensteinian view, deferring Austin's until Chapter 12. I say only "a Wittgensteinian view," because for reasons that cannot detain us here, Wittgenstein himself opposed systematic theorizing in philosophy, and his followers objected to any phrase along the lines of "Wittgenstein's theory of . . ." or "Wittgenstein's doctrine regarding . . . ."[2] I shall merely try to sketch an account based on Wittgenstein's contributions, without attributing that or any other theory to Wittgenstein himself.

If meaning itself is mysterious, one way to reduce the mystery is to enter its domain through something with which we are more directly familiar. In order to get a handle on meaning, let us think of it from the receiving end, the grasp of meaning or understanding of linguistic expressions. And in order to understand understanding, let us think of it as the product of our having been taught our language, and as what one learns when one learns a language.

But as soon as we try looking at it that way, something becomes immediately obvious: that what is learned and taught is a complicated form of social behavior. What you learn when you learn a language is to make moves, to engage in certain kinds of practice, conversational behavior in particular. And primarily, what is taught is the right way to behave when other people make certain kinds of noises, and what kinds of noises to make when circumstances are appropriate for doing so. Linguistic practice is governed by highly complex sets of rules, even though the rules are rarely articulated; small children just pick them up at a colossal rate, learning to obey them without realizing that is what they are doing.

These home truths are obscured by entity theories, which treat meanings as static, inert things. Both Wittgenstein and Austin inveighed at length against entity theories, though here we shall be concerned with a positive account of "use." Wittgenstein also scorned the view that meaning essentially involves referential relations between linguistic expressions and things in the world (though of course he did not deny that there are some such relations).

Wittgenstein offered the key analogy of linguistic activity to the playing of games. (According to the physicist Freeman Dyson, then a Cambridge undergraduate, one day Wittgenstein was walking past a field where a football match was in progress, and "the thought first struck him that in language we play *games* with *words*.")[3] Language is not a matter of marks on the blackboard bearing the expressing relation to abstract entities called "propositions"; language is something that people do, and do in a highly rule-governed and conventional way. Linguistic activity is governed by rules in much the way that the playing of a game is governed by rules.

Moreover, linguistic expressions themselves are like game pieces. Consider chessmen. A "pawn" or a "rook" is defined by the chess rules that govern its initial position and subsequent legal moves; what makes a knight a knight is the way in which it characteristically moves according to the game's conventionally instituted rules. So too, a linguistic expression's meaning is constituted by the tacit rules governing its correct conversational use.

Start with expressions like "Hello," "Damn" (or "Good gracious"), "Oh, dear," "Excuse me," "Amen," "Thanks," "Stop it!," "You're on" (when a bet has been offered), and "Bless you." These do not seem to mean what they do in virtue of standing for anything *or* in virtue of expressing propositions. They are just conventional devices, respectively, of greeting, evincing consternation, deploring, apologizing, endorsing, thanking, protesting, committing oneself to a bet, and blessing. They are noises we make that have socially defined functional roles; there are appropriate occasions for using them, inappropriate occasions for using them, and appropriate responses. When we talk of their meanings, we mean the functions they characteristically perform in the context of our current social practices. On the Wittgensteinian view, this is the locus and natural home of all meaning, though most expressions have vastly more complicated social roles.

To emphasize all this, Wittgenstein coined the term "language-game," as in "the meeting and greeting language-game," "the wedding language-game," "the arithmetic language-game," etc.

Wittgenstein offers a further analogy (1953: 2): a builder and his assistant have just four kinds of building-stones that they use. They speak a little primitive language that has just four corresponding words in it: "block," "pillar," "slab," and "beam." They build things, engaging in their nonlinguistic activities aided by a certain primitive sort of linguistic activity: the builder says "slab," and the assistant brings a stone of the appropriate shape. Now, someone might say, "Of course, that word 'slab' bears the referring relation to a block of this shape, and its meaning is the proposition that the assistant is to bring such a block to the builder." But according to Wittgenstein this would be missing the point. In this little primitive language-game, the word "slab" does have a function that is obviously connected with blocks of that shape, but the point is the function and not the connection. The point of the builder's making the noise "slab" is just to get the assistant to do something, to trigger conventionally (the assistant having learned his trade) a pattern of useful activity. The activity does involve things of this shape, but the primary point is to initiate action, not to refer or to "express" an eternal proposition.

Of course, it is hard to extrapolate this simple picture of meaning as brutely conventional social function to long and complex sentences like "The present queen of England is bald" or "In 1931, Adolf Hitler made a visit to the United States, in the course of which he . . . ," neither of which has any easily identifiable conventional social role (other than, unhelpfully, those of *asserting that* the present Queen of England is bald and that in 1931, . . .). Some additional mechanism must be introduced to accomplish that extrapolation. The Logical Positivists appealed to the notion of verification, but I shall save discussion of that until Chapter 8. Wilfrid Sellars (1963, 1974) invoked the idea of *inferring* as a social act. He spoke too of "language-entry rules," and "language-exit rules," these being respectively rules governing what one is supposed to say in response to certain sorts of nonlinguistic events (such as observations) and what one is supposed to do in response to certain linguistic utterances, but most importantly of "language-language rules," which govern what one is supposed to say as the product of inference from something else that has previously been said. Let us call this the Inferential Theory of Meaning.

It is hard to see how a theory that took "Hello" or "Slab" as its paradigms could succeed in explaining the more refined of the meaning facts. Meaningfulness, synonymy, and ambiguity are not a problem; but what of entailment between complex sentences? The Inferential Theory's appeal to inferring helps, for what might seem to be the static abstract relation of "entailment" between two sentences can be reconstrued as a rule-governed practice of inferring the one from the other. "Harold is fat and Ben is stupid" entails "Ben is stupid" because if someone asserts the former but denies the latter, we apply severe social sanctions; indeed, we at least raise eyebrows if someone asserts the former and then does not go on to behave as if the latter is true. It is this practice itself that makes the inference valid, not (as logic books would have it) any independent guarantee that the inference preserves truth.

Objections and some replies

The beauty of the Inferential Theory is its effortless avoidance of every single objection we have made to each of the three traditional theories (Referential, Ideational, and Proposition). In addition, it is naturalistic, in that it focuses attention on the actual features of language as used in the real world. Still, there are some formidable problems.

Objection 1

All language-games are exactly the same as between Earth and Twin Earth, since those planets are running exactly in parallel; but words on Twin Earth and the rest diverge in meaning from their counterparts on Earth. Of an Earth utterance and its Twin, one may be true and the other false; what more could be required for difference of meaning? Thus, an expression's meaning is not exhausted by the expression's role in a language-game.

Reply

One can classify "language-games" more finely, and deny that we and our Twin-Earth doppelgängers are playing "the same" game, even though what we are doing would look exactly the same if seen on television. For example, we respond to and act upon *water* (H_2O), while our Twins do not, but deal with XYZ; different rules altogether, you see. (This actually was

Sellars' original intention, though he had not yet heard of Putnam's Twin Earth.)

Objection 2

Proper names pose a problem for the "use" theorist. Try stating a rule of use for the name "William G. Lycan," or for the name of your best friend. Remember, it has to be a rule that every competent speaker of your local dialect actually obeys without exception. The only candidate rules that occur to me push the "use" theorist into a description theory of meaning for names. Wittgenstein himself found Descriptivism congenial, but he had not read Kripke.

Objection 3

The Wittgensteinian theory seems helpless in the face of our original datum, speakers' amazing ability to understand long, utterly novel sentences at first hearing without a moment's thought. Chess pieces and the like are familiar, recurring types of object, and the rules for their use are directed one-to-one upon them. And similarly for "Slab," "Hello," "Ouch," and other Wittgensteinian examples of expressions whose uses are defined by local rituals or customs. But our ability to understand and act on long novel sentences cannot be the product of our knowing conventions directed upon those utterances, for no conventions have ever been directed upon those utterances.

The Wittgensteinian must grant that we understand novel sentences *compositionally*, in virtue of understanding the individual words that occur in them and working out the sentences' overall meanings from the way in which the individual words are strung together. (We shall have a great deal more to say about this in Chapter 9.) It follows that what is understood, that is a sentence's meaning, is not *simply* a matter of there being conventional norms directed upon that sentence's deployment, for the sentence's meaning is in large part a function of its internal structure as well.

Objection 4

Could I not know the use of an expression and fall in with it, mechanically, but without understanding it? I have known undergraduates who are geniuses at picking up academic jargon of one sort or another and slinging it around with great facility, but without understanding. I knew one who took a phenomenology course taught by a visiting Parisian, understood none of it, but learned the knack of stringing the jargon expressions together so well that his term paper earned or "earned" an A. Use perfect (or at least graded A); meaning nil.

Objection 5

Many rule-governed social activities – sports and games themselves in particular – do not centrally involve the kind of meaning that linguistic expressions have. Certainly chess moves and tennis shots do not have meaning of that sort. (Contrast the case where spies are using chess moves as an actual secret code; for example, N–Q3 may have conventionally been stipulated to mean "Take the zircon to Foppa and tell him we move tonight.") What, then is supposed to distinguish language-games from ordinary games?

Suppose some community agrees to use certain words – or at any rate sounds and marks – in a peculiar way; say they decide to put only "words" with the same number of syllables next to each other in threes, or they utter "sentences" only in rhyming pairs, where each string begins with a one-letter word and adds one letter successively to each ensuing item. (This might be a sort of community-wide parlor game.) If a newcomer happened upon this whimsical society and knew nothing of the arrangement, s/he would not understand what was going on. The newcomer might, in time, dope out all the rules according to which the various tokens were being used, and yet have no notion what, if anything, was being said. And in this simple case, at least, nothing is being said. Someone might suggest that such a game, like the builders' language, is just too *simple* and/or primitive to qualify. But it is hard to see how the mere addition of further complexity would help.

Reply

Someone might argue that if its rules are rich enough and advert often enough to ambient conditions, *reference* and *predication* will be recoverable from the game description. Suppose there is a rule that, whenever the waiter comes in, every third player shouts "Here, waiter," and is given a martini; whenever any player says "Mix please," s/he is passed the bowl of snacks by whomever is nearest it; and the like. One would then be tempted to conclude that "waiter" refers to the waiter and "mix" means snack food. So the game moves would have meaning after all.

Rejoinder

Perhaps, in that case, the utterances specified by the game rules would have meanings – but only because they do stand for or refer to things and not just because of their conventional deployment behavior.

Let us therefore stipulate that, no matter how complex the game becomes, the players' utterances do not refer to things external to the game; they are only moves in the game. But then it seems even more obvious that the game is not even the beginning of an actual language, and that the moves do not have meaning in the same way that utterances of English sentences do. So the "use" theorist's explicit conditions are not sufficient for something's being a language.

Second reply

Waismann (1965a: 158) anticipates an objection of this kind. He hints at a competing reply: that genuine language-games are "integrat[ed] . . . into life." By contrast, the parlor-game words, like chess moves and tennis shots, "bear a far less close relation to life than words used in earnest." A language-game cannot be encapsulated, something that we keep at arm's length and play just when we feel like it.

Rejoinder

But some language-games, such as the telling of shaggy-dog jokes, are encapsulated and played only occasionally and at will. Also, even if we agree that more serious, multi-purpose language-games are thoroughly integrated into life, we usually think of that close, integrative relation as that of *referring*. The Wittgensteinian does not agree that meaning essentially involves referring, and so Waismann needs to say what the "integration" is instead. The idea seems to be that language-games are integrated with *other social practices*. But it is hard to see how the Wittgensteinian can spell that out (a) in such a way as to explain how the linguistic moves take on propositional content, but (b) without secretly introducing referring.

My use just now of the phrase "propositional content" may suggest an unsuccessfully tacit allegiance to the Proposition Theory. But I am using it, and will continue to use it throughout this book, in a weaker sense, as whatever property of a sentence or other item is somehow expressed by a "that"-clause, as in "means that broccoli will kill you." We need not take that property to be a matter of bearing the "expression" relation to an abstract entity called "a proposition."

Objection 6

One clear sense in which a social practice qualifies as an actual language is that, according to it, one can make noises or inscribe marks and thereby *say that* P for some suitable sentence replacing "P." And one of the things that is surely essential to language is that we can say things in it. But no such indirect discourse is licensed just in virtue of some people's playing chess or the parlor game; none of the players has said or asked or requested or suggested . . . *that* anything at all. There is something missing. We are playing a game, and using tokens according to a set of conventional rules, and engaging in a social practice that may not only be fun but have some larger point; it might even be in some way vital to our way of life. The things the players in these various games have done may have significance in some sense, but nobody has made any assertions or asked anything or advised anyone to do anything.

At this point it is tempting to make some serious concession to the Referential Theory. But that would be to overlook the most recent incarnation of Sellars' Inferential Theory: Brandom (1994), a 700-page monsterpiece, which at least has the potential for evading some of the foregoing objections. Brandom develops a particular conception of "use," according to which a sentence's use is the set of commitments and entitlements associated with public utterance of that sentence. His paradigm is that of *asserting*: when one utters a sentence and thereby makes an assertion, one is committing oneself to defend that assertion against whatever objection or challenge might be made by a hearer. The defense would take the form of giving *reasons* in support of the assertion, typically by inferring it from some other sentence whose uttering is not so readily open to challenge. And in making the assertion one also confers on oneself the entitlement to make further inferences from it. The social game of giving and asking for reasons is governed by rules, of course, and score is kept. (Notions of scorekeeping play a large role in Brandom's system.)

The system is very complex, and we cannot examine it here. But I note that it overcomes some of the objections raised so far against the Wittgensteinian view. Against Objection 5, it does distinguish linguistic utterances from "Slab," chess moves, and so on, since those are not the sorts of things in support of which one gives reasons, rebuts challenges, and so on. (One can of course offer practical reasons for having made a particular chess move or tennis shot, but Brandom means *evidential* reasons, utterances that give us reason to believe some statement of fact. Again, his paradigm is that of an inferential reason, and chess moves etc. are certainly not inferences.) Brandom also recognizes a kind of compositionality, and so he may evade Objection 3. And, admirably, he addresses some fairly detailed semantic phenomena: proper names, descriptions, indexicals, quantification, and anaphora, in terms of their characteristic contributions to the commitment/entitlement potentials of sentences in which they occur.

Now let us move on and look at a considerably different theory of meaning. Paul Grice's theory begins with the outrageous notion that language is a means of communication.

Summary

- "Use" theories have it that "meanings" are not abstract objects like propositions; a linguistic expression's meaning is determined by the expression's characteristic function in human social behavior.
- According to Wittgenstein, linguistic expressions are like game tokens, used to make moves in rule-governed conventional social practices.
- Sellars' version of this idea makes the act of *inferring* central, and it is the complexity of patterns of inference that allows the "use" theorist to accommodate long, novel sentences.
- "Use" theories face two main obstacles: explaining how language use differs from ordinary conventional rule-governed activities that generate no meaning; and explaining how a sentence can mean *that* so-and-so.
- Brandom's "use" theory overcomes some of these obstacles.

Questions

1 Can the Wittgensteinian "Use Theory" as we have sketched it be defended against one or more of Objections 1–4?
2 Adjudicate Objection 5. Can you make a better reply than Waismann's?
3 Come up with a Wittgensteinian reply to Objection 6.
4 Can a red/green color-blind person understand the word "red"? Think about this in regard to "use" theories.

Notes

1 Here are three infrequently noticed ways in which the notion of a "sentence" is quite a considerable abstraction away from real-world linguistic activity. First (you may be

surprised to learn), human utterances do not come broken up into separate words. An acoustical analysis of oral speech production shows a continuous though of course variegated stream of sound. (When . . . we . . . talk . . . we . . . do . . . not . . . pause . . . even . . . briefly . . . between . . . words.) When we hear a stream of sound that constitutes somebody speaking, we put the word breaks in ourselves, automatically and without ever even thinking about it. That is already an abstraction, a theoretical or analytical move that we make.

Second, to think of something as a "sentence" presupposes the notion of grammatical well-formedness. Not just any string of words constitutes a sentence; only the grammatical strings do. And the idea of grammaticality is a sophisticated one, even though it is grasped however dimly by four-year-olds.

Third, consider the category of what linguists used to call "semi-grammatical" utterance. Some of the utterances that people produce are only semi-grammatical, in that if their words were written down on paper, the result would not count as an entirely grammatical sentence by some rule of grammar (it has some grammatical infelicity in it), but it is coherent enough to be understood. In fact, I suspect most people talk that way most of the time. At the very least, we all do things like making false starts, and we all engage vigorously in mid-course editing. Yet not only do we get understood by our hearers; nobody even notices. We correct for semi-grammaticality quite automatically. That correction is a theoretical move made by our brains, and yet another abstraction away from speech events in the real world.

2   Paragraph 43 of Wittgenstein's *Philosophical Investigations* is famously misquoted. It reads, "For a *large* class of cases – though not for all – in which we employ the word 'meaning' it can be defined thus: the meaning of a word is its use in the language." Wittgenstein was very serious about "though not for all"; he did not hold that "meaning is use," period. Indeed, he was allergic to universal generalizations. He thought it a deep defect of philosophy that philosophy seeks universal generalizations; the real world, he contended, is always more complicated than that.

As Georg Henrik von Wright put it, Wittgenstein "lived on the border of mental illness . . . throughout his life" ("Biographical Sketch," included in Norman Malcolm, *Ludwig Wittgenstein: A Memoir* (Oxford: Oxford University Press, 1958)). Wittgenstein also distinguished himself from most twentieth-century English-speaking philosophers by having had quite an interesting life; see Ray Monk's wonderful biography, *Ludwig Wittgenstein: The Duty of Genius* (New York: Free Press, Maxwell Macmillan International, 1990).

3   Reported by Norman Malcolm, op. cit., p. 65. "A central idea of his philosophy, the notion of a 'language-game', apparently had its genesis in this incident."

Further reading

The literature on Wittgenstein is so vast that I hesitate to mention one or two or three exegetical works to the exclusion of others. But: Rhees (1959–60); Pitcher (1964: Chapter 11); Hallett (1967); Kenny (1973: Chapters 7–9).

The *locus classicus* of Sellars' Functional Theory is Sellars (1963); see also (1974). An excellent exposition and defense of the central themes is given in Rosenberg (1974).

Philosophy and Phenomenological Research 57 (1997) contains a symposium on Brandom (1994), with a précis, lead papers by John McDowell, Gideon Rosen, Richard Rorty, and J. F. Rosenberg, and a response by Brandom.

7

Psychological theories: Grice's program

Overview

Grice's basic idea

Speaker-meaning

Sentence meaning

Summary

Questions

Notes

Further reading

Overview

H.P. Grice maintained that a linguistic expression has meaning only because it is an *expression* – not because it "expresses" a proposition, but because it more genuinely and literally expresses some concrete idea or intention of the person who uses it. Grice introduced the idea of "speaker-meaning," roughly what the speaker in uttering a given sentence on a particular occasion intends to convey to a hearer. Since speakers do not always mean what their sentences standardly mean in the language, Grice distinguished this speaker-meaning from the sentence's own standard meaning.

He offered an elaborate analysis of speaker-meaning in terms of speakers' intentions, beliefs, and other psychological states, and refined that analysis in the light of many objections. It is generally agreed that some version of the analysis must be right.

More importantly for our purposes, Grice also offered an analysis of a sentence's (standard) meaning in terms of speaker-meaning. Here he faces severe difficulties, since there are several ways in which sentence meaning obstinately refuses to cooperate with speaker-meaning. Grice has a way of overcoming such obstacles, but it seems likely that that way concedes too much to competing theories of sentence meaning.

Grice's basic idea

We are concerned to arrive at an account of meaning, meaning considered as a remarkable feature of linguistic expressions, of sentences in particular. But suppose we ask ourselves, what are *sentences* really? They are types of marks and noises, individual tokens of which are produced by people on particular occasions for a purpose. When you say something, it is usually for the purpose of communicating. You deliver yourself of an opinion, or express a desire or an intention. And you mean to produce an effect, to make something come of it.

So one might infer that the real natural ground of meaningful utterance is in what mental state is expressed by the utterance. Of course we have already introduced the word "express" as designating a relation between sentences and propositions, but here the term has a more concrete and literal use: sentence tokens are seen as expressively produced by speakers' beliefs, desires, and other propositional attitudes.

Grice (1957, 1969) took these facts as the basis of his theory of meaning. He believed that sentence meaning is grounded in the mental, and proposed to explicate it ultimately in terms of the psychological states of individual human beings. We can think of this as no less than the reduction of linguistic meaning to psychology.

The linchpin of Grice's project was a slightly different notion of meaning, that does not coincide with that of sentence meaning. Here are three examples to illustrate the difference. First, recall Strawson's sentence from Chapter 2, "This is a fine red one." As we saw, the meaning of that sentence itself is not fully determinate; to understand it, we need to know what the speaker is pointing to. One speaker in one context may mean that the pear in her/his hand is a fine red pear, while a different speaker on a different occasion may mean that the third fire-engine on the left is a fine figure of a red fire-engine.

Second, suppose that like some unfortunates I incorrectly believe that the word "jejune" means something like *callow* or *puerile*,[1] and I say "Mozart's 'Piccolomini' Mass is jejune, not good Mozart at all," meaning that the "Piccolomini" Mass is callow and puerile. But "jejune" actually means *meager and unsatisfying* (it is from the Latin word for fasting); the sentence I uttered means that the Mass is meager and unsatisfying, which I would judge to be false even though I do find the Mass callow and puerile.

Third, consider sarcasm, as when one says "That was a brilliant idea", meaning that someone's idea was very stupid. Here too, we get a divergence between the meaning of the sentence uttered and what the speaker meant in uttering it (since the speaker means precisely the opposite). The moral is that what a speaker means in uttering a given sentence is a slightly different kind of meaning from the sentence's own meaning. Grice called it "utterer's meaning"; it is also widely called just "speaker-meaning."[2]

Now, let us turn to Grice's reductive project, the explication of sentence meaning in psychological terms. It proceeds in two importantly different stages. In the first stage,[3] Grice attempts to reduce sentence meaning to speaker-meaning. In the second, he tries to reduce speaker-meaning to a complex of psychological states centering on a type of intention.

On the face of it, the first stage is a plausible idea. As Wittgenstein emphasized, it is very strange to think of sentences as having meanings on their own and in the abstract, as opposed to thinking of sentences as having meaning because of what speakers use them to do. It does seem that linguistic expressions have the conventional meanings they do only in virtue of human communicative practices, and that communicative "practices" boil down to sets of individual speakers' communicative acts. Grice amends that last phrase, focusing on what speakers use sentences to *mean*, in the sense of what the speakers mean in uttering the sentences when they do utter them. For Grice, a sentence's meaning is a function of individual speaker-meanings.

But Grice concentrated his energies on the second stage of the reduction. That speaker-meaning should by explicated in terms of mental states is even more plausible than the first stage. If when I say "That was a brilliant idea," what I mean is that Smedley's idea was very stupid, surely that speaker-meaning is something psychological, something about my mental state. Presumably it is a matter of my *communicative intention*, of what I am intending to convey to you. It does seem that, in general, individual communicative acts are a matter of speakers' having complex intentions to produce various cognitive and other states in their hearers.

Speaker-meaning

Let us start with a plausible and perhaps needlessly specific version of Grice's second-stage analysis, that skips over some of the early footwork contained in or occasioned by his original article (1957). (I offer a paraphrase rather than a direct quotation, to avoid some of Grice's own slightly technical jargon and some complications.)[4] We want to explicate statements of the form, "By uttering x, S meant that P," as in "By uttering 'The "Piccolomini" Mass is jejune', Lycan meant that the 'Piccolomini' Mass is callow and puerile." The analysis runs as follows:

(G1) *S* uttered *x* intending that *A* form the belief that P [where *A* is *S*'s hearer or audience]; and

(G2) *S* further intended that *A* recognize *S*'s original intention [as described in (G1)]; and

(G3) *S* still further intended that *A* form the belief that P at least partly on the basis of recognizing that original intention.

Thus, in our Mozart example, by uttering "The 'Piccolomini' Mass is jejune," I meant that the Mass is callow and puerile, because I uttered it intending that you form the belief that the Mass is callow and puerile at least partly on the basis of your recognizing that I had that very intention.

As advertised, the core of speaker-meaning is an intention, but other mental states figure in the analysis as well, namely the intended future belief of yours and the intended state of recognition.

It may be thought implausible that an ordinary speaker could have such complex intentions at all, much less have them every single time s/he makes an assertion. But Grice is not supposing that these communicative intentions are conscious, or before the mind. Indeed, in daily life most of our intentions are only tacit; we are only occasionally aware of them. So too, you usually say things without explicitly thinking about it, and often you speaker-mean things that you are unaware of.

The foregoing second-stage theory has been under nearly constant revision since 1969, in response to counterexamples of several kinds. I shall review a few of the objections and revisions, just enough to give you the flavor of this subproject.

Objection 1

Speaker-meaning does not in fact require an actual audience. Suppose I am given to soliloquizing. When I have a problem, practical or theoretical or personal, I work through it talking aloud to myself in the privacy of my basement batcave. Not only do I intend no effect on any audience, I would be mortified if I were to find out that someone had been listening. Or consider Paul Ziff's (1967: 3–4) protagonist George and the sentence, "Claudius murdered my father": in a single day, George might utter that sentence first "in the course of a morning soliloquy," again "in the afternoon in the course of a conversation with Josef," and then again "in the evening while delirious with fever" and unaware of his audience even though there was one. Yet George meant the same thing by "Claudius murdered my father" each time. But Grice's analysis requires not only an audience but that the speaker have very specific intentions with respect to that audience, and this is implausible at least for the soliloquy and delirium cases.

Grice (1969: section V) addresses the audienceless cases. He urges a solution in terms of hypothetical or counterfactual audiences: in effect, a speaker should intend that, *were* anyone present and enjoying normal perceptual and other psychological conditions, that person *would* form the belief that P.

Need I, as a speaker, intend this? Perhaps so, since when I speak even to myself I must assume that what I say would make sense to someone. On the other hand, further potential counterexamples come to mind. Suppose I grew up on a desert island, and somehow put together a language all by myself; yet I never formed the concept of "another speaker" or of an "audience." Then I could not intend anything about an audience even counterfactually. But this is a highly controversial case, since many philosophers have denied that it would be even faintly possible for me to make up my own language without having formed the concept of speakers-and-audiences.

Objection 2

Even when there is an actual audience, the speaker may mean something, yet not intend to produce belief by means of intention recognition; requirements (G3) and even (G2) may be too strong. Or the speaker may not even intend to produce the belief at all, since her/his audience *already* has the belief in question and is known by the speaker to have it.

Here is an example of the former type of case. *Conclusion of argument*: one offers an argument, perhaps produces a proof of a geometrical theorem. One certainly speaker-means the argument's conclusion, but does not intend one's audience to reach that conclusion even in part on the basis of recognizing one's original intention. One may firmly intend them not to do so, but rather to form the belief on the basis of the argument's merit alone.

Schiffer (1972: 79–80) approaches the (allegedly) audienceless cases, and *Conclusion of argument* as well, by stipulating that the speaker is her/his own audience. (I personally cannot dismiss this as fanciful, since it has been said of me that I often produce utterances for the simple gratification of hearing myself talk.)[5] This move might do, but for cases of the second type.

For example, *Examinee*: a pupil who correctly answers an exam question means, for example, that the Battle of Waterloo was fought in 1815, but does not intend to *induce* that belief in the examiner(s).

Grice makes essentially two revisions in response to these and a swarm of other counterexamples. First, he suggests invoking the concept of "activated" belief: though some of the audience already believe what the speaker has in mind, their beliefs may not be fully conscious and psychologically active, or even conscious at all. If we beef up (G1), the requirement that the audience be intended to believe that P, to demand that S intends to produce *activated* belief in A, that may account (though not very naturally) for *Examinee*; it does better against some of the other cases.

Grice's second revision is also to amend (G1), this time replacing it by the weaker provision that the audience be intended to believe only that *the speaker* believes that P. (Weakening (G1) in this way is compatible with having strengthened (G1) to require activated belief.)

This second revision seems reasonable. As Grice says, it deals briskly with *Examinee*. And it is not implausible. To say something and mean it, we might hold, is *merely* to express a belief, usually but not always hoping or intending or expecting that one's audience will come to share the belief. (When we inform people of things by telling them those things, we normally expect that informing to work by what informal logicians call "authority": our hearers take our word for what we are saying and believe it because we do.)

Yet as Grice grants and Schiffer emphasizes (p. 43), *Conclusion of argument* is not alleviated by either the first or the second revision. More generally, not all cases of communication succeed *because* the audience takes the speaker's word. Recall the geometrical proof. For an example closer to home, Grice himself has communicated his theory of meaning to us, but not by virtue of having intended us to accept it on the strength of his say-so. It is true that we have come to believe that Grice believes his theory of meaning, so the newly weakened version of (G1) is satisfied; but that does not help here. (We cannot really even assume that Grice does believe the theory; I am afraid philosophers are always writing articles defending views that they do not themselves really believe.)

What about Schiffer's response to *Conclusion of argument*, that the speaker is her/his own audience? I think there are still counterexamples of the same type. Suppose I produce a second proof of my theorem while the first is still sitting on the blackboard. I do not induce a belief in myself, or even activate one that I already held quiescently. Another: suppose two philosophers are having a love-feast over the Direct Reference view of proper names. They are dancing around in a circle and shouting joyfully at each other, "Names only name!" over and over. Each is in a state of fully activated belief in the truth of this dubious assertion, and each knows that the other is; so neither can be said to have the intention of either producing or activating belief in the other. Yet surely they mean by their utterance that proper names only name; it is not a nonsense chant.

Further moves are available here,[6] but I shall drop Objection 2 at this point.

The first two objections were intended to show that Grice's analysis is too demanding. The next two are to the effect that in other respects the analysis is not demanding enough.

Objection 3 (Ziff 1967: 2)

> On being inducted into the army, George is compelled to take a test designed to establish sanity. George is known to be an irritable academic. The test he is being given would be appropriate for morons. One of the questions asked is: "What would you say if you were asked to identify yourself?" George replied to the officer asking the question by uttering ... "Ugh blugh blugh ugh blugh".

George meant to show his contempt, and meant the officer to recognize his contempt on the basis of recognizing his intention to show it. But although Grice's conditions are met, George did not mean anything in any *linguistic* sense (though one might correctly point out that there is a wider sense of "communication" that Grice's analysis still seems to capture).[7]

Objection 4 (Searle 1965: 229–30)

During World War II an American soldier is captured by Italian troops. He wants to get the Italians to release him, by convincing them that he is a German officer. But he does not know either German or Italian. Hoping that his captors do not know German either, he "as it were, attempts to put on a show of telling them that he is a German officer," by officiously barking out the only German sentence he knows, a line of poetry he had learned in school: "Kennst du das Land wo die Zitronen blühen?" ("Do you know the land where the lemon trees bloom?").[8]

Here the soldier uttered his sentence intending to get the Italians to believe that he is a German officer; he further intended them to recognize that original intention; and he still further intended them to form the false belief in part on the basis of recognizing the intention. But it does not seem that in saying "Kennst du das Land ... ," *he means that* he is a German officer.

Grice responds by requiring that the audience be intended to believe there to be a "mode of correlation" between features of the utterance and the intended belief type. Schiffer (1972) makes a different move, in terms of his technical notion "mutual knowledge*." It seems better not to forge on into these arcana for now.

Determined Griceans such as Schiffer (1972) and Avramides (1989) have shown extraordinary fortitude and skill in modifying Grice's original account in such a way as to accommodate all the foregoing problem cases and more, with the result that despite the profusion of objections, a complicated(!) version of the theory remains tenable. And it is generally agreed that speaker-meaning must be in *some* way a matter of speakers' intentions and other mental states. But now we must turn back to the first stage of the Gricean program, the reduction of sentence meaning to speaker-meaning.

Sentence meaning

As may surprise you after you have read the previous section, Grice's (1968) construction of sentence meaning out of speaker-meaning is elaborate and full of tricky details. Rather than plunge into them, I shall reveal some obstacles in advance. Then I shall only outline the way(s) in which Grice tries to surmount them.

It would be natural to start by supposing that a given English sentence means that P just in case when speakers of English utter that sentence, they always or at least normally (speaker-)mean that P. But here come the problems.

Obstacle 1

Ziff (1967) offered the following two examples:

> George has had his head tampered with: electrodes have been inserted, plates mounted, and so forth. The effect was curious: when asked how he felt, George replied by uttering . . . "Glyting elly beleg". What he meant by . . . [that], he later informed us, was that he felt fine. He said that, at the time, he had somehow believed that . . . ["Glyting elly beleg"] was synonymous with "I feel fine" and that everyone knew this.
> (pp. 4–5; by now you will have grasped that George leads a life more interesting than yours or mine)

A man suddenly cried out "Gleeg gleeg gleeg!", intending thereby to produce a certain effect in an audience by means of the recognition of his intention. He wished to make his audience believe that it was snowing in Tibet. Of course he did not produce the effect he was after since no one recognized what his intention was. Nonetheless that he had such an intention became clear. Being deemed mad, he was turned over to a psychiatrist. He complained to the psychiatrist that when he cried "Gleeg gleeg gleeg!" he had such an intention but no one recognized his intention and were they not mad not to do so.

(p. 5)

In the text it is not clear whether Ziff took these cases to be counterexamples to Grice's analysis of speaker-meaning. But I do not understand him in that way and I do not take them as such. It seems to me that, in his altered state, George did mean that he felt fine; and the madman derangedly meant that it was snowing in Tibet. Rather, I take the point to be that if Grice's theory of speaker-meaning is correct, then speaker-meaning comes very cheap: given a suitably disordered mental state, any speaker may mean anything at all by any string of noises s/he happens to utter. If Grice's analysis of speaker-meaning is correct, then, all the worse for the first stage of his project, for there will then be no formal constraint on what speakers *might* mean by any sentence they utter, but only statistics about how often speakers do mean this or that.

In real life, of course, speaker-meaning is not so easily had, for two reasons. (a) Most people are not deranged in the manner of Ziff's patients. Far more importantly, (b) English sentences have the meanings they do have, and one cannot just mean anything by them one likes. Unless I am oddly mistaken about the meaning of the word itself, or some more elaborate stage-setting is in place, I cannot say "It's cold here" and mean by it "It's warm here." (The example is Wittgenstein's.) I could be being sarcastic, of course. But I could not very well mean "I have just rented the video of *Agnes of God*," or "Pigs have wings." The antecedent meaning of a sentence partly controls what a speaker can mean by it in a given context.

(b) further embarrasses Grice's first stage, since if sentence meaning is to be analyzed entirely away into speaker-meaning, we should not have to look to sentence meaning as constraining possible speaker-meanings. (Perhaps "should not" is too strong. There is no flat-out circularity here; and it is certainly possible that one special construct out of speaker-meaning might constrain speaker-meaning in general. But the Gricean will still have to explain why this happens so robustly.)

Obstacle 2

(Platts 1979: 89.) Most meaningful sentences of a language are never uttered at all. Therefore no one has ever meant anything by them. Therefore their meanings can hardly be determined by what speakers (normally, typically, etc.) mean by them.

It is not much use, though tempting, to appeal to what speakers *would have* meant by the unuttered sentences had they uttered them. For one thing, the vast majority of those sentences are ones that the speakers *would never have* uttered. Even for a sentence that the speakers might have uttered even though they did not, the only handle we have on what the speakers would have meant in uttering it is what we already know that sentence to mean.

Obstacle 3

Novel sentences again. Even when a sentence is actually uttered, it may be wildly novel, yet instantly understood by its audience. But if it is novel, then no pre-established expectation or convention has been directed specifically upon *it*. And notice that the first, novel use may be (a) also the last and (b) *itself nonliteral*. (I am pretty sure that the following sentence has never been uttered before, though it may be uttered again: "The President of the United States Philosophy Corporation, who has finally been released from prison and is hurrying here to the aviary on winged feet, will share the riches of her spirit with us at 3:00 p.m. tomorrow.") In such a case, even though the sentence had been uttered, no one would ever actually have meant by it what it literally means.)

Blackburn (1984: Chapter 4) points out that in the right circumstances, a given sentence may be uttered with practically any intention and certainly *without* the intention of displaying one's actual belief. (Blackburn broaches the alternative idea that a sentence S means that P when it is either a conventional regularity or the consequence of a conventional regularity that one who utters S with assertive force "may be regarded as having displayed" that P, this regard-licence being a social fact that obtains independently of any particular utterer's intentions. This is an interesting idea, and calls for much unpacking of "may," "be regarded," and "display," but it is not a Gricean idea, for it self-consciously severs sentence-meaning from speakers' communicative intentions.)

Obstacle 4

Sentences are *often,* and not just abnormally, used with other than their own literal meanings. Even neglecting sarcasm and other forms of indirect speech acts (we shall talk more about such things in Chapter 13), figurative usage is very prevalent (we shall talk more about *that* in Chapter 14). If Grice should want to say that a sentence's own meaning is what speakers "normally" do mean in uttering the sentence, he would have to say what "normally" means independently of the sentence's standard meaning, as well as motivating the claim.

And things get even worse. There are private codes in which a given sentence is *never* used with its literal meaning. The Japanese signal for the 1941 air attack on Pearl Harbor was (the Japanese expression translated as) "East wind, rain," which so far as I know has never been used to mean anything but "It's time to go bomb Pearl Harbor." And even apart from private codes, in everyday life there are many sentences that normally are uttered with other than their literal meanings, and perhaps are never uttered with those literal meanings. ("All right, buddy, where's the fire?" "Can you tell me the time?" "George and Martha buried the hatchet." "Business is business.") And there is the whole question of metaphor, though as we shall see in Chapter 13, Grice himself thinks of metaphor as a species of what is called "conversational implicature."

Now for a sketch of Grice's reduction of sentence meaning to speaker-meaning, and indications of how he would have approached Obstacles 1–4 had he been fully aware of them.[9]

He first concentrates on the narrow notion of sentence meaning *for a particular individual,* that is the meaning that the sentence has in that individual's personal, distinctive speech or *idiolect.* (No two English speakers' idiolects are exactly alike.) And he restricts his initial target further, distinguishing *structured* utterances from *unstructured* ones. A structured utterance has meaningful parts, such as individual words, which contribute to the utterance's overall meaning; any declarative English sentence is an example of this, since it contains words that are individually meaningful and it means what it does in virtue of those words meaning what they do. An unstructured utterance is a single expression or non-verbal gesture, such as "Ouch" or a beckoning motion that means "This way," whose meaning is not compositional in that sense. (Note that Grice uses the term "utterance" very broadly, as including nonverbal communicative acts.)

After some backing and filling, Grice hypothesizes that x [an unstructured expression] means that P in S's idiolect, just in case (roughly) S has in her/his repertoire the following procedure: to utter x if, for some audience A, S intends A to believe that S believes that P. (That last clause is a simplified version of "S speaker-means that P"; Grice argues that the simplification is harmless here.)

Now he expands this analysis to cover utterance meaning for a group of speakers: x [unstructured] means that P for group G just in case (a) many members of G have in their repertoires the procedure of: uttering x if, for some A, they want A to believe that they believe that P, and (b) the retention of that procedure is for them conditional on the assumption that at least some other members of G have that same procedure in their repertoires.

I think what are supposed to overcome Obstacle 1 are (a) and (b), that the relevant procedure is widespread in the community and that individual members of the community rely on the other members to maintain that procedure as well. This seems exactly right.

But now the trick will be to go from the analysis of unstructured-utterance meaning to ordinary sentence meaning, since ordinary English sentences are all structured. Grice brings in the notion of a "resultant" procedure. At this point Grice's article becomes dense and obscure, but I think the idea is this: just as English sentences are made up of smaller meaningful parts – words and phrases – in virtue of which the whole sentences mean what they mean, an individual speaker will have in her/his repertoire a complex, abstract "resultant procedure" made up of the concrete procedures attaching to its respective composite parts. Thus, a sentence's meaning will not be directly a function of speaker-meaning, but rather a function of the individual utterance meanings of its ultimate parts. Only then will the core Gricean idea, and (crucially) his analysis of utterance meaning for a group, be invoked as explicating the utterance meanings of the parts.

I emphasize "*abstract* resultant procedure," because very few of those "abstract" procedures will ever actually occur. And it is that feature that will help Grice with Obstacles 2–3. For the theme of those obstacles is that unuttered and novel sentences do not correspond to any actual speaker-meanings. But at least arguably, they do correspond to the hypothetical speaker-meanings that would be generated by Grice's abstract resultant procedures.

The appeal to abstract procedures may also help to overcome Obstacle 4: even though a certain sentence's literal meaning is never matched by any actual speaker-meaning, it may still correspond to a hypothetical resultant speaker-meaning.

Yet I believe that this absolutely necessary appeal betrays the spirit of the Gricean program. In effect, it gives the game away to a competing theory of meaning; I shall argue that in Chapter 9.

Summary

- According to Grice, linguistic expressions have meaning only because they express ideas or intentions of the speakers who use them.
- "Speaker-meaning" is, roughly, what the speaker in uttering a given sentence on a particular occasion intends to convey to a hearer.
- Grice offers an analysis of speaker-meaning in terms of speakers' intentions, beliefs, and other psychological states, and has tenably refined that analysis in the light of many objections.
- Grice has also offered an analysis of a sentence's own meaning in terms of speaker-meaning.
- That analysis overcomes some severe obstacles, but seemingly only by conceding too much to competing theories of sentence meaning.

Questions

1 Can you help Grice avoid one or more of Objections 1–4?
2 Can you think of further objections to Grice's theory of speaker-meaning?
3 Discuss Grice's "first stage"; will his elaborate method of reducing sentence meaning to speaker-meaning work?

Notes

1 Do not miss Kingsley Amis' tale of this word in *The King's English* (HarperCollins, 1998: 118–19). Amis swears he has seen the word mis-spelled as "jejeune" and even pronounced in pseudo-French as "zherzherne." Come to think of it, do not miss the rest of Amis' book either.
2 There is a tendency in the Gricean literature to assume that speaker-meaning is unique, that a given utterance has but a single speaker-meaning. That assumption is false; we are complex communicators, and we sometimes mean more than one thing at a time by uttering the sentence that we do. Perhaps I mean what the sentence means and also some further conveyed meaning. Or if you are good at puns, your sentence may be itself ambiguous and you intend both meanings at once. Shakespeare could mean as many as five different things in a single utterance.
3 It did not come chronologically first, but was presented in Grice (1968).
4 In particular, let us confine the discussion to declarative sentences, though Grice was careful to address imperatives and others as well.
5 Yes, it has. Can you *believe* that?
6 One possible fix, suggested to me by Wendy Nankas, is to talk not just of activation but of *reinforcement*.

7 Ziff's case is strongly similar to an example of J. O. Urmson's regarding thumbscrews, discussed by Grice (1969: 152–3). In response, Grice offered what he labels "Redefinition I"; but I have never seen exactly how that redefinition was supposed to rule out this kind of counterexample.

There is a set of examples begun in conversation by Dennis Stampe, Stephen Schiffer, and P. F. Strawson, involving deceit and second-guessing of a certain kind. Stampe's version was the first to be addressed by Grice (1969). The counterexamples and responses lead to an indefinite regress of particularly convoluted cases and revisions of the analysis. I doubt that you would thank me for dragging you through even the second example in the regress. (You might even try to return this book and get a fraction of your money back.) So I shall not even expound the first.

8 This is the opening line of a song lyric that appears in Goethe's novel *Wilhelm Meisters Lehrjahre* (1795–6), Book 3, Chapter 1.

9 Schiffer (1972: Chapters V–VI) pursued a different method, employing Lewis (1969)'s theory of conventions.

Further reading

Schiffer (1972) is the classic working-out of Grice's view. See also Gilbert Harman's review (1974a), and Avramides (1989). Related works of Grice's own are collected in Grice (1989).

Bennett (1976) is a valuable defense of the Gricean project by one who was not an insider.

MacKay (1972), Black (1973), Rosenberg (1974: Chapter II), and Biro (1979) are critical of Grice.

8
Verificationism

Overview

According to the Verification Theory, a sentence is meaningful just in case its being true would make some difference to the course of our future experience; an experientially unverifiable sentence or "sentence" is meaningless. More specifically, a sentence's particular meaning is its *verification condition*, the set of possible experiences on someone's part that would tend to show that the sentence was true.

The theory faces a number of objections: it has ruled a number of clearly meaningful sentences meaningless, and vice versa; it has assigned the wrong meanings to sentences that it does count as meaningful; and it has some dubious presuppositions. But the worst objection is that, as Duhem and Quine have argued, individual sentences do not have distinctive verification conditions of their own.

Quine went on to bite that bullet and infer that individual sentences do not have meanings; according to him there is no such thing as sentence meaning. Quine also attacked the formerly widespread view that some sentences are "analytic" in the sense of being true by definition or solely in virtue of the meanings of their component terms.

The theory and its motivation

The Verification Theory of meaning, which flourished in the 1930s and 1940s, was a highly political theory. It was motivated by, and reciprocally helped to motivate, a growing empiricism and scientism in philosophy and in other disciplines. In particular, it was the engine that drove the philosophical movement of Logical Positivism, which was correctly perceived by moral philosophers, poets, theologians, and many others as directly attacking the foundations of their respective enterprises. Unlike most philosophical theories, it also had numerous powerful effects on the actual practice of science, both very good effects and very bad. But here we shall examine Verificationism simply as another theory of linguistic meaning.

As one popular Positivist slogan had it, a difference must make a difference. That is to say, if some bit of language is supposed to be meaningful at all, then it has got to make some kind of difference to thought and to action. And the Positivists had a very specific idea of what kind of difference it ought to make: the bit of language ought to matter, specifically, to the course of our *future experience*. If someone utters what sounds like a sentence, but you have no idea how the truth of that sentence would affect the future in a detectable way, then in what sense can you say that it is nevertheless a meaningful sentence for you?

The Positivists threw out that rhetorical question as a challenge. Suppose I put a line of something that looks like gibberish on the blackboard and I assert that the scribble is a meaningful sentence in someone's language. You ask me what will happen depending on whether the scribble is true or false. I say "Nothing; the world will go on just as it otherwise would, whether this sentence is true or false." Then you should become deeply suspicious of my contention that this apparent gibberish actually means something. Less drastically, if you hear someone utter something in an alien tongue, you presume that it does mean something, but you have no idea what it means; that is because you do not know what would show whether it is true or false.

The Positivists were concerned about the basic property of meaningfulness because they suspected that many of what passed for meaningful utterances in the works of the Great Dead Philosophers were not in fact (even) meaningful at all, much less true. So, their Verification Principle was most notably used as a criterion of meaningfulness-as-opposed-to-meaninglessness: a sentence was counted as meaningful just in case there was some set of possible experiences on someone's part that would tend to show that the sentence was true; call this set the sentence's *verification condition*. (A sentence also has a falsification condition, the set of possible experiences that would tend to show that it was false.) If, in examining a proposed sentence, one could not come up with such a set of experiences, the sentence would fail the test and would be revealed as being meaningless, however proper its surface grammar. (Classic examples of alleged failures: "Everything [including all yardsticks and other measuring devices] has just doubled in size." Eleventh-hour creation: "The entire physical universe came into existence just five minutes ago, complete with ostensible memories and records." Demon skepticism: "We are constantly and systematically being deceived by a powerful evil demon who feeds us specious experiences.")[1]

But the Verificationists did not confine their concern to meaningfulness itself. The theory also took a more specific form, anticipated by C. S. Peirce (1878). It addressed the individual meanings of particular sentences, and identified each sentence's meaning with that sentence's verification condition.

Thus, the theory had a practical use, as an actual test for what an individual sentence does mean; it predicts the sentence's particular propositional content. This is an important virtue, not shared by all its competitors. (The naive Proposition Theory says nothing of how to associate a particular proposition with a given sentence.) The Verification Theory was meant to be used, and has been used – even by people who do not accept it in full – as a clarificatory tool. If you are confronted by a sentence that you presume to be meaningful but you do not entirely understand, ask yourself what would tend to show that the sentence was true or that it was false.

The Verification Theory is thus an *epistemic* account of meaning; that is, it locates meaning in our ways of coming to know or finding out things. To a Verificationist, a sentence's meaning is its epistemology, a matter of what its proper evidence base would be. (On one interpretation, the Sellarsian functional or Inferential Theory of Meaning mentioned in Chapter 6 is Verificationist, for Sellars' inference rules are epistemic devices.)

The Positivists allowed that there is a special class of sentences that do not have empirical content but are nonetheless meaningful in a way: these are sentences that are, so to speak, true by definition, true solely in virtue of the meanings of the terms that compose them. "No bachelor is married"; "If it's snowing, then it's snowing"; "Five pencils are more pencils than two pencils." Such sentences make no empirical predictions, according to the Positivists, because they are true no matter what happens in the world. But they have meaning of a sort because they are true; their truth, however trivial, is guaranteed by the collective meanings of the words that occur in them. Such sentences are called *analytic*.

Verificationism is an attractive view that has been held fervently by many. But like every other theory of meaning, it has its problems.

Some objections

The Positivists themselves never achieved a formulation of the Verification Principle that satisfied even themselves; they could never get it to fit just the strings of words they wanted it to fit. Every precise formulation proved to be too strong or too weak in one respect or another (see Hempel 1950). There is a methodological problem as well: to test proposed formulations, the Positivists had to appeal to clear cases of both kinds, that is of meaningful strings of words and meaningless strings. But this assumes already that there *are* strings of words that are literally meaningless even though they are grammatically well-formed and composed of perfectly meaningful words; and that is, when you think about it, a very bold claim.

These problems do not constitute principled objections to Verificationism, but they suggest two more that do.

Objection 1

Wittgenstein would and did complain that the Verification Theory is yet another *monolithic* attempt to get at the "essence" of language, and all such attempts are doomed to failure. But in particular and less dogmatically, the theory applies only to what the Positivists called descriptive, fact-stating language. But descriptive or fact-stating language is only one kind of language; we also ask questions, give orders, write poems, tell jokes, perform ceremonies of various kinds, etc. Presumably an adequate theory of meaning should apply to all these uses of language, since they are all meaningful uses of language in any ordinary sense of the term; but it is hard to see how the Verification Theory could be extended to cover them.

Reply

The Positivists acknowledged that they were addressing meaning only in a restricted sense; they called it "cognitive" meaning. To be "cognitively" meaningful is roughly to be a statement of fact. Questions, commands, and lines of poetry are not fact-stating or descriptive in that sense, even though they have important linguistic functions and are "meaningful" in the ordinary sense as opposed to gibberish.

The restriction to "cognitive" meaning was fine for the Positivists' larger metaphysical and anti-metaphysical purposes, but from our point of view, the elucidation of linguistic meaning generally, it is damaging. A theory of meaning in our sense is charged with explaining all the meaning facts, not just those pertaining to fact-stating language. Further, the retreat to "cognitive" meaning does not help with Objection 2.

Objection 2

As we noted, the Positivists were working with admittedly preconceived ideas of which strings of words are meaningful and which are not, trying to rule out the intuitively meaningless ones and to rule in the obviously meaningful ones. But it is not only the Positivists that had preconceived ideas about which strings of words are meaningful. Suppose we look at a given string of words, and ask whether or not it is verifiable, and if so what would verify it. In order to do that, we already have to know what the sentence says; how could we know whether it was verifiable unless we knew what it says?

To determine how to verify the presence of a virus, say, we must know what viruses are and where, in general, they are to be found; thus it seems we must understand talk of viruses in order to verify statements about viruses, rather than vice versa. But if we already know what our sentence says, then there is something that it says. And to that extent, it already is meaningful. Thus, the question of verifiability and verification conditions is conceptually posterior to knowing what the sentence means; it seems we have to know what a sentence means in order to know how to verify it.[2] But that is just the opposite of what the Verification Theory says.

A related point is that there is a glaring difference between the sentences that the Positivists wanted to rule out as meaningless ("Everything has just doubled in size," "The entire physical universe came into existence just five minutes ago," etc.) and paradigm cases of meaningless strings, gibberish, or word salad of the sort illustrated in Chapter 1 ("w gfjsdkhj jiobfglglf ud," "Good of off primly the a the the why"). Surely the former strings are not meaningless in the same drastic and obvious way as the latter. Whatever may be wrong with them from an epistemological point of view, they are not mere gibberish.

Reply

The Verificationist must come up with some difference between the two types of string, without admitting that strings of the first type are meaningful after all. Here is a possible move. Strings of the first type are made of regular English words, and because they are grammatical from a superficially syntactic point of view, there is a kind of illusion of under-standing. Since these are the kinds of strings of words that often do say and mean something, they produce in us a feeling of familiarity. We have the feeling that we know what they say. And in a weak sense we do: we can parse them grammatically, and we understand each of the words that occur in them. But it does not follow that these strings of words do, in fact, mean anything as wholes.

Objection 3

The Verification Theory leads to bad or at least highly controversial meta-physics. Recall that a verification condition is a set of *experiences*. The Positivists meant such verifying experiences to be described in a uniform kind of language called an "observation language." Suppose our "observa-tion language" restricts itself to the vocabulary of subjective sense-impressions, as in "I now seem to see a pink rabbit-shaped thing in front of me." Then it follows from Verificationism that any meaningful statement I succeed in making can ultimately only be about my own sense-impressions; if solipsism is false, I cannot meaningfully say that it is. And neither can anyone else.

Even if instead we loosen our notion of "observation" and include what Hempel (1950) called the "directly observable characteristics" of ordinary objects, it remains true that Verificationism collapses a sentence's meaning into the type of observational evidence we can have for that sentence, *without remainder*. For example, we are driven to a grotesquely revisionist view about scientific objects – the instrumentalist view that scientific statements about electrons, memory traces, other galaxies, and the like are merely abbreviations of complex sets of statements about our own labora-tory data. What is the verification condition of a sentence about an electron? Of course it is something macroscopic, something about meter readings or vapor trails in a cloud chamber or scattering patterns on a cathode ray tube or something of the sort. It is observable with the naked eye in the here and now. Are we really to believe that when we talk about subatomic particles we are not really talking about little particles – particles so small that they cannot be observed – but instead about meter readings, vapor trails, and the like? (The Positivists themselves did not consider this instrumentalism grotesque, but thought it importantly true; I think it is grotesque.)

And when we turn to questions about the human mind, we find that a very strong version of behaviorism falls right out: statements about people's minds are merely abbreviations of statements about those people's overt behavior. For the only sort of observational evidence I ever have regarding your innermost thoughts and feelings is the behavior I see and hear you engaging in. If one is a Verificationist, philosophy of mind is over and done with.

Possibly one or more of the foregoing and to me unappetizing theories are true. Perhaps they are *all* true. My point here is just that our theory of linguistic meaning should not show *in one step* that they are. Metaphysics should not be settled by a theory of language, for language is just a late adaptation found in one primate species. (Perhaps it is not even an adaptation, but a pleiotropism.)

Objection 4

How does the Verification Principle apply to itself? Either *it* is empirically verifiable or it is not.

Suppose it is not verifiable. Then either it is *just* meaningless or it is an empty "analytic" or definitional truth. At least one Positivist (I have forgotten which) gallantly embraced the idea that the Principle is just meaningless, a ladder to be kicked away once one has climbed it. Some Positivists took the line that the principle was a useful stipulative definition of the word "meaning," for technical purposes. Hempel (1950) called the Principle a "proposal," hence neither true nor false, but subject to each of several rational demands and constraints, hence not simply *arbitrary*. Of course, any philosopher can stipulate anything at any time; but how does that help those of us who are looking around for a credible, indeed correct *theory of* meaning (as is)? Stipulations have their uses, but when we are trying to come to an adequate philosophical theory of a pre-existing phenomenon, a stipulation is not of much help.

I suppose some Positivists thought of the Principle as a faithful, correct definition that captures the antecedent meaning of "meaning." The trouble with that idea is that we do not know what specifically semantic evidence would bear out the definition as correct. Certainly the Positivists had not subjected the term "meaning" to the sort of analysis that Russell had lavished on the word "the"; and neither ordinary people nor even non-Positivist philosophers shared many *intuitive* judgements in line with the Verification Principle. It does not seem to be analytic, like "No bachelor is married"; I doubt that anyone who understands what the word "meaning" means and what "verify" means knows that to be meaningful is just to be verifiable and that a sentence's meaning is its verification condition.

Suppose the Principle *is* taken to be empirically verifiable. That is, assume it is supposed to be confirmed by our experiences of sentences, their meanings, and their verification conditions, and meaning has been *found* to track verification condition. But (as in Objection 1) that presupposes that we can recognize sentence meanings independently of assigning them verification conditions. And it is not clear just what we should count as the "empirical" data on which the Principle is based. Survey results from street corners? Dictionary definitions? (*Never* that.) One's own linguistic "intuitions"? (Also, the Verification Principle's own meaning would then, by the Principle itself, coincide with its own verification condition, the set of experiences of meanings coinciding with verification conditions; that is a tangle, though I am unsure whether it is ultimately vicious.)

At any rate, the self-application problem is a real one, not just a superficial trick question.[3]

Objection 5

Erwin (1970) offers an argument to show that every statement is verifiable, trivially and in much the same way. Suppose we are presented with a funny-looking machine that turns out to be a marvellous predictor. Namely, when one codes a declarative sentence onto a punch card and inserts it into a slot in the machine, the machine whirrs and klunks and lights up either "TRUE" or "FALSE"; moreover, so far as we are able to check, the machine is miraculously *always right*.

Now consider an arbitrarily chosen string of words, S. The following set of experiences *would* suffice to raise S's probability to a drastic degree: 1. We code S onto a punch card. 2. We feed the card into our machine. 3. The machine lights up "TRUE." (And remember that the machine has never once been wrong.) Thus, there exists a possible set of experiences that would confirm S, even if S is intuitively gibberish. And S's own particular verification condition would be that when it is coded and put to the machine, the machine lights up "TRUE." Thus the Verification Theory is trivialized, since every string of words is verifiable, and it assigns the wrong meanings to particular sentences, because very few sentences mean anything about punch cards being fed into infernal machines.

Something is wrong with that argument. But I have found it very hard to say exactly what.

Objection 6

Any version of the Verification Principle must presuppose an "observation language" in which experiences are described; hence it must countenance a firm distinction between "observational" and (correlatively) "theoretical" terms. As I have mentioned, some of the Positivists restricted their observation language to statements about people's private, subjective sense-impressions. But that did not serve for purposes of intersubjectively checkable science, so most Positivists joined Hempel (1950) in appealing to the "directly observable characteristics" of ordinary objects. There are two problems here. First, the notion of "direct observation" is a vexed one, and seems totally technology-relative *and* interest- or project-relative as well. Is a visual observation "direct" when you are wearing eyeglasses? How about if you are using a magnifying glass? How about through a microscope, at this or that degree of magnification? How about through an electron microscope?

Second, "observations," and statements couched in "observation language," are *theory-laden* at least to a degree; what counts as an observation and what counts as observed and how a "datum" is described are all determined in part by the very theories that are in question.

Both these problems are knotty issues in the philosophy of science; I merely mention them here.[4] But they help to set up a much deeper objection to Verificationism.

The big one

Objection 7

Following Pierre Duhem (1906/1954), W. V. Quine (1953, 1960) argues that no individual sentence *has* a distinctive verification condition, except relative to a mass of background theory against which "observational" testing takes place. This will take some explaining.

There is a naive idea that many people have about science. It is that one puts forward a scientific hypothesis and then tests the hypothesis by doing an experiment, and the experiment shows, all by itself, whether the hypothesis is correct. Duhem pointed out that in the history of the universe there has never been an experiment that could singlehandedly verify or falsify a hypothesis. The reason is that there are always too many auxiliary assumptions that have to be made to bring the hypothesis into contact with the experimental apparatus. Hypotheses do sometimes get disconfirmed, outright refuted if you like, but only because the scientists involved are holding certain other assumptions fixed, assumptions that are disputable and may even be quite wrong. Suppose we are doing an astronomical study, and we are verifying and refuting things by making observations through complicated telescopes. In using such telescopes, the astronomers are assuming virtually all of optical theory, and countless other things besides.

Surprisingly, Duhem's point holds in everyday life as well. Take any good ordinary sentence about a physical object, such as "There is a chair at the head of the table." What is its verification condition? A first thing to notice is that "the" set of experiences that would confirm that sentence is in a way conditional, on one's hypothetical vantage point. We might try something like this: if you walk into the room from the direction of this door here, you will have an experience as of a chair at the head of the table. But even that depends. It depends on whether you have your eyes open, and it depends on whether your sensory apparatus is functioning properly, and it depends on whether the lights are on, and . . . . These qualifications do not foreseeably come to an end. If we try to build in the appropriate hedges ("If you walk into the room . . . , *and* you have your eyes open, *and* your sensory apparatus is functioning . . . , . . . "), more qualifications crop up: are you walking forward rather than backing into the room? Has something been interposed between you and the chair? Has the chair been camouflaged? Has it been rendered invisible by Martians? Has your brain been altered by a freakish burst of Q-radiation from the sky? We can go on like this for days.

The moral is that what we take to be "the" verification condition for a given empirical statement presupposes a massive background of default auxiliary assumptions. Those assumptions are usually perfectly reasonable, and it is no accident that we make them. But a particular "verification condition" is associated with a given sentence only if we choose to rely on such assumptions, almost any of which may fail. Intrinsically, the sentence has no determinate verification condition.

That is (to say the least) an embarrassment for a theory that identifies a sentence's meaning with that sentence's verification condition. But as we shall now see, the matter does not quite end here.

Two Quinean issues

In the 1950s and 1960s, W. V. Quine posed two challenges to the Positivists' philosophy of language. First, he attacked the notion of analyticity (Quine 1953, 1960), that is, he attacked the claim that some sentences are true entirely in virtue of what they mean and not because of any contribution from the extralinguistic world. Quine gives a number of different arguments against analyticity. Some of those are unconvincing. Others are better, and have kept "analytic" a fairly dirty word ever since, or at least till a recent resurgence. I will not itemize them, but only give a general idea of what I think is at the bottom of Quine's repudiation of analyticity.

Quine shares and maintains the Positivists' epistemological bent, and believes that if linguistic meaning is anything it is a function of evidential support. But his own epistemology differs from the Positivists' in being holistic. There are sentences you hold true and sentences you reject as false, but in each case the support for your belief is a complex matter of the evidential relations your sentence bears to many other sentences. Whenever it seems that belief revision is required, you have a wide choice of which beliefs to give up in order to maintain a suitably coherent system (recall Duhem's point). And there is no belief that is completely immune to revision, no sentence that *might* not be rejected under pressure from empirical evidence plus a concern for overall coherence. Even apparent truths of logic, such as truths of the form "Either P or not P," might be abandoned in light of suitably weird phenomena in quantum mechanics. But an analytic sentence would by definition be entirely unresponsive to the world's input, and so immune to revision. Therefore, there are no analytic sentences.

It may seem of little practical consequence whether there are any sentences that occupy the quaint philosophers' category of "analytic." But Quine's rejection of analyticity does have one interesting little repercussion. Suppose two English sentences, S_1 and S_2, are precisely synonymous. Then the conditional sentence "If S_1, then S_2" should be analytic, having the content "If [this state of affairs], then [this very same state of affairs]," which could hardly be falsified by any empirical development. So if there are no analytic sentences, no two English sentences are precisely synonymous, not even "Bambi's mother was a doe" and "Bambi's mother was a female deer."[5]

It gets worse. Here is Quine's second challenge to the Positivists, and indeed to practically everyone. It is not just that there are no analytic sentences, and not just that no two sentences are synonymous. It is that *there is no such thing as meaning.* Quine denies our "meaning facts" in the first place, and urges an eliminativism or nihilism about meaning, in the form of his doctrine of the "indeterminacy of translation."

Here too Quine has given a number of arguments, some more convincing than others. One (from Quine 1969) can be stated very simply: individual sentences do not have verification conditions. But if a sentence had any meaning at all, it would be a verification condition. Therefore, individual sentences do not have meanings at all. Thus does Quine save Verificationism from Objection 5. But it is a desperate lunge, since it saves the village by destroying it, simply eliminating meaning and the meaning-phenomena themselves. The problem with the argument, of course, is in justifying the second premise; if sentences do not have verification conditions, why continue to accept Verificationism when there are so many other theories of meaning on offer?

A better-known argument starts with the hypothesis of a field linguist investigating an alien native language from scratch and trying to construct a "translation manual" or Native–English dictionary. Quine argues that the total evidence available to the linguist fails to determine any one translation manual; many mutually incompatible ones are entirely consistent with that evidence. Moreover the underdetermination here is not merely the standard underdetermination of scientific theories by the evidence on which they are based. It is radical: not even the world's totality of physical fact suffices to vindicate one of the rival translation manuals as against the others. Therefore, no translation is correct to the exclusion of its rival translations. But if sentences had meanings, then there would be correct translations of them, namely the translations that did preserve their actual meanings. Therefore, sentences do not have meanings.

The problem here is to justify the premise that not even the world's totality of physical fact rules in one of the rival translation manuals as correct. The defense of that premise remains obscure.

Summary

- According to the Verification Theory, a sentence is meaningful just in case its being true would make some difference to the course of our future experience; and a sentence's particular meaning is its *verification condition*, the set of possible experiences that would tend to show that the sentence was true.
- The theory faces a number of medium-sized objections.
- But the worst objection is that, as Duhem and Quine have argued, individual sentences do not have distinctive verification conditions of their own.
- Quine attacked the view that there are "analytic" sentences, sentences true solely in virtue of their meanings.
- From Duhem's point, Quine inferred the radical claim that individual sentences do not have meanings; there is no such thing as sentence meaning.

Questions

1   Respond on the Verificationist's behalf to one of Objections 1–6.
2   Try to tackle Objection 7.
3   Have you any further criticism to make of the Verification Theory?

4 Discuss Quine's attack on analyticity, or his defense of meaning indeterminacy. (Some outside reading would be required for either of these.)

Notes

1 The foregoing examples are skeptical hypotheses of a kind that every philosophical tradition has taken seriously; the Positivists had to work hard to argue that those "hypotheses" are meaningless even though the sentences look perfectly meaningful at first glance. The Positivists had less patience and less trouble with the Hegelian idealism of the late nineteenth century, as in "The Absolute is perfect," and with Heideggerian existentialism, as in "The Nothing noths" ("Das Nichts nichtet"). I once received a brochure, advertising a newly published philosophy book. The brochure contained a bulleted list of the book's special features. And one of the bulleted items was: "Eleven new ways in which negation negates itself." I swear I am not making this up.

2 Of course, there are degrees of understanding. We may not understand a term completely. (Do you know exactly what a camshaft is? How about a linear accelerator?) But to understand a sentence even in part, we have to have some idea of what it says. But again, that implies that there already is something that it says prior to anything being determined about its verification conditions.

3 Verificationism flirts with what the late David Stove (1991) called the "Ishmael Effect," the phenomenon of a philosophical theory's making a sole exception of itself. (The reference is to *Moby Dick*: "And I only am escaped alone to tell thee"; actually this is a quotation from Job 1: 15.) For example: "All we can know is that we can know nothing." "The only moral sin is intolerance." "Absolutely everything is relative."

4 See Achinstein (1965) and Churchland (1988).

5 Actually a good thoroughgoing Quinean should not accept this argument. Why not? (*Hint*: see the previous paragraph.)

Further reading

Ayer (1946) is a classic and/but very accessible exposition and defense of Verificationism.

Some influential anti-Verificationist papers besides Quine's were Waismann (1965b), and various collected essays by Hilary Putnam (1975b), especially "Dreaming and 'Depth Grammar'."

Quine's doctrine of the indeterminacy of translation spawned a vast and toxic literature. For one view of the doctrine and the early literature, see Lycan (1984: Chapter 9) (you were expecting me to recommend someone *else*'s view?); also, Bar-On (1992).

The 1970s and 1980s saw an outbreak of neo-Verificationism, due largely to writings of Michael Dummett collected in his (1978). For an oversimplifying but very clear attack on Dummett, see Devitt (1983).

Truth-Condition Theories: Davidson's program

Overview

According to Donald Davidson, we will obtain a better theory of meaning if we replace the notion of a sentence's verification condition with that of the sentence's truth condition: the condition under which the sentence actually is or would be true, rather than a state of affairs which would merely serve as evidence of truth. Davidson offers several arguments, chief among which is that compositionality is needed to account for our understanding of long, novel sentences and a sentence's truth condition is its most obviously compositional feature. As a model of the way in which truth conditions can be assigned to sentences of natural languages such as English, Davidson takes the way in which truth is defined for an artificial system of formal logic. But since English sentences' surface grammar diverges from their logical forms, a theory of grammar and its relation to logic has to be brought to bear; such a theory exists and is supported independently.

Davidson's theory faces many objections. One is that many perfectly meaningful sentences do not have truth-values. Some others are that his program cannot handle expressions (such as pronouns) whose referents depend on context, predicates which are not synonymous but happen to apply to just the same things, and sentences whose truth-values are not determined by those of their component clauses.

Truth conditions

So far, only one of our theories has managed to shed much light on what actually determines the meanings of particular sentences. The Proposition Theory took sentence meanings and just reified them (made them into *objects* of a certain kind), without much further comment and without connecting the object thus reified with anyone's linguistic practices or behavior. Grice attempted to fob off the question into the philosophy of mind, by trying to connect sentences with the contents of people's actual intentions and beliefs, which was not very successful and, more to the point, simply took the intentions' and beliefs' contents themselves for granted.

As we have seen, the Verificationists did better; they offered us a test for the propositional content of any given sentence, that content being (precisely) the sentence's verification-condition. The trouble is that, even if we ignore the Duhem–Quine problem (Objection 7 in the previous chapter), the verification test often seems to predict the *wrong* content (Objection 3).

Donald Davidson (1967b, 1970/1975) argued that we will get where we want to be if we replace the Positivists' notion of a sentence's verification condition with that of the sentence's *truth condition*. On this view, to know a sentence's meaning is to know the conditions under which that sentence would be true, rather than to know how to *tell* whether the sentence is actually true. (Never mind epistemology.) For two sentences to be synonymous is for them to be true under just the same conditions; for a sentence to be ambiguous is for it to be both true and false in the same circumstance yet without self-contradiction; for one sentence to entail another is for it to be impossible that the first be true without the second being true also.

We are already familiar with the truth-conditional approach to meaning, though not by name, from our discussion of Russell's Theory of Descriptions: Russell proceeds precisely by sketching the truth conditions of sentences containing descriptions and arguing on various grounds that they are the correct truth conditions. But more of Russell in the next section.

Davidson begins with two ideas that prove to be related. One is that a theory of meaning should afford guidance as to what determines the meaning of a particular sentence. The other is that of giving central importance to the wondrous phenomenon with which this book began: our ability to understand long novel sentences in a flash. Focusing on the first idea, he asks how one might give a "theory of meaning *for*" a particular language – not a general theory of meaning in our philosophical sense, but a theory of English or of Chinese or of Kwakiutl, that specified the particular meanings of that language's sentences taken one by one.

What form might such a theory take? Davidson offers and motivates several guidelines and constraints. The first is this:

> Since there seems to be no clear limit to the number of meaningful expressions, a workable theory must account for the meaning of each expression on the basis of the patterned exhibition of a finite number of features. But even if there were a practical constraint on the length of the sentences a person can send and receive with understanding, a satisfactory semantics would need to explain the contribution of repeatable features to the meanings of sentences in which they occur.
>
> (1970: 18)

Here he is appealing to our ability to understand long novel sentences, and suggesting an explanation of that ability. How do we understand a potential infinity of English sentences on the basis of our finite vocabulary and limited experience of language? The answer must be that we have mastered "a finite number of features," a relatively small and manageable set of meaningful expressions that serve as meaning "atoms," and also some rules of composition, "patterned" ways of combining those atoms or semantic primitives which generate the meanings of more complex expressions.[1]

Very crudely, the meaning atoms are individual words, and the rules of composition are rules of grammar or syntax that specify how words can be combined in order to project their individual meanings into more complex meanings. Davidson contends that the meaning of a sentence is a function of the meanings of its constituent words.[2] This is the thesis of *compositionality*, as we called it in Chapter 6. Compositionality is the obvious hypothesis to explain our understanding of long novel sentences: we understand complex meanings by decomposing sentences syntactically into smaller meaningful elements, and computing the complex meanings as syntactic functions of the sentences' smallest meaningful parts.

So an adequate theory of meaning in the general philosophical sense should guide us in constructing a systematic "theory of meaning for" any given language, that would specify the meaning of each grammatical sentence of that language by chronicling the sentence's composition out of its constituent words. Thus, it should have the means to generate a list:

"Snow is white" means that snow is white.
"Grass is green" means that grass is green.
"Poltergeists make up the principal type of material

manifestation" means that poltergeists make up the principal type of material manifestation.
"In 1931, Adolf Hitler made a visit to the United States, in the course of which . . . ." [You get the idea.]

And this list is *infinite* or potentially so. Of course, this example specifies the meanings of English sentences in English (and so it sounds a bit uninteresting), but we must also be able to do the same for other languages:

"Der Schnee ist weiss" means [in German] that snow is white.
"Das Gras ist grün" means that grass is green.
"Die Poltergeisten representieren . . ." [etc.]

How might a theory of English or a theory of German generate such a list? Notice first that corresponding to our ability to understand long novel sentences, we have the ability to determine those sentences' truth-values if we know enough facts. For example, if I happen to know that Katherine Dienes' "Ave Maria" setting employs chant segments, drones, overlapping "ora pro nobis" figures, and other devices to suggest the sonority of medieval convent music, and I encounter the sentence

(1) Katherine Dienes' "Ave Maria" setting employs chant segments, drones, overlapping "ora pro nobis" figures, and other devices to suggest the sonority of medieval convent music

(a sentence which I am quite sure is as new to you as it originally was to me); I also know that that sentence is in fact true. And if I had encountered a sentence just like it except that "medieval convent music" had been replaced by "Ice-T's brand of rap music" and a clause had been added, ". . . and Dienes has recently moved to Newark, New Jersey," I would instantly have known it was false.

Thus, it seems we grasp the truth conditions of long novel sentences on sight, as well as understanding them, and the same question arises: how is that possible? Davidson thinks this coincidence is no coincidence. The question has the same answer: compositionality. The truth conditions of long sentences are determined by the truth conditions of the shorter sentences of which they are composed, and the syntactic processes that generate the longer sentences carry truth-related semantic properties along with them, thus compounding simple truth properties into more complex ones.

We have an elegant model for this compositionality of truth conditions, and it serves also as the only model we have for the compositionality of meaning. It is the semantics of a formal language such as the predicate calculus, as formulated by logicians. If you have taken a course in symbolic logic, you will already have seen this coming and will be ahead of me. If you have not, I will try to explain the idea informally, without relying on technical notation.

I shall describe a very simple little language, nearly as simple as Wittgenstein's builders' language but with a crucial distinguishing feature. It has two terms or predicates, "F" and "G," which correspond to the English words "fat" and "greedy"; "F" denotes or applies to all and only the fat things in the world and "G" applies to all and only the greedy things. The little language (which I shall call "Oafish") also has two proper names: "a," which denotes Albert, and "b," which denotes Betty. And it has a semantic rule for forming subject–predicate sentences: a sentence made by prefixing a predicate P to a proper name n is true iff what "n" denotes is included among the things to which P applies. And finally, Oafish contains two further expressions called "sentence connectives": "not," which can be stuck onto any given sentence, and "and," which can be inserted between two whole sentences to make a longer sentence. Each of the connectives is governed by its distinguishing semantic rule. The "not" rule is that a sentence made by sticking not onto another sentence A will be true just in case A itself is not true. The "and" rule is that a sentence of the composite form "A and B" will be true just in case "A" is true and "B" is true also. Thus:

TRUTH DEFINITION FOR OAFISH

"F" applies to fat things.
"G" applies to greedy things.

"a" denotes Albert.
"b" denotes Betty.

A subject–predicate sentence "Pn" is true if and only if what "n" denotes is a member of the class of things that "P" applies to.

A sentence of the form "Not A" is true if and only if the sentence A is not true.

A sentence of the form "A and B" is true if and only if its component sentences A and B are both true.

This is the whole language – all of its vocabulary, all of its meaning rules of any kind. It is of limited interest, and encourages tedious repetitiveness. But its truth definition, even in its brute simplicity, has the twin features that we need: it allows for indefinitely long and indefinitely many grammatical sentences of Oafish, and (nonetheless) it manages to specify the truth condition of every one of them. For example, if an Oafish speaker utters "Fa," we learn from our subject–predicate clause that that sentence is true just in case the denotation of "a," that is Albert, is included in the class of things to which "F" applies, that is, the class of fat things, which is just to say that Albert is fat. (The class of things to which a term applies is called the term's *extension*.) Or one can say that Albert is greedy. Or one can say that he is fat and he is greedy, because our truth rule for "and" tells us that "Fa and Ga" is going to be true just when Albert is fat and Albert is greedy. (Check that for yourself.) And the word "and" can be iterated, that is applied over and over again, to make longer and longer sentences without letup: "Fa and not Fb"; "Fa and not Ga and Fb and not Gb"; "Fa and Ga and not Fb and Gb and Fa and not Fb"; and so on forever. (Of course the later sentences will be repetitious, since Oafish has such a small lexicon, but even the most repetitious sentences are still grammatical and have perfectly clear truth conditions.)

So, just from this trifling little truth definition we have already got infinitely many grammatical sentences, and we have projection rules that tell us, no matter how long a sentence is, the condition under which that sentence is true. Armed with this, we could encounter any novel sentence of Oafish, even if it were five miles long, and compute its truth condition. We have explained a potentially infinite capacity by finite, indeed minuscule, means.

Suppose we have derived a truth condition step by step from our truth definition and made it explicit:

"Fa and not Ga and Fb and not Gb" is true if and only if Albert is fat and Albert is not greedy and Betty is fat and Betty is not greedy.

We have taken a sentence of Oafish and specified its truth condition. But have we not also specified its meaning? Surely what the chosen sentence *means* is just that Albert is fat and Albert is not greedy and Betty is fat and Betty is not greedy. And it means that compositionally, in virtue of what "a," "b," "F," and "G" denote plus the semantic rules for determining complex truth conditions from simpler ones.

Suppose we could do the same for English, that is construct a truth definition that spits out something of the form, "'-----' is true if and only if ____" for each English sentence. (Such products are called "Tarski biconditionals" or "T-sentences," since they were inspired by the form of Tarski's (1956) theory of truth.) And suppose each T-sentence is seen to get its target sentence's truth condition right. Then, Davidson asks, what more could reasonably be asked of a theory of meaning for English?

Consider: a correct assignment of meaning to a sentence should determine that sentence's truth condition; so we know that an adequate theory of meaning for a language should yield at least a truth definition for that language. So if the truth definition also does everything we would expect a theory of meaning to do, it would be reasonable simply to identify a sentence's meaning with its truth condition.

What about the meaning facts, then? I have already mentioned the ways in which the Truth-Condition Theory accounts for synonymy and ambiguity. It accounts for meaning inclusion and especially for entailment as well. "Fa and not Fb" entails "Fa" because, according to our truth definition, "Fa and not Fb" could not be true unless "Fa" were. A truth definition for a language predicts the felt synonymies, entailments, and other semantic relations by reference to the semantic compounding rules it codifies.

And, in part, the contemporary truth-condition theorist studies linguistic constructions in just the same way that Russell worked on descriptions. S/he marshalls a whole bunch of meaning facts about a particular kind or group of sentences in which s/he is interested, facts about synonymy relations, ambiguities, entailment relations, etc., and tries to explain those facts in terms of truth conditions. Russell noted the semantic properties of sentences of this kind or that, especially interesting properties that create logical puzzles, and then asked, how can we put together a theory of such sentences that explains why the sentences exhibit those puzzling semantic features? His answer, as in the Theory of Descriptions, would be a putative truth condition.

The Truth-Condition Theory sees meaning as *representation*. In effect it reverts to the Referential Theory's idea of meaning as mirroring or correspondence between sentences and actual or possible states of affairs; Russell emphasized this idea (and indeed made it a cornerstone of his metaphysics). The truth definition is founded on the referential relations between terms and their worldly denotata or extensions. We saw in Chapter 1 that the crude Referential Theory was far too simple an idea of the correspondence between words and the world; the truth-condition theorist does not posit so strong or simple-minded a correspondence, since s/he does not contend that all words are names. But the truth-condition theorist is back in the business of mirroring nature, of asking what actual or possible states of affairs does a given target sentence depict or represent.

Truth-defining natural languages

Oafish is explicitly truth-defined. Its sentences wear their truth conditions on their sleeves, in the sense that there is no disparity between a sentence's surface-grammatical form and what Russell called its logical form (Chapter 2). And one can just look at an Oafish sentence and, truth definition in hand, work one's way back through the sentence's compositional structure and calculate the sentence's truth condition. That is Davidson's paradigm.

There is a huge "but" (indeed a "But ... !!"), which has probably already occurred to you. It is one thing to provide a truth definition for a made-up formal language, even for a much richer one than Oafish; it is quite another to reveal truth rules allegedly underpinning an already living natural language like English. The natural language was here first. And, much more to the point, sentences of English do not wear their truth conditions on their sleeves. Notoriously, as we saw in Chapter 2, their superficial grammatical forms differ unpredictably from their logical forms.

Well, says the truth-condition theorist, not quite unpredictably. That is where syntax enters the picture. (Indeed, the theorist may say, that is what syntax is *for*.)

I would like to give you an entire course in syntax; failing that, I would like to give you just the basics. But space allows neither. I shall merely gesture toward the fundamental idea and hope that you will pick up some of the rest elsewhere. For simplicity, I will use jargon that recalls the early days of theoretical syntax (roughly, the 1960s) once that discipline had been founded by Zellig Harris and Noam Chomsky.

A syntax or *grammar* for a language, natural or artificial, is a device for sorting well-formed or grammatical sentences from among all the strings made up of words from that language. And again (as with semantics), the model is that of formation rules for a logical system. Recall Oafish. Sentences of Oafish can be parsed, diagrammed by what are called "phrase markers," in a way that directly depicts how they are compounded syntactically out of individual terms. Here is "Fa and not Fb":

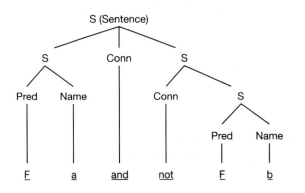

A sentence can be formed by placing a name after a predicate, so "Fa" and "Fb" are sentences. A sentence can be formed by prefixing a sentence with "not," so "not Fb" is a sentence. Finally, a sentence can be formed by placing "and" between two sentences, so the whole thing is a sentence.

Simple English sentences can be diagrammed similarly. Here is a classic: "The boy hit the colorful ball":

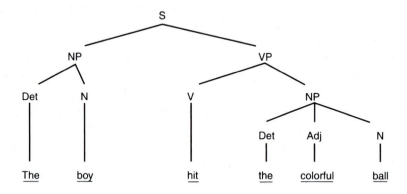

The nodes in such a phrase marker are labelled according to grammatical category, and the lowest ones begin to look like English "parts of speech": noun, adjective, and so on. Higher nodes correspond to more complex grammatical structures such as noun phrases.

But few English sentences are so simple. Most have structures that cannot be entirely rendered by phrase markers of this straightforward type (called "context-free" markers), because there are grammatical relations that are robust and unmistakable that cannot be represented in this form. Chomsky (1957, 1965) argued that the phrase-marker grammar needs to be augmented by a device, specifically a set of rules, that can take one phrase marker and turn it into one of a different and dependent kind; he called such rules "transformations." For example, a *passive* transformation might take the foregoing phrase marker and rearrange its parts into a phrase marker for "The colorful ball was hit by the boy." Transformations are conceived as dynamic, as agents that chop up phrase markers and rebuild their parts into more complicated tree diagrams.

With any luck, then, every grammatical string of English either has a context-free phrase marker or has one that has been derived by a series of one or more transformations from a context-free marker. No other string is grammatical.

(Grammars no longer have this simple architecture, nor do present-day linguists use my antiquated terminology. But to learn more you will have to read up on your own.)

As I said, linguists originally conceived a grammar simply as a machine that separated well-formed strings from gibberish. Some linguists leave it at that, and do not see that that enterprise has much to do with semantics or sentence meaning proper. But as Davidson says, something takes the meanings of individual words and composes or projects them into whole sentence meanings. What is it that does that? Presumably, rules for sticking the words together in some rational order, an order that gives the whole composite a meaning. But notice that one and the same set of words can be arranged in different orders, and two of the resulting strings, even if each is well-formed, can have different meanings: tragically, "John loves Marsha" does not mean the same thing as "Marsha loves John," even though the same three words compose both sentences. So in order to generate different meanings for those sentences, the projection rules must also do some finer tuning; they have got to look, not just at the words themselves, but at some finer distinctions. But the very syntactic rules that compound grammatically acceptable strings out of individual words also seem ideally suited to serve as those meaning-projection rules also. In the late 1960s many linguists came to take that view, and held that transformations preserve meaning (though the latter thesis was qualified and partly abandoned by the Extended Standard Theory of the 1970s and by Government and Binding Theory of the 1980s).

Suppose we have a phrase-structure grammar for an explicitly truth-defined formal language. And suppose we have grammatical transformations that are capable of converting formulas of that language into well-formed strings of English. Then we have a grammar whose phrase-structure component spits out underlying structures (the logic-like formulas) and whose transformational component produces English variations on those underlying structures. Given that transformations preserve meaning, or more narrowly, that transformations preserve *truth* properties, we can then see how English sentences have their meanings. Namely, they have meanings in virtue of having truth conditions, and they have truth conditions in virtue of being transformationally derived from explicitly truth-defined formulas of a logic-like notational system. Synonymous sentences are transformational variations of each other; ambiguous sentences are the products of more than one possible transformational process, and so forth.

Ideally, the truth-condition theorist wants to be empirically more responsible than Russell was. Russell approached truth conditions a priori; he would write an English sentence on the blackboard, write a logical formula next to it, eyeball the two, and judge that the latter seems to get the former's truth condition right. Better, he did appeal to his hypotheses' puzzle-solving abilities as well. But a contemporary truth-condition theorist should want her/his semantical hypotheses to be, in addition, at least somewhat responsible to plausible syntactic theories.

Initial objections

Objection 1

Like the Verification Theory, the Truth-Condition Theory seems to apply only to descriptive, fact-stating language; questions and commands and so on are not true or false at all.

A weak reply

Although we do not ordinarily call questions or commands "true" and "false," they do have bipolar, truth-like semantic values. A question is correctly answered "yes" or "no"; a command is obeyed or disobeyed. Intuitively, a nondeclarative sentence corresponds to a state of affairs that may or may not obtain, even though its function is not to describe or report that state of affairs. And for semantical purposes we may as well treat those semantic values as truth-values. For example, a command is "true" if it does in fact go on to be obeyed, "false" if it does not. Of course this is a nonstandard use of "true" and "false"; we are widening their application to all semantic bipolarity. (Perhaps we should make up a pair of more general semantical terms, such as "positive" and "negative.")

Rejoinder

Not all nondeclaratives are thus bipolar. Consider "wh"-questions, such as "Who robbed the diaper service?," "What time is it?," and "Why did you blow up my boat?" None of these has a "yes" or "no" answer; indeed each admits a very large range of possible correct answers.

Moreover, the difficulty about lack of truth-value is not confined to nondeclarative sentences. First, it has been argued that certain grammatically declarative sentences lack truth conditions and have only epistemic "assertibility" conditions. Most notably, Adams (1965) and others have defended the view that indicative conditionals lack truth conditions and truth-value.

Second, some philosophers hold (following the Positivists) that certain grammatically declarative sentences are *not fact-stating* even though they might be taken by the naive to be so. According to the Emotivists in moral philosophy, moral judgements are only evincings or ventings, semantically just like groans, grunts of protest, cheers, and the like. If so, then such "factually defective" sentences do not have truth-values. So a T-sentence directed upon one ("'Murder is wrong' is true iff murder is wrong") should come out false or anomalous.[3]

Rejoinder

It is easy enough for the truth-condition theorist who is also an Emotivist (or whatever) to restrict her/his truth theory against nonfactual sentences in the first place. But contrariwise, one may argue from the general plausibility of truth-conditional semantics (if one believes in it) to the implausibility of Emotivism and other views that deny truth-value to perfectly grammatical declaratives.

Objection 2

(Stich 1976; Blackburn 1984.) Davidson talks as if the right-hand sides of his T-sentences will be written in English, or in the theorist's own natural language whatever it may be, so that they can be readily seen to be correct or incorrect. Indeed, Davidson touts the T-sentences as empirically test-able consequences of a proposed truth definition for a language. But no actual Davidsonian truth definition could deliver such T-sentences. For such a theory to yield T-sentences – or anything else – as theorems, it must be formulated in a fairly formal and regimented language, some-thing logic-like. (Look again at the truth definition for Oafish.) Moreover, once the theorist gets around to natural-language constructions that do not occur in standard symbolic logics, such as adverbs, belief operators, and the like, the right-hand sides of T-sentences involving those may contain some radically unfamiliar notation. A recent version of Davidson's own (1967a) theory of action sentences generates such T-sentences as:

> "Jones buttered the toast at midnight" is true if and only if
> ($\exists$e)(BUTTERING(e) & PROTAG(Jones, e) & VICTIM(the toast,
> e) & OCCURRED-AT(e, midnight)).

The right-hand side here is to be read much as follows: "There occurred an event, that was a buttering of the toast, performed by Jones at midnight." (By making the underlying subject the whole event rather than the agent Jones, Davidson is able to explain why the target sentence entails such simpler sentences as "Jones buttered the toast," "Jones buttered some-thing," "Something happened to the toast," and "Something happened at midnight," which entailments are otherwise hard to capture.) But what, then, becomes of Davidson's claim of testability? How are we supposed to know whether such arcane T-sentences are correct or incorrect?

Reply

Testability weakens, but not to the vanishing point. For we can still test convoluted T-sentences such as the foregoing against our logical intuitions, and we can still evaluate Davidson's claims to have illuminated striking semantical features of the target sentence.

Objection 3

(Anticipated by Davidson 1967b.) Ferocious technical problems arise once one starts examining sentences with *deictic* elements in them. (A "deictic" or "indexical" element is one whose semantic interpretation varies with context of utterance, like a tense marker or a demonstrative pronoun.) For example, how would one state a truth condition for the sentence "I am sick now"? " 'I am sick now' is true if and only if I am sick now" would never do, since its truth-value depends on who utters it and when and is not in general determined by *my* (your humble narrator's) state of health. Deictic sentences do not even have truth-values, except on actual or hypothetical occasions of their use (a point which would gratify Strawson).

Davidson's own response is to relativize truth to a speaker and a time. The relevant T-sentence would be formulated as, " 'I am sick now' is true as potentially spoken by p at t if and only if p is sick at t." But this is unsatisfactory in each of several ways,[4] not least in that speaker and time of utterance are not the only contextual factors that affect truth-value. (Recall "This is a fine red one.") We shall return to this issue in Chapter 11.[5]

Objection 4

(Reeves 1974; Blackburn 1984.) A Davidsonian truth definition has a hard time distinguishing expressions that happen to coextend (that is, to apply to exactly the same range of referents) but without being mutually synonymous. Consider two single vocabulary items that differ in meaning but that happen to have exactly the same extensions. The standard example of this is the words "renate" and "cordate," meaning respectively "creature with kidneys" and "creature with a heart."[6] A Davidsonian truth theory will not be able to distinguish the meaning of a sentence containing "renate" from that of one containing "cordate," for each term will have been assigned just the same class of objects as its extension.

First reply

In a truth theory of the sort described here, the words used in the right-hand sides of the T-sentences are supposed to correspond as closely as possible to the expressions composing the target sentence. (Look back at the truth definition for Oafish.) Thus, one will write the clause for "renate" as " 'Renate' denotes renates" rather than as " 'Renate' denotes cordates." To derive the latter (albeit true) statement from our truth theory, one would need to add the contingent and nonlinguistic premise, "All and only renates are cordates." And, according to Davidson, the meaning of a target sentence is given, not by just the T-sentence directed upon that target sentence, but by the T-sentence together with its derivation from the axioms of the truth theory. To avoid the suggestion that being cordate is part of the meaning of "renate," we can require that the T-sentence's derivation contain no nonlinguistic premises.

Second reply

"Renate" and "cordate" will be distinguished in sentences containing certain sorts of construction, notably in modal sentences and in belief sentences. Whatever semantics Davidson gives for sentences like "There could be a renate that was not cordate" and "Geoff believes that his pet turtle is renate" would have to accommodate (indeed predict) the noninterchangeability of "cordate" for "renate" in those sentences.

Rejoinder to the second reply

Such sentences – in which coextensive terms cannot be substituted without possibly changing the truth-value of the sentences themselves – are puzzling in their own right. (They are called *intensional* sentences; this is a generalization of the phenomenon that in Chapter 2 was called "referential opacity.") One would expect the substitution to make no difference; after all, even if we are using a different word, we are continuing to talk about exactly the same thing or class of things. We have already encountered a special case of this problem in Chapters 2 and 3, the Problem of Substitutivity for definite descriptions and for proper names. Any theory of meaning must offer some explanation of substitutivity failures. So the phrase "Whatever semantics Davidson gives for sentences like . . ." is not innocent. It will be *hard work* for Davidson to solve that problem given his format for a theory of meaning. (Davidson does address the problem of intensionality here and there, principally in Davidson (1968). His solution is, roughly, to treat intensional sentences as making tacit reference to the very words that occur in them. We shall look at a quite different approach in the next chapter.)

Objection 5

It is all very simple to write a truth rule for a sentence-compounding word like "and". After all, "and" is what logicians call a *truth-functional* connective: the truth-value of "A and B" is strictly determined by the truth-values of its component sentences A and B. But many sentence-compounding expressions do not simply pass truth on in that way. Take the word "because": the truth of "A because B" is not determined by the truth-values of the component sentences A and B, for even if both A and B are true, "A because B" may be false, depending on other features of the world. How, then, might one write a truth rule for "because," parallel to Oafish's rule for "and"? Or take adverbs. How might one write a truth rule for "slowly," or for "very"?

Still worse, consider "believes that" again, as in "Joe believes that Mary believes that Irma believes that the house is burning down." How would we write a truth rule for it? "*n* believes that A" is true if and only if . . ." what?

One obvious strategy is to invoke a domain of helpful entities, such as propositions(!), and write truth rules for non-truth-functional expressions in terms of quantification over that domain. (As we have seen, to deal with some adverbs, Davidson introduced a domain of "events," and made adverbs into adjectival predicates of events.) The main problem with that strategy is that it strains syntax, since the transformations have to work harder to transform the new, zany logical forms into familiar English; as Blackburn points out (1984: 289), a Davidsonian treatment of a non-truth-functional (and intensional) construction such as "because" or "believes that" requires at least a "heavy commitment to concealed logical forms." (But, as before, belief sentences in particular are already an ugly problem for any theory of meaning.)

Objection 6

(Strawson 1970.) Truth-conditional semantics must fully disclose the general notion of truth it is presupposing. (Otherwise it is in the position of analyzing meaning in terms of another concept – call it *krum*, say – and refusing to tell us what "krum" is.) But (says Strawson) the only plausible general analysis of truth is in terms of stating or asserting things, which is to say in terms of communication, which must be cashed *à la* Grice. Thus although the letter of truth-conditional semantics may be unobjectionable, its spirit is broken, for it collapses into Griceanism rather than standing as a superior alternative.

First reply

The notion of truth is *not* like the made-up mystery concept "krum." Whether or not we have an accepted general philosophical analysis of truth, we have the concept expressed by the ordinary English word "true," and we have the formal structure introduced by Tarski, that generates T-sentences. If the notion of meaning can be reduced to that of truth, that is a theoretical economy even if we provide no further philosophical explication of truth; it is not a case of "the concepts of meaning and truth each pointing blankly and unhelpfully at the other" (p. 97).

Second reply

What about all the other general theories of truth that philosophers have offered over the past two thousand years? Notably, there are the classical Correspondence, Coherence and Pragmatic theories. More recently, there is the Prosentential Theory devised by Grover, Camp and Belnap (1975). My best guess as to why Strawson simply ignores these is that he must be assuming that every such theory would somehow have to buy into the Gricean idea at some early stage: for example, since *beliefs* are primarily what cohere or fail to cohere, the Coherence Theory of Truth would have to treat sentences only in so far as they express beliefs, etc. But I do not see why we should grant that assumption (if it is Strawson's) just on his say-so. On this interpretation, Strawson is in the position of insisting, at bottom, "But *surely* some version of Griceanism is correct."

On that note, let me pick up the suggestion Grice made about unuttered and novel sentences, his appeal to abstract "resultant procedures" (see the end of the penultimate section of Chapter 7). It now seems that what he had in mind there was compositionality achieved by syntax. Suppose Grice could deliver a notion of public meaning analogous to sentence meaning but applying to subsentential expressions such as words; call it "expression meaning." Then he could invoke syntax and abstractly construct sentence meanings out of expression meanings (though here again, he would have to work to distinguish the abstract "sentence meanings" from propositions).

How to go about explicating expression meaning? Recall that in Chapter 2 we defined a notion of "speaker-reference" for singular terms, intended in precisely Gricean contrast to the "semantic reference" of the term, understood in terms of speakers' intentions to call hearers' attention to things. Perhaps we could define an analogous concept of "speaker-extension" for predicates in terms of speakers' intentions standing somehow behind uses of those predicates, and so on. Then we could borrow Grice's language about repertoires and procedures from his discussion of unstructured utterances, and use it to fashion corresponding types of expression meaning.

The resulting two-tiered reduction of sentence meaning to speaker-meaning would still face problems, but no longer Obstacles 2–4.

Also, the present idea suggests an interesting research program, for it tosses us back into the theory of reference from a new direction. For example, can the semantic denotation of a proper name really be analyzed in terms of speaker-reference? On the face of it, that idea competes with the Description Theory of names *and* with the Causal–Historical Theory.

But this composite view, the explication of sentence meaning in terms of primitive expression meaning plus a Gricean theory of the individual primitive expression meanings, is to concede that the Truth-Condition Theory is correct, and to add only, though very significantly, a new type of theory of referring that would compete with those considered in Chapters 2–4.

Summary

- Davidson offers several arguments in defense of the Truth-Condition Theory. The main argument is that compositionality is needed to account for our understanding of long, novel sentences, and a sentence's truth condition is its most obviously compositional feature.
- Tarski's style of defining truth for a system of formal logic is a model for the way in which truth conditions can be assigned to sentences of natural languages.
- But since English sentences' surface grammar diverges from their logical forms, a theory of grammar and syntactic transformation is needed.
- Such a theory exists and has independent support.
- Davidson's theory faces many objections. Perhaps the most damaging is that many perfectly meaningful sentences do not have truth-values. Some others are that his Tarskian program cannot handle expressions (such as pronouns) whose referents depend on context, predicates which are not synonymous but happen to apply to just the same things, and sentences whose truth-values are not determined by those of their component clauses.

- It may be possible to fuse Davidson with Grice by providing a Gricean theory of term extensions.

Questions

1 Evaluate Davidson's main argument for his Truth-Condition Theory, that is his appeal to compositionality, and Tarskian truth definitions.
2 Discuss the further argument, given very briefly on pp. 135–6 above, whose premises are that (a) a sentence's meaning should determine that sentence's truth condition, and that (b) a truth definition for a language also does everything we would expect a theory of meaning to do.
3 If you happen already to know something about theoretical syntax, assess the prospects of its being used as a vehicle for connecting English sentences to the right-hand sides of Davidsonian T-sentences.
4 Adjudicate one or more of the objections that we have raised against the Truth-Condition Theory.
5 If you are familiar with the Liar Paradox, explore the problem it poses for the Truth-Condition Theory. (Davidson (1967) addresses this briefly.)
6 Raise a new, further objection to the Truth-Condition Theory.
7 Develop the compositional, "two-tiered" Gricean theory suggested at the end of this chapter. Or, pursue the "first-stage" Gricean reduction of semantic denotation (for names or for predicates).

Notes

1 Here he follows Ziff (1960).
2 "Words" is not quite right. Some meaning atoms are smaller than words: affixes such as "un-" (prefix) and "-able" (suffix). Some words are only pleonastic parts of meaning atoms, as in the French "ne . . . pas." Linguists call true meaning atoms "morphemes." But for convenience and familiarity I shall continue to speak of "words."
3 More sophisticated present-day descendants of the Emotivists include Blackburn (1984, 1993) and Gibbard (1990); but they try to find ways of granting that moral judgements can be called "true" or "false" and figure in T-sentences, without granting that moral judgements state facts about the world.
4 See Lycan (1984: Chapter 3). I should confess that that work is a global defense of the Truth-Condition Theory. I believe the theory is correct and worth paying high prices to hear live in concert.
5 There is also a nasty problem about *ambiguous* sentences; see Parsons (1973) and Lycan (1984: Chapter 3).

6 I have been told by at least one biologist that the two do *not* apply to same things; there are animals with hearts but no kidneys, or the other way around. But ignore this squalid fact and pretend that "renate" and "cordate" do apply to exactly the same animals.

Further reading

Other than Lycan (1984), the best general introduction to the Davidsonian program is Harman (1972). That paper and many other good ones in and about truth-theoretic semantics are reprinted in Davidson and Harman (1975); see also the anthologies, Evans and McDowell (1976) and Platts (1980). Platts (1979) is a good critical discussion of the Davidsonian program.

Harman (1974b, 1982) broke with Davidson to found "Conceptual Role" semantics. For a survey of the ensuing literature, see Lycan (1984b: Chapter 10).

Davidson (1986) is an important criticism of Davidson's own position, based on the phenomenon of malapropism.

An important spinoff from and competitor of truth-theoretic semantics is "Game-Theoretic" semantics, developed by Jaakko Hintikka (1976, 1979). I am unsure how far Hintikka's program competes with truth-theoretic semantics rather than being a variant of it. (The same is true of Edelberg's (1995) perspectival semantics.) The basic papers on GTS are collected in Saarinen (1979).

Baker (1995), Radford (1997), and Sag and Wasow (1999) are excellent introductions to contemporary syntactic theory; see also Hornstein (1995). Larson and Segal (1995) expound the convergence of semantics with contemporary syntax from the viewpoint of theoretical linguistics.

10
Truth-Condition Theories: possible worlds and intensional semantics

Overview

Kripkean possible worlds (as presented in Chapter 4) afford an alternative notion of a truth condition: we saw that a contingent sentence is true in some worlds but not in others. So a sentence's truth condition can be taken to be the set of possible worlds in which the sentence is true. Moreover, possible worlds can be used to construct "intensions" or meanings for subsentential phrases and particularly for individual words or meaning atoms, that are like Frege's "senses" in being independent of actual referents. For example, a predicate has different extensions in different worlds, and its intension can be taken to be the function that associates any given world with the predicate's particular extension in that world. Then a grammar can show how those subsentential intensions combine to make a truth condition, hence a meaning, for a complete sentence of which they are components.

The resulting view neatly avoids several of the objections that beset Davidson's theory, most notably 4, the problem of coextending but nonsynonymous terms, and 5, the problem of non-truth-functional connectives. It also lends a hand with the Problem of Substitutivity. But it inherits the rest of Davidson's difficulties and incurs one or two more.

Truth conditions reconceived

As we saw in the previous chapter, the Truth-Condition Theory understands meaning as representation, as mirroring or correspondence between sentences and actual or possible states of affairs. But we can take the notion of a hypothetical state of affairs more seriously than Davidson is willing to, and consider "possible states of affairs/circumstances/conditions" as Kripkean *possible worlds* (Chapter 4). Recall that a possible world (other than the actual world, our own) is an alternative universe, in which things go otherwise than the way they go here. And because worlds differ among themselves in respect of their component facts, of course the truth of a given sentence depends on which world we are considering.

This affords a new version of the idea of a sentence's truth condition. The sentence is true in some possible circumstances and not in others. Which, in the vernacular of possible worlds, is to say that the sentence is true in some worlds and not in others. When two sentences have the same truth condition, they will be true in just the same circumstances, in just the same worlds. When they differ in truth condition, that means there will be some worlds in which one is true but the other is false, so they will not be true in just the same worlds. As a first approximation, then, let us take a sentence's truth condition simply to be the set of worlds in which it is true.

For the truth-condition theorist, of course, that set of worlds will also be the sentence's meaning. It would follow that synonymous sentences are true in just the same worlds, while for any two nonsynonymous sentences, there will be at least one world in which one of the sentences is true but the other false.

This idea generalizes to the meanings of subsentential expressions. But to show how that works, I must backtrack for a paragraph or two.

I mentioned in Chapter 2 that, unlike Russell, Gottlob Frege (1892) had rejected thesis K3 ("A meaningful subject–predicate sentence is meaningful (only) in virtue of its picking out some individual thing and ascribing some property to that thing"), by positing abstract entities that he called "senses" and arguing that a singular term has one of these over and above its putative referent. And Frege defended compositionality: according to him, the subject–predicate sentence has a composite sense made up of the individual senses of its parts, and is meaningful in virtue of having that composite sense, whether or not its subject even has a referent at all. (Thus did Frege attack the Problem of Apparent Reference to Nonexistents.)

As sketched so far, Frege's view sounds like a version of the Proposition Theory. And so it is; it is prey to the various objections raised against that theory in Chapter 5. But Rudolf Carnap (1947/1956), Richard Montague

(1960, 1970), and Jaakko Hintikka (1961) developed *intensional logic,* giving a possible-worlds interpretation and explication of Fregean senses. Here, roughly, is the idea.

A singular term or a predicate is said to have both an extension (in the sense introduced in the previous chapter) and a Fregean sense or "intension." The trick is to construe a term's intension as a function from possible worlds to extensions. Thus, the intension of a predicate is a function from worlds to sets of things existing in those worlds that are in the predicate's extensions in those worlds. For example, the intension of "fat" looks from world to world and in each world picks out the class of fat things there. "Fat" means not just the actual fat things, but whatever would be fat in other possible circumstances. (To put the idea in more human terms, if you know the meaning of "fat," you know what various hypothetical things would count as fat as well as just the list of which things actually are fat.)

"Individual senses," the intensions of singular terms, are functions from worlds to individual denizens of those worlds. That should sound a bit familiar from Chapter 4; a rigid designator expresses a constant function in that it picks out the same individual in every world. But a flaccid designator changes its referent from world to world: as we saw, "the US President in 1999" designates Bill Clinton in the actual world, but various other people (or other creatures) in other worlds and no one at all in still others. The sense or intension of "the present US President" looks (or hops) from world to world and picks out whoever is currently US President there. As with predicates, if you know the meaning of the phrase "the present US President," you know who would be the President under various hypothetical conditions, even if you do not know who is actually President now.

Functions of this sort combine to make senses or intensions for whole sentences. Take:

(1) The present US President is fat.

In another possible world, (1)'s subject denotes whoever is President there, and "fat" has an extension there that probably differs from the actual class of fat things. So, compositionally, we know how to tell whether (1) is true in that world: (1) will be true in that world just in case the president there belongs to that local extension. Therefore, if we know the intension of "the present US President" and the intension of "fat," we know whether a given world is one that makes (1) true, which is to say that we know how to tell in which worlds (1) is true; for we have in effect a composite function from worlds to truth-values. Therefore we know what set of worlds is (1)'s truth set. (Strictly speaking, the sentence's intension is the function rather than the resulting truth set itself, but I shall ignore this technical distinction hereafter.) And that is to say that we know the proposition expressed by (1), which is to say that we know (1)'s meaning. (Do not be misled: all this talk of our "knowing" things does not mean we are slipping into verificationism. I am speaking metaphorically of how one computes a complex intension given some primitive, simple intensions and subject–predicate grammar.)

If a proposition is in this way construed as a set of possible worlds, then we do after all obtain nontrivial explanations of the meaning facts. Two sentences will be synonymous just in case they are true in just the same worlds. A sentence will be ambiguous if there is a world in which it is both true and false but without contradiction. And the possible-worlds construal affords an elegant algebra of meaning by way of set theory: for example, entailment between sentences is just the subset relation. S_1 entails S_2 just in case S_2 is true in any world in which S_1 is; that is, the set of worlds that is S_2's meaning is a subset of S_1's meaning.

Thus, the implementation of truth conditions in terms of possible worlds saves this sophisticated version of the Proposition Theory from Harman's Objection 3 (Chapter 5), for it tells us what a "proposition" is, in terms that we can work with independently: a proposition is a set of worlds. (One may have metaphysical qualms about the idea of a "non-actual possible world," but at least one already knows what a world is supposed to be.) The present view also avoids our second objection to Ideational Theories, which carried over to the Proposition Theory, for it tells us what an abstract "concept" is: a function from worlds to extensions. (Shortly I shall introduce a complication.)

Finally, there is a direct argument for the possible-worlds version of the Truth-Condition Theory, given very briefly in Lewis (1972):

> In order to say what a meaning is, we may first ask what a meaning does, and then find something that does that.
>
> A meaning for a sentence is something that determines the conditions under which the sentence is true or false. It determines the truth-value of the sentence in various possible states of affairs, at various times, at various places, for various speakers, and so on.
>
> (p. 22)

I believe the idea is this: if you understand a certain sentence S, and you are shown a possible world at random – we fly you there and dump you down in that world, miraculously making you omniscient as regards its facts – then right away you know whether S is true or false. (If you know every single fact of that world and you still cannot tell whether S is true there, then you cannot understand S.) So one thing that a meaning does is to spit out a truth value for any world it is given. Which is to say that a meaning is *at least* a truth condition in the sense of a particular set of worlds. (This leaves it open that a meaning may include more than just a truth condition.)

Advantages over Davidson's view

The possible-worlds view has some important advantages over Davidson's version of the Truth-Condition Theory. Specifically, it avoids Objections 4 and 5 that we made against Davidson.

Objection 4 was the problem of coextending but nonsynonymous terms. On the possible-worlds view, that is no problem at all. "Renate" and "cordate" differ in meaning because, although they apply to just the same things in the actual world, their extensions diverge in other possible worlds; countless worlds contain renates that are not cordates and vice versa. End of story (though shortly we shall resurrect Frege's solution to the Problem of Substitutivity).

Objection 5 was the problem of non-truth-functional sentence connectives. Here the possible-worlds view displays a unique strength. For it enables us to state truth conditions for certain connectives directly in terms of worlds. Take the simple modal operator "It is possible that," as in "It is possible that the present US President is fat." The latter sentence will be counted as true just in case *there is a world in which* the present US President is fat. And if we wanted to say "Necessarily, if there is a US President, the United States exists," intensional semantics would count that as true just in case *in every world*, if there is a US President, the United States exists.

From this we can see that our original formula needs qualification: not every simple expression's sense or intension can be cast as a function from worlds to an extension or referent. Some are functions from intensions to other intensions; "It is possible that" takes the intension of the sentence to which it is applied and turns it into a different intension. Another, subsentential example would be adverbs, such as "slowly." "Jane swims" is true in a world just in case the referent of "Jane" in that world is among the things that swim there, because the extension of "swims" is just the class of that world's denizens that swim. But what about "Jane swims slowly"? Grammatically, "slowly" modifies the predicate "swims," making it into the complex predicate "swims slowly." And the intensional semanticist maintains that the semantics follows in just the same way: the intension of "slowly" is a function from intensions to intensions; it picks up the intension of "swims" and turns it into a modified intension, namely the function that looks at a world and picks out the class of things that swim slowly in that world.[1]

The possible-worlds theory has a deft way with belief sentences also. Let us return for a moment to Frege. As a solution to the Problem of Substitutivity, Frege proposed that a belief sentence can change its truth-value as a result of substitution of coreferring terms because, even though the two terms have the same referent, they may have different senses, and so a different composite sense may result from the substitution. As always with unexplicated versions of the Proposition Theory, that sounds right but does not really explain anything so long as "sense" is merely taken for granted. But the possible-worlds theorist can give the explanation more content: although the two terms corefer in the actual world, they diverge in other worlds, so their intensions differ. Therefore the composite intensions of otherwise similar sentences in which they appear will differ also. If believing is a relation between the believer and a proposition, that is a sentence intension, then of course the believer may believe the one intension without believing the other.

At this point an adjustment is needed. As I noted above, the present version of the possible-worlds theory counts two sentences as being synonymous when and only when the two are true in just the same worlds. But what of necessary truths that hold in every world? It would follow that every such truth is synonymous with every other; for example, "Either pigs have wings or they don't" and "If there are edible mice, then some mice are edible" would mean exactly the same, which they obviously do not. Moreover, any sentence would be counted as being synonymous with any other sentence necessarily equivalent to it: "Snow is white" would be said to mean just the same as "Either snow is white or pigs have wings and pigs are mammals and no mammals have wings"; and whoever believed the former would be automatically counted as believing the latter. Something has to give.

The source of the problem seems to be that complex intensions can be necessarily coextensive even when they are made up out of quite different concepts. The cure, then, as Carnap saw, was to require that for synonymy, sentences should not only have the same intension but have that intension composed in the same way (or much the same way) out of the same atomic intensions. This is what he called *intensional isomorphism*, and it rules out all the foregoing problem cases. For example, "Either pigs have wings or they don't" and "If there are edible mice, then some mice are edible" are composed out of entirely different intensions (those of "pig" and "wing" in the first case and those of "mouse" and "edible" or "eat" in the second).

Remaining objections

The possible-worlds theory inherits several of the objections raised against Davidson's version: 1 (nondeclaratives and non-fact-stating sentences), 2 (testability), and 6 (taking truth for granted); an intensional theorist would make much the same range of replies as we did on Davidson's behalf. Objection 3 (deixis) arises in a different way, since the possible-worlds approach does not involve T-sentences, but it does arise, since no provision has as yet been made for deixis in the intensional apparatus. Objection 3 will be the main business of the next chapter.

The possible-worlds view also inherits the first two objections made against the Proposition Theory in Chapter 5: weirdness and alienness. As I noted in Chapter 4, it is one thing to take "possible worlds" as a metaphor or heuristic for explaining a way of looking at things, as I did in explaining Kripke's view of proper names. It is another to appeal to them directly in serious theorizing, as the intensional semanticists do. In what sense *are there really* alternative worlds that *do not really exist*? But this is a large subject and I cannot go into it here.[2]

The possible-worlds view is also subject to Objection 4 against the Proposition Theory (neglect of meaning's "dynamic feature"). At the time, we replied simply that even if propositions do not help in the explanation of human behavior, behavior is not the primary thing that needs explaining; rather, the meaning facts are. But the objection has been pushed further against both versions of the Truth-Condition Theory.

Objection 7

Many Davidsonians and some intension theorists tend to think of the kind of semantically charged syntax I have been describing as a machine program for computing large meanings from smaller ones, a program that is in some sense being run in the brains of speakers and hearers. But that idea is problematic. Here is a more specific worry about the "dynamic feature," pointed out by Michael Dummett (1975) and by Hilary Putnam (1978). Dummett's and Putnam's own writings are dense and somewhat obscure, but here is a simple way of putting one of their concerns: a sentence meaning is what one knows when one knows what a sentence means. But to know what a sentence means is just to understand that sentence. And understanding is a psychological state, one that inheres in a flesh-and-blood human organism and affects that organism's behavior. Now, how can knowledge of a truth-condition *per se* affect anyone's behavior, when (as is easily shown by Twin-Earth examples) truth is a "wide" property of sentences in the sense that it "ain't in the head" and knowledge of truth is a conspicuously wide property of people? The truth-condition of "Dogs drink water," here, differs from that of "Dogs drink water" on Twin Earth, but the difference is irrelevant to behavior and cannot affect it. But understanding (= knowing meaning) must and does affect behavior. Therefore understanding is not, or not merely, knowledge of truth-condition, and so meaning is not, or not simply, truth-condition.

First reply

Put in this way, the argument assumes that "understanding" must itself be a "narrow" or "in the head" concept. That is, to say the least, not obvious. (I leave to you the exercise of constructing a Twin-Earth counterexample.) Realizing that the argument needs a narrow concept of understanding also should make us reconsider the simple equating of "knowing meaning" with understanding and vice versa, truistic as that equating may have sounded at first.

Second reply

Further, the argument assumes that wide concepts cannot *per se* figure in the etiology of behavior. As is made clear by the "intensional causation" literature of the past decade,[3] "figuring in" can be done in many ways. There is no doubt that behavior depends counterfactually on wide states of people, and I think that is the strongest etiological notion guaranteed by common sense. If anyone thinks that understanding affects behavior in a stronger sense of "affect" than just that the behavior depends counterfactually on the understanding, we would have to hear some defense.

Objection 8

(A similar one.) If, Quine to the contrary, individual sentences ever have meaning at all, then whatever meaning is must be accessible to the translator; for translators are precisely people who compile translation manuals from scratch. But the truth-conditions of sentences are not accessible to the radical translator. A Martian visiting Earth and Twin Earth would necessarily translate Earth English and Twin English into Martian in exactly the same way, since all her evidence would be exactly the same.

Reply

It is not true that all the evidence would be the same. If the Martian finds that "water" is a natural-kind term (and she buys Putnam's account of natural-kind terms), she will know that if water and Twin water are different stuffs, the two words mean different things; she can then ask a chemist whether the stuffs are different stuffs. There are, of course, deep problems in the epistemology of translation, but they do not afflict truth-conditional semantics in particular.

The "use" theorist is not quite finished with the truth-condition view. We shall begin Chapter 12 by considering a further objection.

Summary

- A sentence's truth condition can be taken to be the set of possible worlds in which the sentence is true.
- More generally, possible worlds can be used to construct "intensions" for subsentential expressions, that will combine compositionally to determine the containing sentence's truth condition.
- The resulting view avoids both the problem of coextending but nonsynonymous terms and the problem of non-truth-functional connectives.
- The possible-worlds theory also deepens Frege's solution to the Problem of Substitutivity.
- But the theory inherits a number of Davidson's original difficulties and incurs one or two more.

Questions

1   Evaluate Lewis' direct argument for the possible-worlds version of the Truth-Condition Theory.
2   Discuss the possible-worlds theory further, pro, con, or both. (If you do not already know some possible-worlds semantics, you will want to do at least a bit of outside reading; I recommend Lewis (1970).
3   Adjudicate Objection 7 and/or Objection 8.

Notes

1   Montague (1960) built up a structure of such higher- (and higher-)order intensions corresponding to more and more abstract parts of speech. In fact, out of a desire to one-up Quine, Montague explicitly assigned very rarefied individual intensions to "sake,"

"behalf," and "dint." As I mentioned in Chapter 1, in this way he meant also to strike a blow on behalf of the Referential Theory. (But it is at best a glancing blow: the words are not taken as *denoting* their intensions as if they were proper names.)

2 See again Lewis (1986) and Lycan (1994).

3 See, for example, Heil and Mele (1993).

Further reading

The simplest and most natural introduction I know to the Possible-Worlds version of truth-conditional semantics is Lewis (1970). Then work up to Cresswell (1973). (Tough stuff, requiring knowledge of formal logic and set theory; but it all came from something much tougher, collected posthumously in Montague (1974).) Two good textbook introductions to Montague Grammar are Chierchia and McConnell-Ginet (1990) and Weisler (1991).

PART III

Pragmatics and speech acts

11
Semantic pragmatics

Overview

Semantic vs. pragmatic pragmatics

The problem of deixis

The work of semantic pragmatics

Summary

Questions

Notes

Further reading

Overview

Linguistic "pragmatics" is characterized as studying linguistic expressions' uses in social contexts. But there are two importantly different ways in which an expression's use "depends on context." First, due to the presence of such "deictic" elements as personal pronouns and tense, a sentence's propositional content varies from context to context (recall that "I am sick now" says different things depending on when it is uttered and by whom). Second, even once the sentence's propositional content has been fixed, there are several other important aspects of its use that will still vary with context. "Semantic pragmatics" studies the former phenomenon, the determination of propositional content by context; "pragmatic pragmatics" studies the latter.

Davidson deals with the problem of deictic elements by complicating the standard form of his T-sentences. The possible-worlds theorists deal with it by relativizing truth to a set of content-affecting contextual factors such as speaker and time. But both approaches need to be liberated from having to list a fixed set of contextual features.

Semantic pragmatics has a complicated range of data to deal with. It must not only chart the complicated uses of pronouns, tense, and the like, but must solve the general problem of disambiguation: given that nearly every English sentence has more than one meaning, how does a hearer identify the correct one upon hearing the sentence uttered?

harles Morris (1938) divided linguistic study into *syntax, semantics*, and *pragmatics*. Impressionistically put, the distinction was supposed to be this: syntax is the study of grammar, the study of which strings of words are well-formed sentences of a given language and why. Semantics is the study of meaning, construed primarily (though as we know not uncontroversially) as a matter of the relations that linguistic expressions bear to the world in virtue of which they are meaningful. In contrast, pragmatics studies the uses of linguistic expressions in various social practices including, of course, everyday conversation and communication, but not only those. On this usage, Wittgenstein's view (Chapter 6 above) can be put by saying that either "semantics" is entirely misguided or it collapses into pragmatics.

Semantic vs. pragmatic pragmatics

The single word we hear most often in the study and practice of pragmatics is the word "context," meaning *context of utterance.* Pragmatics is specifically about the functioning of language in context. This marks a significant contrast, because syntax and semantics have generally aspired to be contextless. Syntax is about whether a sentence is grammatical or whether a string of words constitutes a grammatical sentence, period. Semantics has always focused on sentence meaning, the meaning of a sentence type in abstraction from any particular use to which the sentence might be put. But there are always pests like Wittgenstein, Strawson, and J. L. Austin reminding us that the very idea of a "sentence type" is a violent abstraction from linguistic reality. When a sentence is uttered, it is invariably uttered in a particular context by a particular speaker for a particular purpose. And this is something that cannot be ignored, for solid reasons that I shall try to make clear in the remaining chapters of this book.

I said that the distinction between semantics and pragmatics was supposed to be that the former deals with the acontextual meanings of sentence types, while the latter addresses the social uses of linguistic expressions in context. But there are two reasons why that characterization is too simple. The first reason is that there is an important sense in which most sentence types simply do not have acontextual meanings. The second is that, as we shall see later on, social-use factors interpenetrate in certain special ways with what we would otherwise think of as propositional meaning.

Here is the sense in which most sentence types lack acontextual meanings. Recall the phenomenon of deixis, brought up in Objection 3 against the Truth-Condition Theory, and consider a heavily deictic sentence. Suppose you and I come into an empty classroom and find the following words written on the blackboard: "I have never been to a karaoke bar, but you and I will visit one tomorrow morning." Unless we can find out who had written those words when and to whom, we do not know what exactly has been said (even though we know *something* about what has been said); we do not know what proposition has been expressed. In terms of the possible-worlds theory, we do not know the sentence's intension. In fact, if the sentence had been scribbled on the board merely as a linguistic example and no referents had even tacitly been assigned to its deictic elements, it would not express any proposition at all and would not even have an intension.

The common moral of the original Objection 3 and of this last argument is that a sentence's complete truth condition depends on contextual factors. And even if one does not accept the Truth-Condition Theory of meaning, one can see that a sentence's meaning, in the sense of its propositional content, depends on context in just the same way.

Cresswell (1973) distinguished between two kinds of pragmatics: "semantic pragmatics" and "pragmatic pragmatics." Semantic pragmatics deals with those elements of meaning in the sense of propositional content that simply do depend on context. It is the discipline that tells us how propositional content is determined by contextual features. But before we say more about it and explain the contrasting notion, let us deal with Objection 3.

The problem of deixis

Returning to Davidson's problem: he needs to find a way of formulating T-sentences that accommodates deictic or indexical elements without getting truth conditions wrong. I mentioned Davidson's own proposal for doing this. Other notable attempts have been made by Weinstein (1974) and especially Burge (1974), but here I shall present a simple idea suggested by Harman (1972).[1]

We saw that one drawback of Davidson's proposal was its limiting the potentially relevant contextual factors to speaker and time. There are many others. An obvious example is objects indicated by the speaker's pointing gesture, as when the speaker says, "This one is more expensive than that one," successively pointing to two different objects on display. To take a more exotic example, *hemisphere*.[2] "It is autumn" is true as I write this in North Carolina, USA, but it would not be true were it uttered simultaneously in Sydney or in Buenos Aires. (Nor is the relevant hemisphere determined by the speaker's location; it depends on the audience and on conversational purposes as well. If I am conversing with an Australian about Australian affairs – even if we are both currently in North Carolina in November – I may say, "Because it's spring, the students will be just starting to think about their final exams.") So we need an approach to deictic target sentences that does not presuppose a fixed number of contextual variables.

Let us get the whole job done in one stroke. We can relativize "true" to contexts – since we already know that the truth of a sentence type does vary with context – and introduce a function, α, that will look at a deictic element occurring in a context and tell us what that element contributes in that context to propositional content. For example, if (as is generally thought) the first-person pronoun "I" always denotes the speaker, α will look at an occurrence of "I" in a particular utterance and map that expression onto the person who did the uttering. For short, α("I",C) – read as "what α assigns to 'I' in the context C" – is the speaker in C. Likewise, if "now" denotes roughly the time at which an utterance is itself uttered, then α("now",C) is that time. And α("tomorrow",C) would be the day immediately following the uttering in C.

Then we can write the right-hand sides of Davidson's T-sentences in terms of what α assigns in the context C to each deictic element in the target sentence. Thus:

"I am sick now" is true in C if and only if α("I",C) is sick at α("now",C).

"I have never been to a karaoke bar, but you and I will visit one tomorrow morning" is true in C if and only if α("I",C) does not go to a karaoke bar during α(perfect tense, C)[3] but α("you",C) and α("I",C) visit a karaoke bar during the morning of α("tomorrow",C).

Problem solved. Davidson's technical problem of formulating T-sentences, that is; further philosophical questions can and will be raised about α.

The intensional logicians dealt with deixis by relativizing truth to an "index," which was a fixed set of contextual variables. Montague (1968) and Scott (1970) took an index to be a set of eight standard elements consisting of a possible world, a time, a place, a speaker, an audience, a sequence of indicated or demonstrated objects, a "discourse-segment," and a "sequence of assignments to free variables" (never mind what those last two mean). In this system, a truth condition assignment would look like this:

"I am sick now" is true at $<w,t,l,p,a,i,d,s>$ if and only if in w, p is sick at t.

But this shares the drawback of Davidson's method, though not as severely, in that it arbitrarily restricts the number of contextual features that can be cited.[4] We have no way of foreseeing what further such features might become relevant to the truth of an utterance.

For example, we have already introduced one unexpected variable, *hemisphere* (as between southern and northern). There are plenty of others, seemingly without limit. The truth of "It is 5:00 p.m." depends on *time zone*, an entirely conventional construct. (As Wittgenstein once noted, time zones are bound to our planet; "It is 5:00 on the sun" has no truth-value.) And some locutions presuppose a kind of *vantage point*, often distinct from the place of actual utterance, that can shift even within a single sentence (Fillmore 1975; Taylor 1988). Take

(1) a. Zonker went to Uncle Duke's party
    b. Zonker came to Uncle Duke's party.

(2) I'm going out to clean the pasture spring; . . . . – You come too.
    (Robert Frost, "The Pasture")

(1a) and (1b) can have the same truth condition, but (1b) can be said properly only by a speaker whose assumed vantage point is the party location itself. (Note too that what counts is the vantage point at the time of the party under discussion, not at the time of utterance; this is yet another context variable, usually called the *reference time*.) In (2), the vantage point shifts fluidly from the place of utterance to the pasture spring, or at least to somewhere along the journey at which the speaker is pictured as ahead of the hearer.

Arriving at Princeton to give a talk, I am met by a former colleague whom I last saw teaching at Wellesley. I ask, "Are you here now?," asking not whether she is physically located in Princeton (duhh) but whether she is now employed in the Princeton philosophy department (Nunberg 1993: 28); thus truth-value can vary with *employing institution*. Or take

(3) Tomorrow is always the biggest party night of the year.

uttered on the Friday before classes begin (Nunberg 1993: 29; Nunberg credits Dick Oehrle with the example). "Tomorrow" in (3) cannot refer, as it usually would, to the day or night following the date of utterance; it refers to a *type* of date on the students' academic calendar, namely to the annual Saturday before classes begin.

I could go on and on. The moral is that we cannot ever be sure we have anticipated all the context variables that can affect truth-value. So I would advise the intension theorists to avail themselves, instead, of my mighty assignment function α.

The work of semantic pragmatics

The trick is to find out *how α is computed*, that is, what rules we use in particular contexts to fill in the missing chunks of propositional content corresponding to deictic elements. Presumably each such element in the language is governed by an appropriate rule.

For example, we might look at the pronoun "I" and suggest that in a context, "I" always denotes the speaker. Turning to "now," it seems reasonable to say that "now" always refers in context to the time of the utterance. In fact, these first attempts are too simple. "I" can be used as a device of deferred reference to a position or role, as when the condemned prisoner says "I am traditionally allowed to order whatever I like for my last meal" (Nunberg 1993: 20). Sometimes "I" is used as a bound variable, as in "If I'm a music department, I'm a snake pit." The temporal reference of "now" can be deferred also, as when we are looking at a time-line representation of the evolution of life and, pointing, I say, "Now the dinosaurs appear," or when you leave a message on your answering machine that says "I am not home now." "Now" is sometimes spatial rather than in any way temporal – "Now Hillsborough Road crosses Airport Road and becomes Umstead Drive" – and sometimes not even spatiotemporal – "Now comes the first prime number whose square is greater than 1,000." But one job of semantic pragmatics is to refine such rules until they are adequate to the data.

The intensional logician David Kaplan (1977) thinks of such rules as functions. As an intension is a function from worlds to extensions, a semantic–pragmatic rule is a function from contexts to intensions. At the level of the sentence, the intension is a function from worlds to truth-values. Kaplan calls that the sentence's "content," and as before, it corresponds to the traditional notion of a proposition. The composite semantic–pragmatic rule is a function from contexts to contents; Kaplan calls that "character." Content is what is left undetermined by the deictic sentences in our examples; character is what does determine content given all the relevant contextual features of a context of utterance. Thus, when we come upon the karaoke sentence, character tells us to look for the speaker (to find α("I",C)), and the hearer and the date of utterance; once we know those, we will know what has to obtain in a possible world in order for the sentence to be true in that world.

I said that when we encounter the karaoke sentence unprepared, we do not know (in full) what it says. And I was right. But there is another perfectly good sense in which we understand the sentence itself, and virtually any English speaker understands "I am sick now" entirely out of context. Kaplan argues that the "m"-word should be reserved for character rather than for content, on the entirely reasonable ground that ordinary English speakers surely know the meanings of everyday deictic sentences even when they do not know the contextual parameters that would fix those sentences' contents. Yet content in his sense is also still a perfectly good thing to mean by "meaning." It is hardly a matter for heated dispute.

Computing α and/or characterizing character is not the only task of semantic pragmatics. Another and horribly vexed one is *disambiguation*. Many sentences, like "Visiting philosophers can be boring," "Ted is lying about meditating," and (Paul Ziff's example) "The mouse tore up the street," are obviously ambiguous. And in fact, almost every sentence we ever encounter in life is technically ambiguous, in the sense that it has one or more possible if farfetched meanings in addition to the one that would normally be intended by an utterer. Yet we rarely pause to think, or even notice that we are choosing from among a range of possible meanings (not merely filling gaps in an otherwise unique propositional content). How we do this is a deep question, much deeper than that of how we compute α. Certainly too deep for this book, though some hints will be furnished in Chapter 13.

That is semantic pragmatics. In contrast, "pragmatic pragmatics" takes propositional content for granted, and asks wider questions about the use of sentences in contexts. One and the same sentence with an already fixed propositional content can still be used to do interestingly different things in different contexts. As we shall see in our remaining chapters, there is considerably more to producing and understanding language than just grasping propositional meaning, hard as the latter is to explain.

Summary

- Linguistic "pragmatics" is characterized as studying linguistic expressions' uses in social contexts.
- "Semantic pragmatics" studies, in particular, the determination of propositional content by context.
- Davidson deals with the problem of deictic elements by complicating the standard form of his T-sentences.
- The possible-worlds theorists deal with it by relativizing truth to a set of content-affecting contextual factors such as speaker and time.
- But both approaches can be freed from having to list a fixed set of contextual features, if we avail ourselves of the assignment function α.
- In addition to tracking the complicated uses of particular deictic expressions, semantic pragmatics is charged with solving the terrible problem of disambiguation.

Questions

1 Is there a better way for Davidson or for the possible-worlds theorist to solve the problem of deixis than by importing Harman's assignment function α? In particular, does α create new difficulties of its own?
2 Take an expression such as "I" or "now" (or "tomorrow" or "recently" or "west" . . .) and try to state the *exact* rule according to which it affects the propositional content of a sentence in which it occurs.
3 Make at least a feeble start on the problem of disambiguation. (Do not expect impressive results.)

Notes

1 It is further developed in Chapter 3 of Lycan (1984).
2 This was once pointed out to me by Peter van Inwagen.
3 This treatment of tense is a fudge, for convenience; for a fuller treatment of tense, see Lycan (1984: 55–62).
4 There is a more serious objection to it as well, pointed out by Burge (1974).

Further reading

For a somewhat less technical discussion of indexicals than Kaplan (1978), see Kaplan (1989). Recanati (1993) takes up the DR approach to indexicals.

Yourgrau (1990) is a good collection on demonstratives.

Taylor (1988) and Nunberg (1993) contain excellent examples of unusual indexical constructions.

12
Speech acts and illocutionary force

Overview

Performatives

Rules and infelicities

Force, content, and perlocution

Cohen's problem

Summary

Questions

Notes

Further reading

Overview

J L. Austin called our attention to what he called a "performative" utterance of a declarative sentence, whereby one performs a conventional social act but does not state or describe anything – for example, "I apologize" or (in a game of bridge) "I double." The kinds of acts that can be performed in this way are called "speech acts." Each type of speech act is governed by rules of two sorts: constitutive rules, which must be obeyed if the act is to have been accomplished at all, and regulative rules, violation of which merely renders the act defective or, in Austin's word, infelicitous. There are many and surprisingly various ways in which a given speech act can be infelicitous.

But Austin came to see that there is no principled distinction between performative utterances and those of ordinary declaratives. Rather, every utterance has a performative aspect or "illocutionary force," which determines the type of speech act performed, and virtually every utterance has a descriptive or propositional content as well. Further, many utterances have features which incorporate their distinctive effects on hearers' mental states; these features are called "perlocutionary."

Jonathan Cohen has raised a nasty problem about the truth conditions of sentences that contain explicit performative prefaces that specify the type of speech act to be performed, for example, "*I admit that* I had several private conversations with the defendant." No satisfactory solution to that problem has been found.

Performatives

Consider the following sentences.

(1) I promise to pay you for the diapers.
(2) I pronounce you husband and wife.
(3) I christen this ship the *Ludwig Wittgenstein*.
(4) I apologize.
(5) I double. [A bid in bridge.]
(6) Raise you five. [A bet in poker.]
(7) Nay. [A vote on a formal motion.]

Except possibly for the last two, these are declarative sentences, so (in particular) the Verificationist must address them; what are their respective verification conditions? Perhaps that question is too hard, or unfair in view of Quine's Duhemian objection. But what are their truth conditions?

We could direct T-sentences upon them. For example,

"I promise to pay you for the diapers" is true if and only if I promise to pay you for the diapers.

Really? (No, not really.)

"I double" is true if and only if I double.

Possibly; perhaps "I double," as said by me on the appropriate occasion, is true if and only if I do double on that occasion. But it seems that we are leaving something out, something that is more important than the utterance's slightly degenerate truth condition. As J. L. Austin (1961, 1962) might have put it, when I say "I double," I am not *describing myself as doing some doubling*; I am actually doubling, and nothing more. (Doubling is a move in the game of bridge. It is part of a real language-game, in the literal sense.) And no one could acceptably rejoin, "That's false, you don't double." If someone else then says of me, "He doubled," that is a true report of what I did. But when I originally say it, simply as a move in the game, it does not seem like a candidate for truth or falsity.

"Nay" is true if and only if nay.

Forget it; that "T-sentence" is not even grammatical.

We have here the basis for a further objection to Verificationism and to the Truth-Condition Theory, a compound of a Wittgensteinian objection and our first objection to the Truth-Condition Theory. A Wittgensteinian might look at (4), (5), and (7), especially, assimilating them to the builders' primitive ("Slab!") language, and remind us again of the many devices such as "Hello" and "Oh, dear" that have conventional social uses and are perfectly meaningful without having anything to do with verification or with truth itself. Even when we turn to the more highly structured (1)–(3) and (6), it seems that although each is declarative in mood, none is in the business of stating a fact or disclosing a truth. They are in different lines of work; so they seem to count as "factually defective."

In Austin's original article (1961), he called sentences like (1)–(7) "performatives," to distinguish them from "constatives" (constatives being just the usual sorts of descriptive, fact-stating, true-or-false sentences that philosophers like). In uttering a performative one is not, or at least not ostensibly, describing anything or stating a fact, but performing a social act. When I utter (1), I am actually making the promise. When I utter (4) I am simply apologizing. When I utter (6) I add to my bet, making a financial commitment. When I utter (3), in the proper context with a bottle of the appropriate kind of champagne, I actually perform the christening. Austin called such social actions "speech acts," and so gave birth to the branch of linguistics and philosophy of language that ever since has been called "speech-act theory."

Whatever the outcome for anyone's theory of meaning, we must study the phenomenon of (in Austin's title phrase) "doing things with words," on pain of leaving out a very important range of linguistic phenomena. (There are two further reasons as well. One is that speech-act theory is the most effective cure for philosophers' otherwise overmastering tendency, vividly exemplified in this very book so far, to think that declarative sentences are the only ones that matter. The other is that many mistakes have been made and fallacies committed in areas of philosophy other than philosophy of language, through ignorance of speech-act theory; but space does not permit.)

Rules and infelicities

Speech acts are conventional acts; just as any "use" theorist would have it, they are embedded in and defined by social customs, practices, and institutions. Their performings are governed by rules of many kinds. The rules are usually unwritten, merely implicit in normative social behavior.

Searle (1965, 1969) divides speech-act rules into *constitutive* rules and (merely) *regulative* rules. As I interpret this terminology,[1] a constitutive rule is one, violation of which aborts the purported speech act. Suppose I utter a sentence with the intention of performing a certain type of speech act, A. If I violate a constitutive rule, it follows that I have simply failed to perform an act of type A. For example, if tomorrow I utter (3) and break a bottle over the prow of the USS *North Carolina*, I do not succeed in christening her, for I have not the standing or authority to do so. (The US Navy has explicit rules for appointing the dignitaries who christen battleships. There is also the fact that the *North Carolina* has been christened already, on 12 June 1940.)[2] If a clergyman utters (2) to a young couple standing before him in a Chicago chapel, but is not licensed to perform marriages in the state of Illinois, or if one of the couple is not of legally marriageable age, the wedding does not succeed (indeed is not a *wedding* at all, despite the organ music, rings, and rice). To raise someone five by uttering (6), I have to be playing poker at the time, and five has to be within the agreed-upon betting limit.

Violation of a regulative rule is less grave. If I utter a sentence intending to perform a speech act of type A, and violate no constitutive rules but do violate some regulative rule, the result is that I do perform an act of type A, but defectively or, in Austin's official vocabulary, "infelicitously." If the wedding did succeed, but the resulting marriage is only one of crass convenience and the couple were lying their heads off when they spoke their vows, the wedding was defective; it is a regulative rule of marriage that the couple love each other and sincerely intend to remain married. Promising is a closely related example: if I utter (1) insincerely, having no intention of paying you your money, it is an infelicitous promise. For that matter, if I shout (1) to you across a crowded room, and you cannot hear me, that is an infelicity of a different sort.

There are borderline cases between constitutive and regulative rules. What if I utter (4), but in a flauntedly unrepentant, jeering, sneering tone? Is that a grievously infelicitous apology, or no apology at all?

Austin was greatly concerned to emphasize the multifariousness of infelicity. An utterance can go wrong in any one of any number of quite different ways. It can be an ill-advised move in a game, as when one utters (6) because one has miscalculated the odds. Or it may be insincere. Or one may lack the standing or authority to perform an act of the kind intended. Or it may be very rude. Or it may be made too softly and go unheard. Or it may be made, tactlessly, in front of the wrong people. Or it may be verbose and pompous and blather on and on. Or it may presuppose something false, as if I were to apologize for doing something that my hearer had wanted done, or that was not in any way a bad thing to have done, or that

I did not even do at all. This great variety of defects will become philosophically important later on.

Force, content, and perlocution

Naturally, Austin began seeking a workable, fairly precise test for performativity. He tried to characterize the notion syntactically, and ran into various kinds of trouble that need not detain us. But he settled fairly comfortably on the so-called "hereby" criterion: an utterance is counted as performative if one could fairly interpolate the word "hereby" before the main verb. Thus, (1) is performative because the speaker could as well have said, "I *hereby* promise to pay you . . . ." The "hereby" emphasizes that the act in question, here the giving of a promise, is constituted by the speaker's very utterance itself. The criterion works well for (2)–(6) also: "I hereby pronounce . . . ," "I hereby christen . . . ," and so on. "I hereby double" would be stilted, but its meaning would be perfectly in order.

Certainly the criterion marks off performatives from constatives. If I utter a paradigmatic constative, such as "The cat is on the mat," I could not have inserted "hereby." "The cat is hereby on the mat" is nonsensical or at least false, because the cat is (or is not) on the mat regardless of my saying that it is. My saying it does nothing to make it so.

Austin noticed a pesky class of clear non-constatives, apparent performatives, that are too simple to pass the "hereby" test. Actually (7) might be taken as an example, since "Hereby nay" is ungrammatical. But it is plausible to say that "Nay" is just a laconic form of "I vote nay," which does meet the "hereby" condition.

However, what about "Hooray!," "Shame!," and "Damn!"? None of these admits "hereby," and they are harder than "Nay" was to hear as merely short for declaratives containing performative verbs. One might try arguing that "Hooray!" really means, "I hereby cheer"; Lewis (1970: 57–8) proposed to understand "Hooray for Porky" as "I cheer Porky." Perhaps "Shame!" means "I hereby castigate you" and "Damn!" means "I hereby curse." But these hypotheses are not obviously correct.

Austin grew far more deeply dissatisfied with the "performative"/ "constative" distinction when he noticed another type of sentence. Consider:

(8) I state that I have never traveled to a Communist country.

(8) passes the "hereby" test, and so should be counted as performative. When I say it, I thereby do perform a certain speech act: an act of stating.

But it is also indelibly fact-stating, descriptive. Indeed – whether or not the speaker has in fact ever traveled to a Communist country – that is its whole point; the operative verb is "state." The speaker's statement is true or false. If (8) is uttered under oath and the speaker has traveled to a Communist country, the speaker can be indicted for perjury. So (8) seems to be either both performative and constative, or neither.

And there are more:

(9) I judge that we are overextended in the area of sealskin futures.
(10) I report that the Committee has voted unanimously to expel Grannie.
(11) I advise you that it would be very stupid to buy more Amalgamated Amalgam stock.
(12) I warn you that that Rottweiler has been starved for three days and is peevish.

Even (1) has a paraphrase with similarly constative features: "I promise that I will pay you for the diapers," which at least *asserts* that I will pay you.

Such examples made Austin realize that a single utterance can have both a performative part or aspect and a constative part or aspect. In fact, virtually every utterance does, even if it lacks an explicit performative preface like those that begin (8)–(12). If instead of (8), I testify merely "I have never traveled to a Communist country," I still perform an act of stating, in addition to merely expressing the propositional content that I have never traveled to a Communist country. Whenever I make an assertion – that is, whenever I make an utterance having the force of an assertion – I perform an act of asserting.

Declaratives can be uttered with other forces as well. If I were to delete the performative prefaces from (9)–(12) and say only "We are over-extended . . . ," "The Committee has voted . . . ," and so on, in the same contexts, those utterances would have the forces respectively of a judge-ment, a report, an advising, and a warning. Austin called this type of feature "*illocutionary* force," and he contrasted it with "locutionary" or propositional content.[3]

In different contexts, the same declarative may have different illocutionary forces. "That Rottweiler has been starved for three days and is peevish" could have the force of a threat rather than a warning; or it could be merely an observation; or (notice) it could be a soothing reassur-ance. Even children recognize differences in potential force: a complaint such as "If you don't quit it I'm going home" is met by the gibe, "Is that a threat or a promise?"

Turning to nondeclaratives, it is considerably more obvious that they have distinctive varieties of forces. In fact, the point of moods such as interrogative and imperative seems to be to indicate ranges of illocutionary force.

(13) Are you a member of the Salvation Army?

could be paraphrased as "I (hereby) ask you whether you are a member of the Salvation Army," and likewise for "wh"-questions such as "Who let Fluffy out of her cage?"

(14) Go to the Music Library and find a copy of Lana Walter's *Petite Mass*

could have the force of a command, an order, a mere request, or just a suggestion, depending on the intentions and purposes of speaker and hearer and on whatever power relation or institutional authority may obtain between them.[4]

Thus did Austin's original distinction between performative and constative utterances turn into a distinction between force and content as aspects of a single utterance. Austin (1962) elaborated a massive catalogue of different illocutionary forces and the factors that distinguish them. Here are a few further examples of distinct illocutionary acts: admitting (in either of two senses); announcing; assuring; authorizing; censuring; committing; complimenting; conceding: confessing; congratulating; defining; denying; granting; hypothesizing; inquiring; insisting; pardoning; pleading; pledging; predicting; proposing; reprehending; thanking; urging; vowing.

Constitutive and regulative rules still govern the performance of illocutionary acts. Austin continued to emphasize the great variety of these and the corresponding variety of possible defects and infelicities. And now that we have recognized that some speech acts are acts of stating, asserting, and the like, we see that *falsity* is one common besetting defect of such acts; a regulative rule regarding acts of that class is that what is said should be true.

Austin complains at length that philosophers are obsessed with "the true–false fetish," the misguided idea that truth-value is all that matters in speech. In particular, we often mistake other kinds of infelicities for falsity; when we hear a sentence that is somehow defective, we tend to assume, fallaciously, that the sentence is not true. (In Chapter 13 we shall scout two instances of this fallacy.) There are many ways in which utterances can go wrong – badly wrong – without being false. Falsity is just one form of infelicity among many others.[5]

*

Austin introduced a third feature of utterances, in addition to illocutionary force and locutionary content: perlocutionary effect. Some verbs are like performative verbs in meaning a kind of social act performed by linguistic means, but fail the "hereby" test because they describe the act in terms of its actual effects on the hearer rather than in terms of the speaker's intention. Take "frighten," and "convince." I cannot rightly say "I hereby frighten you" or "I hereby convince you that Grannie did it," because whether you are respectively frightened or convinced depends in part on you and is in no way guaranteed (much less constituted) by my utterance itself. Acts of frightening and convincing are what Austin calls perlocutionary acts; they are things we do with words, but not in the same intimate sense as are illocutionary acts. Here are a few more examples of perlocutionary acts: alarming; amazing; amusing; annoying; boring; embarrassing; encouraging; deceiving; distracting; impressing; informing; inspiring; insulting; irritating; persuading.

The Verification and Truth-Condition Theories of meaning identify a sentence's *meaning* with the sentence's propositional or locutionary content alone. But is not illocutionary force a kind of meaning? Certainly, if you do not understand distinctions of force, then there is an important aspect of language that you have not yet mastered. So it seems that the Verificationists and truth-condition theorists have left something out.

They may reply: "Important, of course; pragmatic properties are important in real life. But they're not part of *meaning*." I believe this is just a schoolyard scuffle over the "m"-word, which is often used more generally as an umbrella term for whatever aspects of linguistic activity are considered important. We already know that there are kinds of meaning besides locutionary sentence meaning – speaker-meaning, for example. Now we can add that here is now an illocutionary kind of meaning, force, which is not the same thing as locutionary meaning either. Each of these kinds of meaning is perfectly real and indispensable to language use.[6]

Cohen's problem

Jonathan Cohen (1964) raised a nasty problem about sentences like (8)–(12). It is a problem about truth conditions. Take (8) ("I state that I have never traveled to a Communist country"). What is (8)'s truth condition?

Cohen says (p. 121), "It is tempting at first to suppose that in Austin's view the meaning of our utterance is found totally in the clause that follows the performative preface." Substituting "truth condition" for "meaning," it is indeed tempting to read the truth condition out from under the performative preface. For what an utterer of (8) states is that s/he has never traveled to a Communist country, not that s/he is stating something. One could hardly evade a perjury charge by responding "The sentence I uttered was true, not false: I did indeed *state that* I had never traveled to a Communist country; the fact that I actually had traveled to a Communist country is irrelevant." Likewise, surely (9)–(12) are not automatically true simply because I did respectively so judge, report, advise, and warn. (Though Lewis (1972) took exactly that bold position.) The locutionary content, or at least the truth condition, is just that I have never traveled to a Communist country, and the "I state that" is just the performative preface that makes the force explicit.

Some philosophers of language, such as Cresswell (1973) and Bach and Harnish (1979), have questioned Austin's vehement denial that the agents of speech acts are describing themslves as performing those acts; these philosophers have suggested that, in addition to the main acts, the utterers are also describing themselves as performing them. Thus, if I utter

(15) I order you to attack and capture the University of Chicago,

my main speech act is that of giving an order, and as such does not involve truth-value, but in addition I do describe myself as giving the order, and so my sentence is true in that degenerate sense.

On this hypothesis, such sentences as (8)–(12), which differ from (15) in that their associated main speech acts are truth-liable, would have two truth-values each: a primary truth-value attaching to what was stated, asserted, or whatever, and a self-descriptive truth-value that would nearly always be automatically "true." Fine, I suppose, but it seems a pointless qualification of the position Cohen calls tempting.

A further argument for the tempting view is that formal, explicit performatives such as (8)–(12) and (15) seem to be just verbose, inflated equivalents of the simpler statements, warnings, orders, etc. one could have issued without the performative prefaces. The difference between (15) and just "Go attack and capture the University of Chicago" seems only one of style.

But Cohen raises a serious objection to the tempting view. Consider any of (8)–(12). Suppose Eleanor utters (12) to Franklin, and Lucy, overhearing, says "She's warned him that that Rottweiler has been starved . . . ," or "Eleanor has warned Franklin that that Rottweiler has been starved . . . ." In each case, Lucy refers to just the same individuals and predicates just the same relation between them, and only the tense has changed. Surely, in particular, "warn" in (12) means *warn*. The words that occur in (12)'s performative preface have their standard senses and referents. So, the preface is not just a tag or flag meant to signal force. (There are such tags and flags; grammatical mood is basically that, a simple range-of-force indicator. But "I warn you that" and the other prefaces in (8)–(11) are not just force labels; they have internal grammatical structure and their parts have their own meanings and referential properties.) So why, then, would we get to pretend that those parts of the sentences do not exist, and read the locutionary meaning out from under them?

It gets worse. As it turns out, the idea that performative prefaces are merely force labels is simply untenable. For such prefaces can have *a lot* of structure. For example, they can contain adverbial modifiers. Long adverbial modifiers.

(16a) I admit freely that I had several private conversations with the defendant.
(16b) I admit with reluctance that I had several . . . . [Notice that "with reluctance" modifies "admit," not "had several . . . ."]
(16c) I admit gladly and with the greatest pleasure that I had . . . .
(16d) Because I am concerned to tell the whole truth, I admit that I . . . .
(16e) Mindful that there is a just and mighty God in Heaven who punishes those who withhold information in courts of law, and in mortal fear of the worm that dieth not and the fire that is not quenched, I admit . . . .

According to the tempting view, the only locutionary content in (16a)–(16e) is that of their common complement clause ("I had several private conversations with the defendant"). But that claim grows less plausible as we work our way down the list. (16d)'s performative preface contains an entire clause that the speaker asserts, though in passing, as fact. (16e)'s contains several somewhat controversial assertions; if I were to utter (16e) seriously, you certainly could describe me afterwards as having expressed a highly contentful theological view. And not just expressed; the theology certainly seems to be part of what is said.

It seems the tempting view cannot be sustained. What becomes tempting at this point is instead to go back and admit that the sentences' locutionary contents include their performative prefaces. (Call this the "liberal" view.) What is so bad about that?

Here is what is so bad, in case we have forgotten. If the liberal view is correct, then (8)–(12) are simply and automatically true whenever they are uttered and the relevant constitutive rules are not violated. No perjury charge could be made to stick, if the witness were careful to testify only in explicit performatives such as (8). Notice that semantically, (8)–(12) would not even entail their complement clauses (because one can state, report etc. things that are not so). My uttering of (10) would not commit me semantically to the claim that the Committee has voted unanimously to expel Grannie.

The two-truth-value hypothesis, which I said seemed a pointless qualification of the tempting view, no longer seems so pointless, for in light of examples like (16a)–(16e), neither the tempting truth-value nor the liberal truth-value seems expendable. And we can make the two-truth-value hypothesis more palatable by arguing that the two truth-values attach to slightly different sorts of thing. Notice that in uttering (8) I make a statement. What statement? The statement that I have never traveled to a Communist country. So, although I made that statement by uttering a sentence that, taken liberally, does not entail its propositional content, I nonetheless made it. And if the fact is that I have traveled to a Communist country, my statement is false even though the sentence I uttered, taken liberally, is a true sentence. I could be convicted of perjury, not for having uttered a false sentence, but for having made a false statement.

(16d) and (16e) would require some elaboration. One feels that the utterer of (16e), in particular, has made two or three assertions in addition to that which is expressed by the complement clause. Yet the earlier examples in the list are borderline cases; would an utterer of (16a) *assert that* her/his admission was given freely? A full theory of speech acts would have to sort out such subtleties at length.

Summary

- Austin called our attention to "performative" utterances and speech acts more generally.
- Each type of speech act is governed by rules of two sorts: constitutive and regulative.
- Violation of a regulative rule renders a speech act defective or infelicitous. There are many and varied ways in which a given speech act can be infelicitous.
- There is no principled distinction between performative utterances and those of ordinary declaratives; rather, every utterance has an illocutionary force, and virtually every utterance has a propositional content as well.
- In addition, many utterances have perlocutionary features.
- Cohen's problem about the truth conditions of sentences that contain explicit performative prefaces has not been solved.

Questions

1   Are all speech acts like "I double" in that they are constituted entirely by convention? (See Strawson (1964).)

2   Can every speech act be assigned a locutionary content? Discuss our apparent counterexamples and argue pro or con.

3   Choose a particular type of speech act and try to enumerate its constitutive rules and its characteristic regulative conditions. (Searle (1969) does this for the act of promising.)

4   Spot some difficulties for Austin's distinction between locutionary, illocutionary, and perlocutionary features. Find some troublesome borderline cases.

5   Lewis (1970) defends the anti-Austinian idea that when one tokens (even) a "pure" performative, one at the same time states that one is performing the act in question – or at least the sentence one utters is true if and only if one is performing that act. Examine this view.

6   Go more deeply into Cohen's problem.

Notes

1   Searle's own usage is not consistent.

2   Just to save you looking: she was christened by Isabel Hoey, daughter of the then Governor of North Carolina. I am told that Hoey did use the traditional bottle of champagne, while a band played "Anchors Aweigh."

3   Austin took propositional content nearly for granted. He strongly opposed entity theories, so by "locutionary content" he did not mean anything about propositions as things. He merely gestured towards "sense and reference," alluding to Frege but evidently not using "sense" to mean a kind of theoretical entity. Austin was offhand about propositional content because his focus was on the other thing, illocutionary force, that varies independently.

By contrast, William Alston (1963) tried seriously to work Austin's speech-act pragmatics into a theory of locutionary meaning itself, identifying a sentence's meaning with the sentence's "illocutionary act-potential," the range of illocutionary acts the sentence could be used to perform. If you are able to use a sentence in every illocutionary way that it affords, you know its meaning, and that is all there is to sentence meaning. But in fact this did nothing to illuminate locutionary meaning, since potential-speech-act descriptions such as "assert that gorillas are vegetarians" already presuppose a notion of propositional content. (Also, as Maureen Coyle once observed to me, sentences that share their locutionary contents can differ violently in their illocutionary act-potentials: "Mother will eat the oyster"/"Will mother eat the oyster?"/"Mother, eat the oyster!")

4   In a recent *Kudzu* comic strip, the preacher Will B. Dunn resists the urging of a liberal parishioner that the Ten Commandments be renamed "The Ten Suggestions."

Strawson (1964), Schiffer (1972), and Bach and Harnish (1979) argue convincingly that not all illocutionary force is as purely conventional as that of (1)–(7), the comparatively "pure" performatives with which we began. Some force, say that of being an advising or being a question-asking, is more a matter of Gricean speaker-intentions.

5 Linguists have missed the fact that Austin used "infelicitous" as the broadest possible umbrella term. They generally use the word as applying to sentences, and neologistically mean something like "nonsyntactically and nonsemantically but pragmatically defective [in a way that is supposed to be fairly specific but is never specified]."

6 Moreover, there is evidence that some semantical phenomena cannot be explained except by reference to illocutionary factors; see Barker (1995).

Further reading

The acknowledged classic on speech-act theory following Austin is Searle (1969). But considerably better is Searle (1979a), a collection of essays. See also Travis (1975) and Holdcroft (1978).

Two excellent works (in addition to Schiffer (1972)) that connect speech-act theory to other issues in pragmatics and to current research in linguistics and psychology are Bach and Harnish (1979) and Gazdar (1979). See also Cole and Morgan (1975), Levinson (1983), and Green (1989).

Ginet (1979) is an excellent paper, and illuminates Cohen's problem. Ways out of the problem (none of them entirely satisfactory) have been offered by Cresswell (1973), Bach and Harnish (1979), and Lycan (1984: Chapter 6).

13
Implicative relations

Overview

Conveyed meanings and invited inferences

Conversational implicature

"Presupposition" and conventional implicature

Indirect force

Summary

Questions

Notes

Further reading

Overview

Sentences entail other sentences, and in that strong sense *imply* them. But there are several ways in which sentences or utterances also linguistically imply things they do not strictly entail. First, very often a speaker uses a sentence to convey something other than what that sentence literally means, as for example in sarcasm or in broad hinting. According to Grice's theory of "conversational implicature," such implications are generated by a set of principles that govern cooperative conversation. Hearers pick up the implications either by assuming (contrary to appearances) that speakers are being cooperative and drawing inferences from that assumption, or by noting that speakers are being deliberately uncooperative and drawing inferences from that assumption. However, it is not clear how we are supposed to do this as rapidly and as accurately as we do.

Second, Strawson's criticism of Russell's Theory of Descriptions suggests a notion of "presupposition" distinct from entailment in that, when a sentence's presupposition fails, the sentence is not false but lacks truth-value entirely. But it is hard to find clear examples of this relation.

Third, some implications are carried by the choice of a special word, such as "but" as opposed to "and," in that "but" means just the same as "and" except for carrying a contrastive connotation. Grice calls this phenomenon "conventional implicature."

Fourth, there are some sentences that would standardly be used to perform speech acts other than the acts indicated by their grammatical moods and semantic contents. To explain this anomaly of "indirect force," Searle tries an extension of Grice's theory of conversational implicature. But that strategy falls short of accounting for all the data, and there is no very satisfactory alternative.

D avidson talks of a semantics' capturing the "felt implications" of target sentences, by which he means the sentences' entailment relations. But Grice (1975) has taught us that implication comes in different kinds. There are a number of phenomena that fall naturally under the label of "implication" but are not, or not obviously, cases of entailment. In this chapter I shall survey four of them.

Conveyed meanings and invited inferences

First, there are what we might call "conveyed meanings" of utterances. It is natural (though not obligatory) to describe this phenomenon in terms of speaker-meaning: in many cases – this is quite prevalent in ordinary conversation – a speaker utters a sentence that means that P but it is obvious to all that the speaker's main communicative intent is to convey something different, that Q. For example, I say to an obstreperous visitor, "There's the door," meaning that the visitor is to leave now. But the sentence "There's the door" does not mean "You are to leave now," nor could I be described as having come out and said that the visitor is to leave. I say one thing, I mean another; and this is perfectly clear to both parties without either of them having to think about it for a moment.

In Chapter 7, of course, we have discussed mismatches between speaker-meaning and sentence meaning. But there we tended to focus on pathological cases in which, for example, a speaker has a bizarre belief about the meaning of the word or about someone else's understanding of the word (or a reasonable belief about somebody else's bizarre understanding of the word). But in the case of what I am calling conveyed meaning, there is no pathology; it is a perfectly normal conversational phenomenon. Suppose you ask me whether Smedley is a good philosopher, and I say:

(1a) Smedley summarizes texts pretty accurately and has very nice handwriting,

or, less subtly:

(1b) Smedley is very good at ping pong.

Clearly, what I am conveying to you is not what my sentence literally means. What my sentence means may or may not be true, but that is immaterial. What I convey is something different, that Smedley is very bad or at least not very good at philosophy. My hearer should grasp that immediately; and indeed, competent hearers do grasp such conveyed meanings without ever realizing that that is what they are doing.

Here, then, we have come upon another linguistic phenomenon that (like illocutionary force) is part of what anyone would have to understand in order to be counted as a fully competent speaker of the language. If you were a foreigner well versed in English or at least had learned the lexical meanings of the words and enough grammar to understand the literal meanings of sentences, but you took utterances like the foregoing examples literally, there would still be something important that you were missing.

Another kind of "implication" that has exercised linguists is what Geis and Zwicky (1971) originally called "invited inference." One example is the perfection of conditionals into biconditionals: suppose I say,

(2) If you mow my lawn, I'll give you ten dollars.

Taken literally, (2) is only a one-way conditional; without logical impropriety I could have added, "Come to think of it, if you don't mow my lawn I'll give you ten dollars anyway." But upon hearing (2) alone, you would immediately fill in that if you do not mow my lawn then I will not give you the ten dollars. You hear the mere "if" as an "if and only if."

Another example would be the elevation of what are only conjunctions into causal claims. Thus:

(3) Martha watched the Education School burning and smiled with pleasure.

Anyone would hear (3) as implying that Martha was *caused* pleasure by seeing the Education School burning; some people would hear (3) as actually saying that. But (3) does not say that. (3) literally says only that one thing happened and then another did (compare "Martha watched the Education School burning and scratched her nose"). Likewise, "and" is often heard as carrying a temporal implication. There is a difference that most people would hear in the meanings of

(4a) John and Marsha fell in love and they got married

and

(4b) John and Marsha got married and they fell in love.

Even though (4a) does not entail that John and Marsha fell in love and got married *in that order*, the temporal inference is invited.

Conversational implicature

Grice (1975) addressed himself to phenomena of the foregoing kinds. Seeing speaker-meaning as communication of the contents of one's mental states, he began thinking about mechanisms of conversation and the social norms that govern cooperative conversation. He went on to develop the theory of what he called *conversational implicature*.

According to Grice, the conversational norm-in-chief is the *Cooperative Principle*:

(CP) Make your conversational contribution such as is required, at the stage at which it occurs, by the accepted purpose or direction of the talk-exchange in which you are engaged.

(CP) may sound vacuous, but it summarizes a set of corollaries that are anything but. Grice calls the corollaries "conversational maxims." Here are a few.

(M1) Make your contribution to a conversation as informative as is required (for the current purposes of the exchange). [The Maxim of Strength]
(M2) Do not make your contribution more informative than is required.
(M3) Do not say what you believe to be false.
(M4) Do not say that for which you lack adequate evidence. [The Maxim of Evidence]
(M5) Be relevant. [The Maxim of Relevance]
(M6) Avoid ambiguity.
(M7) Be brief (avoid unnecessary prolixity).

The maxims' function is to expedite the giving and receiving of information, in fairly obvious ways.

The maxims afford explanations of how a speaker can say one thing and be correctly perceived as meaning another. Grice (p. 50) offers a template for such explanations, in the form of a standard pattern of reasoning meant to be engaged in by the hearer:

> He [the speaker] has said that p; there is no reason to suppose
> that he is not observing the maxims, or at least ... [CP]; he
> could not be doing this unless he thought that q; he knows (and
> knows that I know that he knows) that I can see that the suppos-
> ition that he thinks that q is required; he has done nothing to
> stop me thinking that q; therefore he intends me to think, or is
> at least willing to allow me to think, that q; and so he has
> implicated that q.

("Implicate" is Grice's technical term for this indirect means of communication.)

When I utter "There's the door," I intend my visitor to reason in Grice's way. Roughly: "The door? The door has nothing to do with anything I currently have in mind. So, by the Maxim of Relevance, the door must be relevant to something he has in mind. And he knows (and knows ...) that I must have worked that out. So he has deliberately shown me that he wants me to know where the door is. Why might that be? Egad, he must want *me* to *go out* the door." Of course, all this reasoning takes place subconsciously and at very high speed.

Contextual information may help with the reasoning too. In this case, the visitor may realize that he has been being fairly offensive, that I have not offered him a drink, that I am not smiling, and that it is 6:45 p.m. In any conversation, background information is mutually assumed, and vast funds of assumptions are assumed by both parties to be shared by both parties; Stalnaker (1978) calls such material "common ground."

When I utter (1a) or (1b), I imply by way of the Maxim of Strength and the Maxim of Evidence that I am not in a position to say anything stronger about Smedley's ability. But since (we may suppose) the reason I was asked is that I am the person who is in an ideal or at least good position to assess Smedley's ability, this deliberately invites my hearer to conclude that there is nothing good to say about it.[1]

When I utter (2), I intend my hearer to reflect that if I were going to give her ten dollars in any case, uttering (2) would violate both the Maxim of Relevance (why mention the lawn in particular?) and the rule against prolixity. (There is also the background information that people do not often go around giving out money when no service has been rendered and no charitable purpose is evident.)

(3) and (4a) are a little harder to explain. What prompts us to infer from (3) that Martha smiled *because* she saw the Education School burning is probably some combination of the Maxim of Relevance with our know-ledge of the effects of burning, of Martha's likely attitude toward schools of education, and of the connection between desire-satisfaction and facial musculature. (4a) may have to do with some deep narratological assump-

tion. Such matters, and the otherwise dangerously vague notion of "relevance" generally, have been investigated in some depth by Sperber and Wilson (1986), a work which departs from Grice in some ways and has spawned a considerable industry.

Grice mentions that one can also generate an implicature by *flouting* a conversational maxim, that is, by violating it blatantly. My favorite Gricean example (paraphrased from pp. 55–6):

(5) Ms X produced a series of sounds that corresponded quite closely to the score of Handel's "I Know That My Redeemer Liveth."
    [Said by a concert reviewer]

Why has the reviewer dribbled out all this prolix stuff, instead of saying simply that Ms X sang "I Know That My Redeemer Liveth"? "Presumably, to emphasize a striking difference between . . . [Ms] X's performance and those to which the word 'singing' is usually applied." A more common type of example is when the speaker's sentence is too obviously false; Grice cites sarcasm there.

Grice suggests that his theory will account for metaphor, since metaphorical utterances typically flout (M3):

> Examples like "You are the cream in my coffee" characteristically involve categorical falsity, so the contradictory of what the speaker has made as if to say will, strictly speaking, be a truism; so it cannot be *that* that such a speaker is trying to get across. The most likely supposition is that the speaker is attributing to his audience some feature or features in respect of which the audience resembles (more or less fancifully) the mentioned substance.
>
> (p. 53)

We shall assess this suggestion in Chapter 14.

Two features are characteristic of conversational implicature. First, an implicature must be something one works out, or could work out, using reasoning of the kind illustrated above. If no such reasoning is available, then the implication must be of some other kind. Second, an implicature is *cancellable*, in the sense that a speaker who wanted to could forestall the inference that would otherwise be reasonable: "Smedley is very good at ping pong. But don't get me wrong – he's a terrific philosopher too. I mentioned the ping pong first because we've just been playing and I'm exhausted."[2]

In the previous chapter I noted Austin's complaint that when a philosopher perceives infelicity in an utterance, the philosopher tends too quickly to reject the sentence uttered as false. During the 1950s and 1960s, this was even a fashionable style of argument: from "This sentence would sound funny if uttered" to "This sentence is false/incoherent/ meaningless." Grice is in part concerned to eradicate that argument form. And we are now in a position to appreciate an example of it (a slightly convoluted example, because it is itself *about* falsity). Recall, from Chapter 2, Strawson's first objection to Russell's Theory of Descriptions. He says that no one would ever respond to an utterance of "The present King of France is bald" by saying, "That's false." And he is right about that. But from it he infers that the sentence uttered *was not* false, that is that "That's false" would itself be false. And that does not follow. The obvious reason we would not say "That's false" is that to do so would be misleading by way of the Maxim of Strength: you are in a position to say something much stronger and more informative and a better contribution to the conversation, namely, "Hold on; there is no king of France." So even if Strawson's own competing thesis (that statements with nonreferring singular terms in them should be taken as nonstatements rather than as false statements) is actually correct, his argument does not show that.

Grice's theory of conversational implicature is widely accepted, as are most of its standard uses in philosophy. I know of only two main direct complaints that have been lodged against it. First, some philosophers are suspicious of the amount of complex but nearly instantaneous and almost entirely unconscious reasoning posited by Grice's theory. (Read through Grice's template again, and see how long it takes you.)[3] But then, in many walks of life we do a great deal of reasoning very quickly and subconsciously.

The second complaint is Wayne Davis' (1998) (foreshadowed in Harnish (1976) and in Sperber and Wilson (1986)). Most cases of Gricean reasoning divide into two stages, an initial negative stage and a subsequent positive stage. In the negative stage, the hearer detects that the speaker's meaning diverges from sentence meaning. In the positive stage, the hearer comes to a conclusion regarding what the speaker does mean instead. Appeals to the Maxim of Relevance certainly work that way. So does any Gricean reasoning that starts with "[The speaker] couldn't mean *that* [because it is too obviously false and we all know that]." We know that something is up; but then there is the positive part of figuring out just what it is that is up. Davis objects that Grice gives us very little help with the positive part.

Take (3). I suggested some background knowledge of causal relations that would help a hearer calculate the implicature. But why is it obvious that the needed relevance is causal relevance in the first place? It does seem that causal relevance is the obvious candidate, but nothing in Grice's theory predicts or even hints at that. Or consider Grice's suggestion about metaphor. It is indeed obvious that the speaker means something other than what "You are the cream in my coffee" (literally) means, but what signals that "the speaker is attributing to his audience some feature or features in respect of which the audience resembles [cream in coffee]"? Why is *that* "the most likely supposition"?

Davis points out that philosophers of language have missed this important lacuna in Grice's theory because, whenever we look at an example, we *already know* what would normally be implicated by an utterance of the sentence in question, and so we are not moved to ask ourselves how the positive calculation is worked out. The cure for this is to pretend that we do not already know, and just look at the utterance in context and try to hit upon clues that would show an entirely uninitiated hearer what the speaker meant to convey. It is not easy.

Practitioners of the "relevance" literature have discovered what they argue is a new kind of implication, called "explicature," intermediate as between conversational implicature and entailment, in that the explicatum is cancellable but, if left uncancelled, is counted as said rather than merely implied – see Carston (1988) and Recanati (1989). An alleged example would be "She put down the letter, shed a single tear, and walked slowly but steadily to the cliff's edge; then she jumped." That sentence does not strictly entail that its subject jumped off the cliff, because one could cancel the implication without contradiction, for example adding "– not off the cliff, mind you, just up and down near the edge." But, Carston and Recanati maintain, if the speaker *does not* cancel the fatal implication within a conversationally reasonable time, the speaker will be counted as having said, and not merely implicated, that the subject jumped off the cliff. But there are tenable arguments on both sides of this issue.

Relevance theorists now think of their program as a competitor rather than a development of Grice's model. They reject the idea that there is a specifically linguistic process that generates implicatures, and in particular that there are particular conversational maxims of Grice's sort. Rather, they maintain, implicatures are the product of all-purpose cognitive processing that aims at efficiency of information transfer more generally.

"Presupposition" and conventional implicature

A second species of implications that are not entailments was suggested by Strawson's position on definite descriptions. Recall that in response to

Russell, Strawson said that "The present King of France is bald" does not entail the existence of a present king, but merely presupposes it. The mark of this, according to Strawson, was that when there is no king, "The present King of France is bald" is not false, but lacks truth-value entirely. The same goes for "The present King of France is not bald."

A few philosophers and many more linguists took up Strawson's idea, and have made it a little more formal: when a sentence S_1 entails a sentence S_2, and S_2 is false, then necessarily S_1 is false and S_1's negation is true. But when S_1 presupposes S_2 and S_2 is false, then S_1 does not go false, but lacks truth-value, and so does S_1's negation.[4] Notice that presupposition in this sense (called *semantic presupposition*) is like entailment and unlike conversational implicature in being *noncancellable*. Both S_1 and S_1's negation necessitate S_2 in the absolute way characteristic of entailment.

There are actually no uncontroversial examples of semantic presupposition. But here are a few candidate sentence pairs.

(6) a. It was Grannie who robbed the diaper service.
    b. Someone robbed the diaper service.

(7) a. Have you stopped beating your spouse?
    b. You have beaten your spouse.

(8) a. Rocky realized that his fly was open.
    b. Rocky's fly was open.

(9) a. Fred, who was fat, could not run.
    b. Fred was fat.

(10) a. She was poor but she was honest.
    b. Being poor inhibits [or somehow contrasts with] being honest.

In each case, it has been claimed, the "a" sentence necessitates the "b" sentence, and so does the "a" sentence's negation; if the "b" sentence is false, the "a" sentence is not false but goes to zip. And indeed, in each case the "a" sentence's negation does intuitively seem to carry the same implication as does the "a" sentence itself.

But in some cases, although the "a" sentence does necessitate the "b" sentence, the "a" sentence's negation does not. This is true of (6). For

(6′) It was not Grannie who robbed the diaper service; no one robbed it,

though perhaps peculiar, is not self-contradictory. If (6′) is not self-contradictory, then the negation of (6a) does not necessitate (6b) in the strong sense required for semantic presupposition. (6a)'s negation does conversationally implicate (6b), by way of the Maxim of Strength; someone who utters "It was not Grannie who robbed the diaper service" is in a position to make a stronger and more usefully informative denial, namely that of (6b) itself. But conversational implicature is cancellable, as necessitation is not; no necessitation, no semantic presupposition.

(7), though interrogative, meets a similar fate. If you are married and you are asked (7) (and you have never beaten your spouse), here is the correct answer: "No."[5] Because one can stop doing a thing only if one has at some time been doing it. (Of course the answer "No" is misleading, because via the Maxim of Strength, it implicates that one has beaten one's spouse and continues to do so. The correct *and nonmisleading* answer would be, "No, because I never have beaten her/him in the first place.")

(8) is possible to dismiss in this way, but harder.

(8') Rocky did not realize that his fly was open; he could hardly have realized that, because his fly wasn't open

does not seem contradictory either; but there is not so obvious a Gricean explanation of (8a)'s negation implicating (8b).

(9) is perhaps the best alleged example of semantic presupposition on our list.

(9') It's false that Fred, who was fat, could not run, because Fred wasn't fat

does sound contradictory or at least semantically anomalous.

Yet to my ear, if Fred was not fat, (9) does not go truth-valueless. I hear (9) as strictly speaking false, because the speaker has (though unemphatically) called Fred fat. But that does not explain what is wrong with (9').

Our remaining case, (10), is more distinctive, and I shall postpone it briefly.

If the Direct Reference Theory of proper names is correct, then perhaps Strawson is right and sentences containing nonreferring names lack truth-value. Of course, that is what gave rise to the problems of Apparent Reference to Nonexistents and Negative Existentials. But if so, then sentences containing proper names at all do semantically presuppose the existence of referents for those names.

Some linguists have distinguished a looser notion of "pragmatic presupposition" from that of semantic presupposition. But that term has not been clearly defined, and no one type of pragmatic implication has been meant by this to the exclusion of other types.

To return to (10):

(10′) It's false that she was poor but she was honest; being poor does
not inhibit being honest

is not contradictory, but is awkward. And (10a)'s implication of (10b) is
noncancellable. Suppose the person spoken of was both poor and honest.
Then, intuitively, the speaker has said two true things about her. But if
being poor does not at all inhibit (or somehow contrast with) being honest,
something is still very wrong with (10a) (compare "Wilt is 7′2″ but he's
tall"). One feels the speaker has chosen the wrong word: "but" is like
"and," *except* that "but" carries a special connotation that "and" does not;
very likely that is "but" 's *raison d'être*.

Grice (1975) had a third classification for (10), neither conversational
implicature nor semantic presupposition. He called it *conventional implicature*. Conventional implicature is implicature, in that a speaker implicates something rather than actually saying it, but it differs from conversational implicature in two ways. First, conventional implicatures are not
worked out; they are grasped immediately, not on the basis of reasoning.
Second, they are not cancellable (I cannot say "George is a linguist but he's
smart – don't get the wrong idea, though; I didn't mean anything about
linguists not being smart"). Conventional implicatures are normally
carried by tendentious choices of particular words, as of "but" over "and."

Grice's original example was "He is an Englishman; he is therefore
brave."

> [W]hile I have said that he is an Englishman, and said that he is
> brave, I do not want to say that I have *said* . . . that it follows
> from his being an Englishman that he is brave, though I have
> certainly indicated, and so implicated, that this is so. I do not
> want to say that my utterance of this sentence would be, *strictly
> speaking,* false should the consequence in question fail to hold.
>
> (pp. 44–5)[6]

Further examples involve the words "too" and "either": "Jonnie is a
linguist and her husband is very smart too"; "Grice was a philosopher and
his wife wasn't very smart either."

Here, as in many cases, a good way to investigate the nature of these
different kinds of implications is to ask about the *penalty* or sanction that
ensues when an implicatum is false. When S_1 entails S_2 and S_2 is false, the
penalty is that S_1 is false. When S_1 semantically presupposes S_2 and S_2 is
false, then S_1 is sent ignominiously to zip. When someone utters S_1, thereby conversationally implicating S_2, and the conveyed meaning or invited

inference S_2 is false, then the penalty is that, even if S_1 is true, the speaker's utterance is misleading. If S_1 conventionally implicates S_2 and S_2 is false, then S_1 is misworded, even if not false.

A further type of "pragmatic presupposition" not already mentioned here might be called "illocutionary implication": the performing of a speech act in some sense implies the satisfaction of its distinctive felicity conditions. For example, my promising to return your champagne glasses implies that I intend to return them, and does so noncancellably (I cannot add, " . . . but don't get me wrong; I have no intention of returning them"). To our penalty catalogue, we might add that if someone utters S_1, thereby performing a speech act having S_2 as a distinctive felicity condition, and S_2 is false, then the speech act is infelicitous in a distinctively illocutionary way.

Indirect force

As I mentioned in the previous chapter, the three principal English moods correspond to three broad illocutionary genera of which individual types of speech act are species: the normal use of a declarative is to make a statement, that of an interrogative is to seek information, and that of an imperative is to issue a directive of some kind. But the correspondence is far from perfect:

(11) I want you to go to the Broccoli Festival with me.
(12) Can you pass the salt?
(13) Believe me when I say I'll never again mix Glenfiddich and paregoric.
(14) Tell me how you saved Kate Winslett from the giant tree frog that ate Pittsburgh.
(15) I want you to tell me what has become of my children three.

(11) is grammatically declarative but would normally be used to issue a request or even an order. (12) is interrogative but would normally be heard, not literally as an information-seeking question about the hearer's abilities, but as a request also. The imperatives (13) and (14) would normally be used respectively to make a statement and to ask a question. (15), though declarative, would also be used to ask a question.

Grammatical mood in itself is hardly sacred. The real problem is deeper: each of (11)–(15) also has a more literal reading that does correspond to its grammatical mood. For example, (11) could be uttered as a purely factual answer to "Please tell me what desire is uppermost in your mind right now, so that I can begin your psychoanalysis." These more literal readings exist, but are uncommon and hard to hear. What needs explaining is why (and how) the nonliteral uses are the normal uses. This sort of illocutionary displacement is called "indirect force."

Searle (1975) advocates what I shall call the conservative approach to indirect force. Namely, he maintains that an utterance's indirect force can be predicted using just general principles of speech-act theory that we already know together with Gricean mechanisms that we already know. No new apparatus need be introduced.

Searle begins by putting forward some generalizations about ways of performing particular speech acts indirectly. For example: "S can make an indirect request (or other directive) by either asking whether or stating that a preparatory condition concerning H's ability to do A obtains"; "S can make an indirect directive by stating that the sincerity condition obtains, but not by asking whether it obtains." Searle illustrates and explains such generalizations by deriving instances of them using only principles of speech-act theory and Gricean conversational reasoning.

Take (12), literally a question about the hearer's ability but normally used to make a request. According to Searle, the hearer first infers in Gricean fashion that the speaker intends to convey something other than (12)'s literal meaning (the speaker obviously lacks theoretical interest in the hearer's fine muscle coordination, etc.). Then the hearer cleverly notes two things: that the speaker has alluded to the satisfaction of a preparatory condition for a request, and that the request in question is one whose obedience the speaker very probably wants the hearer to bring about. That is how the hearer identifies the speaker's utterance as a request to pass the salt.

The conservative view inherits the two main objections incurred by Grice's theory of conversational implicature: there is skepticism regarding the posited instantaneous subconscious reasoning, and Davis' (1998) complaint arises with a vengeance: the negative stage, that of recognizing that there is some ulterior force, is easy, but the positive stage is much harder.

Davis' problem is aggravated for the case of indirect force, because the hearer faces a greater challenge – not just to identify an implicated content, but in addition to pick out the unexpected force. (Here again, the difficulty is masked by the fact that when we look at examples, *we already know* what indirect force they would have.) In the case of (12), what cues lead the hearer to identify it as a request?

Searle acknowledges the problem. The hearer has to notice that the speaker has alluded to a preparatory condition for requesting. But what cue would tip the hearer off to that? Moreover, the ability condition is also a felicity condition for speech acts of many different sorts; so how would the hearer single out requesting in particular? Perhaps s/he could narrow it down to directives. Within the class of directives we could perhaps exclude orders, commands, suggestions, and others on grounds of power relations and tone of voice. We also have corroborating information about the obedience conditions being ones in which the speaker may well have an interest. But at each substage of this reasoning, there is plenty of room for error.

At one point Searle suggests that there is a convention at work in addition to the purely Gricean reasoning. The words, "Can you . . . ?" do have a sort of conventional ring. But if so, it cannot be such a brute convention that it makes the locution in question amount to an idiom like "kick the bucket" or "bury the hatchet." Requests beginning with "Can you . . ." are, if you like, idiomatic, but they are not idioms, for they admit of literal answers. The hearer could say, "I can, yes, but are you sure you should be putting any more salt on your food?" This could be a smart-aleck answer ("Do you have the time?" – "Yes, I have it"), but it need not be; perhaps the hearer knows the speaker to have high blood pressure. One is at least able to reply to the sentence's literal, compositional content, even if that is not entirely felicitous given that the speaker's utterance was an indirect request. If "Can you . . ." has conventional force of some kind, the kind badly needs explaining.

Morgan (1978) makes an important attempt at explaining the only quasi-conventional mechanism involved here. Bach and Harnish (1979) argue for a less convention-like device of "standardization." Both think of indirect force as "short-circuited" implicature, that is, as an implicature so common as to have become in some way automatic.

There is a further problem about indirect force, called to our attention by Gordon and Lakoff (1975): there are syntactic marks of indirect force. That is, there are surface-grammatical features that demand indirect inter-pretation of the sentences in which they occur.

(16) Why paint your house purple?
(17) Why don't you be nice to your brother for a change?/Be nice to your brother for a change, why don't you?
(18) Would you get me a glass of water?
(19) I would like a dry martini, please.
(20) Here, I need that wrench.

None of these sentences can have the force associated with its grammatical mood. Unlike "Why are you painting your house purple?" (16) cannot be an innocent question, but must be a discouragement. (17) must be a reproach; (18) and (19) must be requests; unlike the simpler "I need that wrench," (20) must be a request or something stronger.

Searle's conservative approach is balked here. It has no way of predicting these data. Worse, it cannot even apply to them because, *à la* Grice, it posits calculation; indirect force is to be worked out. But with (16)–(20), there is nothing to work out. They wear their indirect forces on their sleeves.

Other theories of indirect force have tried to cope with this problem; none has been uncontroversially successful. The data themselves are not entirely uncontroversial: Bach and Harnish (1979: Chapter 9) dispute some of them, most explicitly that (19) is grammatical.

Summary

- Often a speaker uses a sentence to convey something other than what that sentence literally means.
- According to Grice's theory of conversational implicature, such implications are generated by a set of principles that govern cooperative conversation. But Davis has offered a significant challenge to this view.
- Relevance theorists reject the idea that implicatures are generated by a set of conversational maxims. They hold instead that implicatures are the product of all-purpose cognitive processing that aims at efficiency of information transfer more generally.
- Strawson's criticism of Russell's Theory of Descriptions suggests a notion of "presupposition" distinct from entailment. But it is hard to find clear examples of this relation.
- A third type of implication, conventional implicature, is carried by the choice of a special word.
- There are sentences that are normally used with indirect force. To explain this, Searle tries an extension of Grice's theory of conversational implicature. But that strategy falls short of accounting for all the data, and there is no very satisfactory alternative.

Questions

1 Think of some more examples of conveyed meanings and invited inferences, and try to explain them using Grice's principles.
2 State some traditional philosophical issue and show how the notion of conversational implicature illuminates it.
3 Adjudicate one of our two objections to Grice's theory of conversational implicature, or come up with a further objection of your own.
4 Is there anything to the notion of "presupposition" in a natural

language that cannot be accounted for in terms of implicature? Less tendentiously, is there more to the notion of "presupposition" in natural language than I have admitted in this chapter?

5   Discuss the notion of conventional implicature, and try to think of more examples. Is Grice right in contending that it differs both from ordinary entailment and from conversational implicature?

6   Say something helpful about the puzzle of indirect force.

Notes

1   Notice, by the way, that if you ask me a question and I then produce an utterance, you automatically assume that my utterance is intended as an answer to your question. Suppose you ask, "Why are you late for class?," and I say, "We had spaghetti at our house last night." You would think: What? How does having spaghetti impede getting to class on the following day? Was it tainted? If you did start thinking along those lines, notice that you would simply have assumed that I was cooperating by producing an answer to the question you asked.

One thing you will gradually learn, the more you think about conversational cooperation, is how pathetically easy it is for a trained linguist or philosopher of language to mislead, deceive, cheat, and hoodwink other people without ever saying anything false. Advertising copywriters and politicians are masters of conversational implicature, having worked it out instinctively, because it allows them to convey falsehoods without breaking the law by uttering false sentences.

2   Grice adds a third feature, "detachability". Since his form of conversational reasoning proceeds from the propositional content of the sentence uttered, any logical equivalent of the sentence should generate the same implicatures in the same context. But there are obvious objections to this, as when the rule against prolixity is exploited.

3   Philosophers impressed by the Connectionist approach in Artificial Intelligence will be especially suspicious, not to say derisive. But such philosophers are also skeptical of syntax, and of semantics conceived as explaining anything about human beings.

4   Of course this formulation is unfaithful to Strawson's original intent, because he did not want us to replace our two-valued logic for sentences with a three-valued logic for sentences; it was not that instead of having these two possible truth values, "true" and "false," a sentence now can have a third one, "zip" or "neuter." Strawson's point was that it is not sentences that have truth-values at all.

5   There; was that worth the price of this book, or what?

6   Ironically, I myself doubt that Grice's own sentence is an example of conventional implicature, because I believe the implication is carried by the semantic meaning of the word "therefore." "Therefore" means "for that reason." And so Grice's sentence is synonymous with "He is an Englishman, and for that reason, he is brave," which in my speech entails that his being an Englishman is a reason or ground of his being brave. Fortunately, there are plenty of better examples.

Further reading

Grice (1978) is a sequel dealing with stress and irony. Grice's posthumous collection (1989) contains that and other important papers on related topics.

Davis (1998) is a comprehensive critique of Grice's theory of conversational implicature. It also discusses indirect force.

The "relevance" literature spawned by Sperber andWilson (1986) has gotten very large. See also Blakemore (1992) and Carston (2002).

Seeds of the "explicature" literature are in Cohen (1971). See also Bach (1994).

A good expository pro-presupposition paper is Karttunen (1973). Two very good books on the "presupposition" literature are Kempson (1975) and Wilson (1975); for a scorched-earth critique, see Lycan (1984: Chapter 4).

Sadock (1975) explores the distinction between conversational and conventional implicature. The containing volume, Cole and Morgan (1975), is a splendid one, and contains several other nice works on implicature; see also Cole (1978). Karttunen and Peters (1979) is good on conventional implicature, as is Warner (1982). But the best general treatment of conventional implicature is Lycan (1984: Chapter 5).

Bach (1999) iconoclastically but tenably disputes the very existence of conventional implicature.

The classic papers on indirect force are in Cole and Morgan (1975); see particularly the papers by Gordon and Lakoff, Georgia Green, and Alice Davison.

Morgan (1978)'s theory of indirect force is developed further in Lycan (1984: Chapter 7).

Bach and Harnish (1979) offer an imposing master theory of communication, incorporating all the phenomena we have surveyed in this chapter and the last.

Levinson (1983) is a good general work on pragmatics. Davis (1991) is an excellent anthology.

PART IV
The dark side

14
Metaphor

Overview

The phenomenon of metaphor is far more prevalent than is generally admitted by philosophers, and it raises two main questions: what is "metaphorical meaning"? And how do hearers grasp metaphorical meaning as readily as they do?

Most theorists have thought that metaphor is somehow a matter of bringing out similarities between things or states of affairs. Donald Davidson argues that this "bringing out" is purely causal, and in no way linguistic; hearing the metaphor just somehow has the effect of making us see a similarity. The Naive Simile Theory goes to the opposite extreme, having it that metaphors simply abbreviate explicit literal comparisons. Both views are easily seen to be inadequate.

According to the Figurative Simile Theory, rather, metaphors are short for similes themselves taken figuratively. This view avoids the three most obvious objections to the Naive Simile Theory, but not all the tough ones.

Searle treats metaphorical meaning as speaker-meaning that is also conveyed meaning, and invokes Gricean apparatus to explain it in much the way he explained indirect force. This has some plausibility and overcomes Davidson's leading objections to metaphorical meaning, but incurs other objections.

A further theory of metaphor is based on the phenomenon, important in its own right, of single words' analogical differentiation into hosts of distinct though related meanings.

A philosophical bias

Philosophers like language to be literal. The previous thirteen chapters have concentrated on theories of literal reference and literal meaning, and even our discussions of indirect force and conversational implicature have viewed those phenomena as merely speaker-meanings derived by some discrete mechanisms from literal sentence meaning. I have barely mentioned *metaphor* and other figurative uses of language.

That bias reflects standard philosophical practice. Philosophers tend to think that literal speech is the default and metaphorical utterances are occasional aberrations, made mainly by poets and poets manqué. But the bias is only a bias: sentences are very often used in perfectly ordinary contexts with other than their literal meanings. Indeed, virtually every sentence produced by any human being contains importantly metaphorical or other figurative elements.

My use just now of the word "element" was at least in part metaphorical. Or consider the number of times in a day that someone utters the word "level." "Level" is almost invariably metaphor, unless the speaker is actually talking about a horizontal layering of some physical thing. Nonliteral usage is the rule, not the exception.

The letter of the claim that almost every sentence contains figurative elements is widely conceded, because everyone grants that among the literal expressions are many "dead" metaphors, that is phrases that evolved from what were originally novel metaphors but have turned into idioms or clichés and now mean literally what they used to mean metaphorically. We speak of a river's "mouth," but no one in the present century thinks of this as a metaphorical allusion to human or animal mouths. Likewise "inclined to [do such-and-such]," "rich dessert," "dead microphone," and, for that matter, "dead metaphor." *Perhaps* "level" as in "higher/lower level" is now literal too. "Level" in "carpenter's level," meaning the tool, is certainly dead; there is no other term for that tool, and in a dictionary it would be listed as a separate meaning of the word.

However, as has been emphasized by Lakoff and Johnson (1980), the distinction between novel or fresh metaphor and "dead" metaphor is one of smooth degree, not of kind. Fresh metaphors get picked up and become current, and then only very gradually – sometimes over centuries – sicken, harden, and die.

(Exactly how many expressions in the previous paragraph were used metaphorically rather than literally, assuming the distinction is *not* one of degree?)

So it seems intellectual honesty requires us to confront metaphor.

The issues, and two simple theories

There is some variation in taxonomy as to how metaphor is classified with respect to other figures of speech. Some theorists use the term "metaphor" very broadly, as almost synonymous with "figurative." Others use it very narrowly, as naming one very specific figure alongside many other ones. I will not try to make fine distinctions here.

The main philosophical questions concerning metaphor are two: what is "metaphorical meaning," broadly construed? And by what mechanism is it conveyed, that is how do hearers grasp that meaning, given that what they hear is only a sentence whose literal meaning is something different? Metaphor raises many further important philosophical questions, as to the rationale for expressing oneself metaphorically instead of directly, the distinctive effectiveness and power of metaphor as a figure of speech, and the centrality of metaphor in each of several walks of life, but in this chapter I shall confine my attention to the more specifically linguistic questions.

A few examples to work with:

(1) Simon is a rock.[1]
(2) Juliet is the sun. [Said by Romeo, after asking (tendentiously) what light through yonder window broke. Juliet also "hangs upon the cheek of night / Like a rich jewel in an Ethiop's ear," but that was back in Act I and I hope he thought better of it.]

A more complex solar metaphor:

(3) Now is the winter of our discontent / Made glorious summer by this sun of York.[2]
(4) When the blood burns, how prodigal the soul / Lends the tongue vows.[3]

What seems to characterize (1)–(4) and other sentences called metaphorical? Beardsley (1967) identifies two features working in tandem: within such a sentence there is a conceptual "tension" (human beings differ categorially from rocks or suns, and souls and tongues are not the kinds of things that could interact commercially); yet the sentence is not only intelligible but perhaps even exceptionally informative or illuminating, and may express an important truth. Other theorists have expressed the first of these two features more strongly, saying that a metaphorical sentence interpreted literally is incoherent, absurd, or at best transparently and wildly false – though we shall see below that that is not always so.

Davidson's causal theory

Figurative language was thoroughly disdained during the Logical Positivist period, presumably on account of the Positivists' Verificationism.[4] Since such sentences as (1)–(4) – at least as they are intended – are not verifiable in the ordinary empirical way, they were judged not to be cognitively meaningful. On this view, there is no such thing as "metaphorical meaning" if by "meaning" one means linguistic meaning; there is only emotive or affective significance. Donald Davidson (1978) too rejects "metaphorical meaning" and denies the existence of linguistic mechanisms by which metaphorical significance is conveyed. Unlike the Positivists, he thinks sentences like (1)–(4) do have meanings; but he contends that the meanings they have are just their literal meanings (however strange). "[M]etaphors mean what the words, in their most literal interpretation, mean, and nothing more" (p. 30). When Romeo uttered (2), he was saying only that Juliet was, literally, the sun, though doubtless he was *doing* more than just expressing that ludicrous falsehood.

Davidson's article is largely devoted to his negative case against "metaphorical meaning"; he gives several critical arguments, two of which we shall consider later on. But he does sketch a positive account of the significance of metaphor. It is fairly brutely causal:

> A metaphor *makes* us attend to some likeness, often a novel or surprising likeness, between two or more things.
>
> (p. 31, italics added)

> [A] simile tells us, in part, what a metaphor merely *nudges* us into noting.
>
> (p. 36, italics added)

There is no logic to it, Davidson seems to be saying, much less any linguistic mechanism that indicates the likeness to be "noted." A pill or "a bump on the head" (p. 44) could do as well and as properly. Obviously the effect of metaphor is far from random, or poetry and other literature would not make the sense they do, much less succeed brilliantly; but the psychological means by which they do succeed are not in the linguist's domain.

Davidson's view implies that the only relevant difference between (1)–(4) and nonsense strings such as Chapter 1's "Good of off primly the a the the why" is that, for whatever reason, (1)–(4) have psychological effects that word salad does not. But surely there is a huge *cognitive* difference between (1)–(4) and the word salad: we often not only understand them but can paraphrase them more literally; we draw inferences from them; we sometimes take ourselves to have learned new empirical facts from having heard metaphorical utterances. That cognitive value manifestly does not derive from their usually bizarre literal meanings. Moran (1997) adds the example of embedding in conditional antecedents ("If music be the food of love, play on," or even "If music is the food of love, I'm going to buy some records").

A cognate point is that if Davidson is right, one can never misinterpret a metaphor.[5] If in response to Romeo's utterance of (2), some eavesdropper had chirped, "I get it! – Juliet depresses him because she's so stupid and she smells horrible," on the Causal Theory this would not have been an incorrect account of Romeo's metaphorical utterance, but only evidence that the eavesdropper's mental architecture was causally different from Romeo's and from ours.

Moreover, as Goodman (1981) urges, Davidson cannot allow for metaphorical truth. If metaphorical utterances have only literal meaning, there being no other candidate for a bearer of truth-value, they will normally be false and only occasionally and accidentally true. But remember (however reluctantly) the prevalence of nonliteral usage. Even if we discount uncontroversially "dead" metaphor, few human utterances are entirely free of metaphorical elements. If metaphorical utterances are rarely true, then utterances are rarely true.

Finally, Moran (1997: 263) notes that when a metaphor dies, the relevant expression acquires a new literal meaning and accordingly gets an additional dictionary entry. This would be inexplicable, or at least arbitrary and odd, if the metaphor had previously had no sort of meaning at all.

And there are contemporary views that reject metaphorical sentence meaning but give more plausible accounts of metaphorical communication. Given the availability of such accounts, there is no reason to accept Davidson's purely causal theory.

The Naive Simile Theory

Philosophers beginning with Aristotle have noticed a striking similarity between metaphors and similes: it seems that both metaphors and similes express or invite comparisons of their topics to something a bit unexpected. Simon was *like* a rock, Juliet is like the sun in one or more respects, and Edward IV resembled the sun in perhaps a different way. This suggests an even closer kinship: the idea that a metaphor is just an abbreviated simile. According to the Naive Simile Theory in particular, a metaphor derives from the corresponding simile by ellipsis. Thus, (1) is *short for* "Simon is like a rock," and (2) is short for "Juliet resembles the sun."

(3) is considerably trickier, since although its grammatical subject can be translated as "Our discontent, which is like a winter," the concluding referent (Edward IV) is not mentioned in any literal way; one would have to render that last part of (3) as something like "by x, a Yorkist who resembles the sun," where the reference of "x" to Edward is somehow determined by context. "Made glorious summer" would have to be interpreted as something like "alleviated in a manner similar to a winter's giving way to a glorious summer." But probably all this can be worked out. ((4) is still tougher; I shall return to (4).)

This simile view reconciles Beardsley's two features: it accommodates the "conceptual tension" characterizing a metaphor, while explaining the metaphor's intelligibility. The intelligibility is straightforward, since statements of likeness or resemblance are obviously intelligible. The tension arises from the move from likeness to actual ascription ("Juliet *is* the sun").

The Naive Simile Theory has seemed plausible to, and even taken for granted by, many literary theorists and philosophers alike. But it faces objections, of which here are three.

First, Beardsley (1967) complains that although the theory does explain the distinctive tension in the way I have noted, that explanation is very shallow. If a metaphor is only *short for* the corresponding simile, then it is simply synonymous with the simile and should not be heard as anomalous or puzzling in the first place. On this view, the tension is the merest surface appearance. But that seems wrong. There is no particular tension in "Juliet is like the sun," even if one wants to be told more about the respects in which Juliet resembles the sun. One feels that a metaphor *works by* containing an inherent tension that is more substantive. (Davidson (1978) and Searle (1979) will go on to argue that, in particular, the metaphor works by having the anomalous literal meaning that it does.)

Second, Searle complains that a simile taken by itself is almost entirely uninformative. "Similarity is a vacuous predicate: any two things are similar in some respect or other" (p. 106; see also Goodman 1970). In what way is Juliet supposedly like the sun? Not by being a gigantic ball of gas, or by consisting in large part of nuclear fusion, or by being 93 million miles from the earth. As Searle points out, those properties are salient and well-known features of the sun; yet the Naive Simile Theory gives no hint as to why Romeo's metaphor imputes different properties to Juliet rather than those. Thus, the theory fails to offer any mechanism by which metaphorical significance might be conveyed.

Third, even when we have identified the relevant respects of similarity, they often prove to be themselves metaphorical. Searle gives the example, "Sally is a block of ice." How, according to the naive simile theorist, is Sally like a block of ice? Perhaps she is hard and very cold. But not, of course, *literally* hard or cold; "hard" and "cold" are themselves used metaphorically here. So Sally is only *like* something that is hard and cold. In what ways? Perhaps she is unyielding, unemotional, and unresponsive. But, Searle points out (p. 107), there is no sense in which blocks of ice are unyielding, unemotional, and unresponsive but many other inanimate things are not. Bonfires too are unyielding, unemotional, and unresponsive; but neither "Sally is like a bonfire" nor "Sally is a bonfire" is metaphorically compatible with the original sentence. The naive simile theorist would have to insist that there is a further underlying literal similarity between cold things and unemotional things. But we are given no evidence for that claim. Searle conjectures that due to heaven knows what psychological factors, "people [just do] find the notion of coldness associated in their minds with lack of emotion" (p. 108).

This last objection suggests a simple but radical modification of the Naive Theory, that preserves the central claim that metaphors are compressed similes but avoids most of our six objections. It is articulated and defended at length by Fogelin (1988): that metaphors abbreviate, not similes taken literally, but similes themselves taken figuratively.

The Figurative Simile Theory

Similes are often, perhaps usually, figures of speech. Sally is only figuratively like a block of ice, for she is only figuratively hard and cold. Simon is only figuratively like a rock, and Juliet is only figuratively like the sun. One way to see this (not Fogelin's own way) is to note that *literal* similarity is symmetric: if A is literally similar to B, then necessarily B is literally similar to A. But a block of ice is not literally like Sally, nor a rock literally like Simon, nor the sun literally like Juliet. And no one would propose such comparisons as similes, as in "The sun? – Oh, the sun is like Juliet." It is when similes are themselves nonliteral that they best paraphrase metaphors. This suggests the hypothesis that a metaphor is just an abbreviated *figurative* simile, deriving from the corresponding simile taken figuratively.

This Figurative Theory easily sidesteps our three objections to the

Naive Theory. *First objection*: Since the figurative theorist does not reduce metaphors to literal and near-trivial assertions of similarity, it cannot be said that the Figurative Theory treats the metaphors' conceptual tension as superficial. There is already conceptual tension in the underlying simile. *Second objection*: Taken figuratively, the simile already carries one or more particular respects of similarity. So it does not fail to explain how the metaphor brings out those same respects. *Third objection*: Of course the figurative theorist is not committed to literal similarities between Juliet and the sun, Sally and a block of ice, etc.

These three advantages come at an obvious price. In each case, the Figurative Theory remedies a deficiency of the Naive Theory by lodging the needed material in the now figuratively interpreted corresponding similes and letting the respectively derived metaphors inherit it. But the danger here is that of only putting off the problem. For now the explanatory work is being done by the figurative nature of the underlying similes, and so their figurative interpretations need explaining in turn. Indeed, our original two main questions arise for figurative similes: what is it for such sentences to have figurative meanings, and how are those meanings conveyed to hearers?

Fogelin exploits the notion of a *salient* feature of a thing.[6] In that way he is able to mobilize a *non*symmetrical similarity relation (p. 78): "A is similar to B just in case A has a sufficient number of B's salient features." A may share a sufficient number of B's salient features without B's sharing a sufficient number of A's *salient* features, since the particular features of B that A shares need not be salient in A. For example, a chipmunk is very like a rat, except for being cute or perceived as such by humans; it has most of the rat's salient features, being a small scavenging rodent of loose morals. But one would not say that a rat is like a chipmunk, because the cuteness of chipmunks is highly salient to humans and rats are not cute.

According to Fogelin, the difference between a figurative comparison and a literal one is in the standard of salience, which in a way *reverses*. It is (Fogelin says, p. 90) literally true that Winston Churchill looked like a bulldog, but literally false that Churchill *was* like a bulldog (he having been human rather than canine, two-legged, lacking in fur, given to talking rather than barking, far too big to crawl into burrows, etc.). Yet it is figuratively true that he was like a bulldog. In calling him one, Fogelin says, "we compare him to a bulldog (as opposed, say, to a French poodle), while at the same time trimming the feature space in terms of the subject's [Churchill's] salient features" (p. 91). Unfortunately Fogelin does not go into detail about "trimming the feature space." I believe the idea is that, having rejected the simile as literal, the hearer nonetheless charitably assumes that the alleged similarity does obtain, and now ignores the salient features of bulldogs that most obviously make the literal comparison false and looks for features that match the salient features of Churchill. (I am not sure what these would be; toughness, tenacity, earthiness, and looking like a bulldog?)

On this view, sentences have metaphorical meanings in context that differ from their literal meanings; yet it does not follow that any expression in the sentence has *changed* its meaning from literal to figurative use, or that the metaphorical meanings are spooky or magical. Rather, *resemblance* is always and everywhere relative to a standard of similarity, a "feature space" that determines which properties are to be matched with which. The standard of similarity is like an indexical in being determined by contextual factors, but also can take more than one value within a single context. That is why the sentence can be both true (metaphorically) and false (literally) on one and the same occasion of utterance: because two different standards of similarity are in play – much as "Muffie is small" can be both true and false if Muffie is an undersized moose. This is a nice advantage of Fogelin's theory.

However, Fogelin faces at least three more difficulties. First, a statement may continue to be accepted as metaphorically true even when the corresponding simile has proved to be false. Searle (pp. 102–3) offers the example, "Richard is a gorilla," which the Naive Simile Theory would parse as "Richard is like a gorilla." Let us suppose that what is meant is that Richard is like a gorilla in being fierce, nasty, prone to violence, and perhaps not very bright. But primatologists tell us that, in fact, gorillas are not nasty or prone to violence; they are shy, rather sensitive, and very intelligent animals. Likewise pigs, which figure in many metaphors imputing messiness, filth, greed, obesity, crassness, or some combination of those: I myself know of no evidence that pigs are either dirty or particularly greedy, or that they are fatter relative to their skeletal size than other animals are.[7]

One might think that Fogelin has easily avoided this new objection, for when a *simile* is figurative it does not require the actual correctness of the relevant stereotype. "Sam acts like a gorilla" and "Merle eats like a pig" are correctly expressed and understood despite the fact that the two stereotypes are respectively simian and porcine slanders, because in the similes, "gorilla" and "pig" are themselves being used figuratively rather than literally. But Fogelin's picture of "trimming the feature space" presupposes or at least strongly suggests that the features relevantly shared by, say, Churchill and a bulldog are possessed literally by each of the two. And in that sense, on Fogelin's theory a metaphor must still bottom out in a literal sharing of genuine properties. In examples such as Searle's (in which the stereotype is just wrong) it is far from obvious what the properties would be.[8]

Second, consider that many sentences individually admit of either literal or metaphorical interpretation. ("Adolf is a butcher"; "The worm has turned.") Even when a sentence seems anomalous, often we can imagine circumstances in which it would be literally true; as Davidson notes (1978: 41), "You are pigs" would have been literally true if addressed by Odysseus to his men in Circe's palace. Very likely there has never been a sentence that does not admit of some metaphorical understanding. For any sentence that does bear metaphorical interpretation, even one that would almost always be heard literally rather than metaphorically (say, "Ernest is lost"), any simile theorist will have to call it semantically ambiguous, as between its literal meaning and its simile-abbreviating meaning (that Ernest resembles a lost person). But such a proliferation of supposedly genuine semantic ambiguities is surely implausible.

The third new objection is that some metaphorical statements are too convoluted to be parsed as similes. (4) above is such an example. It is not literally about anyone's blood, and blood cannot literally burn (while still within the body under even faintly normal conditions); "the soul" is probably itself being used metaphorically, and even if not, souls cannot literally lend anything to tongues; but "tongues" is not being used to mean tongues, either, and vows are not the sorts of things that can be lent. So any simile theorist faces the daunting task of translating all of those things at once into resemblance talk. One would have to make free use of the sort of contextual placeholder that I used in explicating (3). A first pass might be: "When x, which is like a person's blood, does something that resembles burning, how prodigally y, which is like a person's soul, does something similar to lending some things that are vowlike to z, which resembles a person's tongue." We are not much the wiser. And refinement is needed, because for "the blood" metaphorically to burn is probably something distinctive to a bloodlike substance, not for it to do something that resembles the literal burning of, say, a piece of wood. It is no wonder that simile theorists have in the main stuck to simple subject–predicate examples like (1) and (2).

The Pragmatic Theory

Unlike the causal view, the Naive Simile Theory supplied a notion of "metaphorical meaning"; sentences had metaphorical meanings in addition to their literal ones, even though the former meanings proved to be shallow and unsatisfactory. And as we have just seen, Fogelin's version of the figurative view endorses an even more robust notion of metaphorical meaning, in that his metaphorical meanings are (even if ineffable) more substantive and illuminating. As I mentioned earlier, Davidson argued globally against metaphorical meaning, indeed seems to enact a scorched-earth policy; so we should address his arguments. But he gives five or six, and I have space to discuss only the two that I take to be most pertinent as directed against the other theories discussed here.

First:

> There are no instructions for devising metaphors; there is no manual for determining what a metaphor "means" or "says"; there is no test for metaphor that does not call for taste.
>
> (p. 29)

Second: it is almost universally conceded that although some metaphors can be paraphrased in literal terms without great loss, many are open-ended in that the relevant set of similarities is vague and indefinite, and some (as in the poetry of e. e. cummings)[9] cannot be paraphrased at all. These striking facts are neatly explained by the claim that there is no metaphorical meaning, for on that view there is nothing to paraphrase or circumscribe (p. 30). Fogelin argues that the Figurative Simile Theory explains those facts as well. But Davidson adds that our uptake of a metaphor, "what we notice or see" "is not, in general, propositional in character [at all] . . . . Seeing as is not seeing that" (p. 45). Moreover, if a given sentence did have a metaphorical meaning, we would expect that that content could be fairly accurately expressed by some paraphrase, even if the paraphrase were cumbersome, prolix, flat, boring, or all of those.

Now, Davidson's attack on metaphorical meaning can be exaggerated, as it is in spots by his own rhetoric. As I said, it is presented as a scorched-earth or zero-tolerance policy. But in fact Davidson concentrates his critical arguments on the idea that *linguistic expressions* change their meanings in metaphorical usage; his bête noire is the positing of linguistic ambiguity. And at one important point he is careful "not to deny that there is such a thing as metaphorical truth, only to deny it of sentences" (p. 39). This leaves open the possibility that there is a middle way or compromise position.

Searle (1979) proposes an account of metaphor that joins Davidson in deflating "metaphorical meaning" even further than did the Naive Theory, and in rejecting a linguistic ambiguity view. But as against Davidson it takes seriously the idea that metaphorical utterance is genuinely linguistic communication rather than mere causation, and it posits a cognitive mechanism that computes something well worth calling metaphorical meaning.

I shall call Searle's view the Pragmatic Theory, for, bluntly, he sees metaphor as simply a species of indirect communication in the sense of

Chapter 13.[10] Recall from that chapter that Searle (1975) had offered a "conservative" account of how indirect speech acts are performed and understood. The speaker utters a sentence grammatically marked for one range of illocutionary force but primarily means something by it that has a different force or at least a characteristically different locutionary content. The hearer first uses Gricean reasoning to determine that the speaker is trying to convey something other than what her/his sentence literally means; then the hearer uses further Gricean reasoning augmented by principles of speech-act theory and by mutually obvious contextual assumptions to work out the intended force and content of the utterance.

According to Searle:

> The problem of explaining how metaphors work is a special case of the general problem of explaining how speaker meaning and sentence or word meaning come apart. . . . Our task in constructing a theory of metaphor is to try to state the principles which relate literal sentence meaning to metaphorical [speaker's] utterance meaning.
>
> (pp. 92–3)

Searle breaks down the interpretive process into three steps (parallel to the process he had posited for the interpretation of indirect speech acts). First the hearer must determine whether to look for a nonliteral interpretation in the first place. Second, if the hearer has decided to seek a metaphorical interpretation, s/he must then mobilize some set of principles or strategies for generating a range of possible speaker meanings. Third, s/he must employ a further set of principles or strategies for identifying which meaning or meanings from among that range are most likely to be in play on the present occasion. (Note that if this further set cannot pare the likely meanings down to one or two, that would explain the frequent open-endedness of metaphor.)

The obvious strategy underlying the first step is Gricean: when an utterance would be obviously *defective* if taken literally, look for a different speaker meaning. Our (1)–(4) all fit this model, since considered literally, each is false to the point of conceptual confusion. (As Searle says, however, not all metaphorical sentences are outrageous falsehoods or even false at all. The defect in literally uttering "Rocky is a real man," "The quality of mercy is not strained," or Mao Tse-Tung's "A revolution is not a dinner party," is their utter pointlessness due to their excessively plain truth.)

The Gricean strategy is not the only first-step option. Some metaphorical utterances are not in any way defective; there are other contextual cues, such as the kind of discourse that is taking place. Searle observes that "when reading Romantic poets, we are on the lookout for metaphors" (p. 114). Kittay (1987: 76) notes that metaphors are sometimes explicitly flagged as such: a victim is tied against a wall by thieves. "He realized that both literally and metaphorically . . . he was up against the wall, and . . . his hands were tied."

The principal general strategy for the second step, Searle unsurprisingly says, is to look for similarities or comparisons. Searle offers eight principles according to which the uttered phrase can call to mind a different meaning "in ways that are peculiar to metaphor." For example (Principle 2), the different meaning can be a "salient or well known property" of the thing or state of affairs mentioned. Or (Principle 3), as in our "gorilla" and "pig" examples, the intended property can be one that is only often imputed to the thing.

Searle mentions just one strategy for the third step: to consider which of the meaning candidates are likely or even possible features of the subject under discussion. Juliet could not be a giant ball of gas, or consist largely of nuclear fusion, or be 93 million miles from the earth. Of course, hearers also know things about what ideas particular speakers are likely to be expressing.

There remains the task of distinguishing metaphor as a species of indirect communication from others such as ordinary implicature, irony, and what Searle calls "indirect speech acts" proper. Searle contrasts metaphor with indirect speech acts by contending (p. 121) that in the latter case the speaker means what s/he says in addition to meaning something more as well. (He does not address ordinary implicature, but he might well say the same in its regard.) The difference between metaphor and irony seems to be just that with metaphor the second and third stages of interpretation work by similarity or comparison, while with irony there is a simpler sort of reflex: the utterance taken literally is defective in that either the opposite is clearly true or the speaker may be expected to believe the opposite, so the "natural" choice of indirect meaning is just the opposite.

Davidson and Searle agree more than they disagree. Both deny that linguistic expressions have special metaphorical meanings, and both hold that metaphor can be understood using apparatus already on hand in mainstream philosophy of language. (Fogelin aptly classifies the Causal and Pragmatic Theories together as "fecund falsehood" theories.) Moreover, I do not see why Davidson should, or how he could, dispute Searle's view that there is metaphorical speaker-meaning. He does argue, contrary to Searle's view, that what some metaphors convey is not propositional at all. But the biggest disagreement is over rules, principles and cognitive mechanisms, Davidson stoutly denying any and Searle eagerly proposing quite a few. So let us see how Searle might rebut Davidson's two arguments against "metaphorical meaning."

Davidson first argued that there are no instructions or rules for generating or for interpreting metaphors. As if directly inspired by that passage, Searle produced quite a number of such rules, and so far as they go they are plausible. Davidson added the qualification, "no test for metaphor *that does not call for taste*"; very likely Searle would concede that point, since he makes no claim to completeness and does not predict that even a final set of principles will give perfectly determinate results. But he wins this round on points.

Davidson's second appeal was to open-endedness, unparaphrasability and downright nonpropositionality. Searle's account predicts open-endedness, since we may expect that his second and third stages will often fail to tamp down the possible speaker-meanings to just one or two. As for unparaphrasability, Searle grants that often we use metaphor precisely because there is no handy and accessible literal expression that means the same thing, but he argues that if something is a linguistic meaning at all, in principle it could be formulated (however cumbersomely) in some language or other.

I think Searle wins that round also, but there is a deeper issue about nonpropositionalness. Searle's account is propositional to the core, since all speaker-meaning is meaning *that* so-and-so. If Davidson is right that what we notice or see in metaphor "is not, in general, propositional in character," then by Searle's own principle aforementioned, it is not a linguistic meaning of any kind, not even a speaker-meaning.

Davidson's "in general" makes his claim fairly ambitious, indeed false. Perhaps many poetic and other literary metaphors are so rich as to be nonpropositional in their purport, but everyday metaphors used casually by ordinary people are often perfectly paraphrasable in context. Quite often, just as Searle says, the speaker certainly does mean something, possibly something quite specific. Hans comes into his apartment and finds it a disgusting mess[11] – dirty underwear on the floor, four days' worth of dishes festering in the sink, other items not to be mentioned in a family publication such as this book – and Hans accosts his room-mate: "You pig!" He means fairly precisely that his room-mate is a filthy slob. (Had he instead found the apartment neat and clean but all the good food gone because his room-mate had scarfed it, he might have said "You pig!" meaning that his room-mate is a glutton.) So I think Davidson has overstated his case by overlooking facts of speaker-meaning.

On the other hand, just as Davidson says, writers who strew fresh literary metaphors, far from always having determinate speaker-meanings, may have no speaker-meanings or other propositional intent at all. That does not make the metaphors any less good or useful, because metaphor

222 THE DARK SIDE

does sometimes have the quasi-perceptual character noted by Davidson; in some cases metaphor affects one's literally perceptual set. (In other, intermediate cases, the metaphor just puts one in a different intellectual frame of mind for thinking about the topic at hand.) And that is a telling point against Searle.

Thus, each view has at least one advantage over the other. I believe that a rapprochement is possible, a hybrid view that combines the advantages of the Causal Theory and the Pragmatic Theory. But I leave that to you as an exercise, and merely note three further objections made against Searle.

First, Cooper (1986) and Moran (1997) point out that if metaphorical meaning is simply speaker-meaning, then it is determined by and confined to the speaker's intentions. Yet in cases of fresh metaphor, as Cooper says (p. 73), "even a quite definite speaker-intention does not finally determine the meaning of a metaphor." Moran adds that "the interpretation of the light [the metaphor] sheds on its subject may outrun anything the speaker is thought explicitly to have had in mind" (p. 264).

Second, Davis' criticism from Chapter 13 applies as before: Searle makes his second and third steps look far easier than they would be in real life, but we have been prevented from noticing this by the fact that we already know the right answer to the calculation. Notice that his problem about Searle's third step is exacerbated by Searle's own point that the similarities that underwrite metaphors are themselves usually metaphorical.

Third, Ross (1981) and Kittay (1987) call our attention to a class of metaphor phenomena, sometimes called "analogical," that indisputably involve meaning and meaning shift but are addressed neither by Davidson's view nor by Searle's. They are pervasive; they occur in nearly every sentence that comes out of our mouths. I will try to acquaint you with them; unfortunately, the theories of metaphor that exploit them are very dense and complicated, and I will not have the space to expound them.

Metaphor as analogical

As a way into the area in question, I introduce the "infinite polysemy" thesis defended by Weinreich (1966), Lyons (1977), Cohen (1985), and Davidson (1986), as well as by Ross and Kittay. That doctrine concerns *lexical meaning*, the meanings of words and short phrases rather than those of whole sentences. It is that virtually any word, even a pronoun, may take on any number of novel and distinct lexical meanings without limit, given a suitable variety of environments within sentences in which they occur. Indeed, one and the same word, depending on the subsentential context and under strange enough external circumstances, can mean almost anything. Moreover – what is most surprising – words do this in such a way that the novel meanings can be grasped on the spot by normal hearers.

All this is because novel word meanings are generated in context from existing ones by intricate but fairly tractable mechanisms of "analogy" that are mobilized automatically by every normal speaker.[12] For the same reason, very few such differences of word meaning are utter, brute ambiguities such as that of "bank" (financial vs. flying technique) or "die" (to perish vs. as used in craps and in board games); the polysemous meanings are systematically interrelated.

Consider the following sets of examples. (a) "She *dropped* a stitch"; "She *dropped* her hem-line; "She *dropped* her book"; "She *dropped* a friend"; "She *dropped* her courses" (Ross, p. 33); "She *dropped* her eyes" (Kittay, p. 154). Each occurrence of "dropped" in this list means something at least slightly different (and we may add the further noun forms "letter *drop*," "parachute *drop*," and "*drop* of blood"). Moreover, Ross says, "[t]he meanings . . . are appropriate, *fitted* to the completion words . . . ." (b) "He picked a date"; "He appointed a date"; "He fixed a date"; "He wanted a date"; "He borrowed a date" (pp. 80–1). Ross notes that each of these sentences is still ambiguous, and the ambiguity could be reduced only by the addition of wider contexts. (c) "He charged the gun"; "He charged the jury"; "He charged her with murder"; "He charged him with responsibility"; "He charged more than the law allowed"; "He charged the boy too much"; "He charged the battery"; . . . (paraphrased from Ross, p. 100). (d) My own example: "Dead man"; "dead duck"; "dead silence"; "dead ringer"; "dead march"; "dead eye"; "dead end"; "dead head"; "dead assets"; "dead heat"; "dead bolt"; "dead language"; "dead wrong"; "dead drunk"; "dead tired," "dead boring"; "dead set (on)"; "the dead of winter." (e) Prepositions such as "in" and "on" notoriously have no constant meaning from context to context. (Lakoff and Johnson (1980) make this point trenchantly.) (f) It occurs to me that even affixes and case markers are thus polysemous. The possessive in particular denotes seemingly countless different relationships, only some of them expressible as "ownership" in any sense at all.

It is true that we are making very fine distinctions here. Someone might well deny that *all* the foregoing word uses actually differ in meaning, and it may be suggested that some of the differences are only of tone or of connotation. But when we ask, as a diagnostic, whether a sentence of the sort listed can simultaneously have more than one truth-value depending on disambiguation, the answer is obviously yes. Kittay (p. 111) reminds us of Peggy Parish's children's books, whose main character, the house-maid Amelia Bedelia, is deaf to such variations. "When asked to 'dust the furniture', she uses a powder-puff to spread face powder on the furniture;

when required to 'draw the curtains', she produces a sketch of them; and when asked to 'dress the chicken', she puts a miniature pair of trousers and shirt on a bird intended for that night's dinner." "Dust," "draw" and "dress" each have different senses, however closely those senses may be related to each other.

Unfortunately for our purposes, each of the two leading theories of analogical meaning differentiation, Ross' and Kittay's – much less their extension to a theory of metaphor in particular – are far too complicated even to be sketched here. I can only refer you to their works, and hope you have enjoyed this limited look at the dark side of philosophy of language.

Summary

- The phenomenon of metaphor is far more prevalent than is generally admitted by philosophers, and it raises two main questions: what is "metaphorical meaning"? And how do hearers grasp metaphorical meaning as readily as they do?
- Most theorists have thought that metaphor is somehow a matter of bringing out similarities between things or states of affairs.
- Davidson argues that the stimulation of comparisons is purely causal, not linguistic. At the opposite extreme, the Naive Simile Theory has it that metaphors simply abbreviate literal comparisons. Both views are easily refuted.
- According to the Figurative Simile Theory, rather, metaphors are short for similes themselves taken figuratively. This view avoids a few of the objections to the Naive Simile Theory, but not others.
- Searle mobilizes Gricean apparatus to explain metaphorical meaning as speaker-meaning. This has some plausibility and overcomes Davidson's leading objections to metaphorical meaning, but incurs other objections.
- A further theory of metaphor is based on the phenomenon, important in its own right, of single words' analogical differentiation into hosts of distinct though related meanings.

Questions

1   Is there more to be said for Davidson's causal theory, or for the Naive Simile Theory?
2   Pursue Fogelin's Figurative Simile Theory, attacking or defending.

3 Try to come up with a compromise view between Davidson and Searle.
4 Defend Searle against one or more of our objections, or make a further objection.
5 If you are willing to do some outside reading, discuss Ross' and Kittay's "analogy" phenomena. (Not for the faint of heart.)

Notes

1 "Thou art Peter, and upon this rock I will build my church" (Matthew 16: 18).
2 There is a shaggy-dog story, told to me by Jane Lycan, whose punch line is the most elaborate I have ever heard: "Now has the wizard of our discothéque made Gloria slimmer by this ton of pork."
3 *Hamlet*, I. iii. 116–17. But the most elaborately mixed of Shakespeare's metaphors known to me is patriotic:

> This royal throne of kings, this sceptred isle,
> This earth of majesty, this seat of Mars,
> This other Eden, demi-paradise,
> This fortress built by Nature for herself
> Against infection and the hand of war,
> This happy breed of men, this little world,
> This precious stone set in the silver sea,
> Which serves it in the office of a wall,
> Or as a moat defensive to a house,
> Against the envy of less happier lands,
> This blessed plot, this earth, this realm, this England,
> This nurse, this teeming womb of royal kings,
> Feared by their breed and famous by their birth . . .
>
> (*Richard II*, II. i. 40–52)

He got away with it.
4 And by earlier empiricists as well. Blackburn (1984: 172) offers a pungent quote from Hobbes' *Leviathan*.
5 I owe this observation to Franklin Goldsmith.
6 Here and elsewhere he draws on Tversky (1977).
7 If you want greed, try cats. But no one ever calls someone a cat as a metaphorical way of saying that that person is greedy.
    A further example is "bastard." I know of no evidence that a male person whose parents were not married when he was born is any more likely to be callous or unscrupulous than is anyone else.
8 Fogelin addresses this objection (pp. 44–5), but I think weakly. He complains that "gorilla" is not a metaphor but a *dead* metaphor; if so, that seems inessential to the example. Then he suggests that either the ellipsis is larger than usual, including "what most people think —s are like," or the speaker "speaks from the perspective of common belief which he and his listener know contains false beliefs they do not share." The first of these moves is semantically desperate; the second, in the absence of some independent motivation, is *ad hoc*.

9 According to cummings' poem, "Anyone lived in a pretty how town" (cited in Chapter 1), its protagonist [A]nyone "sang his didn't he danced his did" (line 4).

10 Searle himself reserves the term "indirect" for types of communication, such as indirect force and some conversational implicature, in which one conveys a second meaning in addition to meaning what one's sentence says.

11 A real-life example, I am sorry to say, brought up by a graduate student during a seminar.

12 This idea is actually very old; Aristotle explored it, and it was vigorously elaborated by the medieval philosophers.

Further reading

Black (1954/1962) was a seminal paper and attracted wide commentary.

Johnson (1981) is a useful anthology.

Cohen (1975), Stern (1985), Elgin and Scheffler (1987), and Tirrell (1989) offer further approaches to metaphor.

Glossary

Analytic A sentence is analytic if its truth, however trivial, is guaranteed by the collective meanings of the words that occur in it.

Anaphoric expression An anaphoric expression inherits its meaning from another expression, its *antecedent*, which usually occurs earlier in the sentence or in a previous sentence.

Antecedent (of an anaphoric expression) The antecedent of an anaphoric expression is the expression from which the anaphoric expression inherits its meaning.

Compositionally, compositionality A characteristic of how we understand novel sentences, namely that we understand such sentences in virtue of understanding the individual words and how they are strung together; presupposes that the meaning of a sentence is determined by the meanings of its component words together with their syntactic relations to each other.

Context of utterance The setting in which a piece of language is used by a speaker.

Contextual definition A type of definition, to be contrasted with explicit definition, whereby one exhibits the role played by the word to be defined by showing how one can paraphrase whole sentences in which the word occurs.

Conventional implicature Conventional implicature is implicature, in that a speaker implicates something rather than actually saying it, but it differs from conversational implicature in that conventional implicatures are grasped immediately, not on the basis of reasoning. Normally they are carried by tendentious choices of particular words.

Conversational implicature Conversational implicature is implicature which one works out, or could work out, using reasoning based on something like Grice's conversational maxims.

Deictic A deictic element is one whose semantic interpretation varies with the context of utterance, such as a tense marker or a demonstrative pronoun. Deictic elements are also called "indexicals."

Description theory of proper names The thesis that names are equivalent in meaning to descriptions.

Domain The class of things over which a quantifier ranges.

Extension A term's extension is the class of things to which the term applies; the extension of "red" is the class of red things.

Flaccid designator A singular term which designates different things in different possible worlds.

General terms Terms, such as "dog" and "brown", which are meant to apply to more than one thing.

Ideational theories Theories which hold that meanings are mental entities.

Identity statement An identity statement contains two singular terms. If the statement is true, both its terms pick out or denote the same person or thing.

Idiolect The personal and distinctive speech of a particular individual.

Intensional isomorphism There is an intensional isomorphism between two sentences when the sentences have the same intension and have it in virtue of being composed in the same way (or much the same way) out of the same atomic intensions.

Intensional logic A formal system delineating the logic of Fregean senses.

Intensional sentences Sentences in which coextensive terms cannot be substituted without possibly changing the truth-value of the sentences themselves.

Lexical meaning The meaning of a word or short phrase, as contrasted with sentence meaning.

Modal Concerning possibility and necessity.

Natural-kind terms Common nouns, such as "gold" and "tiger," which refer to natural substances or organisms.

Possible world A world, or universe, which might have been the actual world.

Quantifiers Words, such as "all" or "some," which quantify general terms.

Referential Theory of Linguistic Meaning This theory attempts to explain the significance or meaning of all linguistic expressions in terms of their having been conventionally associated with things in the world, and attempts to explain a human being's understanding of a sentence in terms of that person's knowing what the sentence's component words refer to.

Restricted quantification A feature of most quantified statements whereby the domain over which the quantifiers range is not the entire universe. The domain is restricted in some way typically indicated by context.

Rigid designator A singular term which denotes the same thing in every possible world (more strictly, in every possible world in which that thing exists).

Semantic presupposition A sentence S_1 semantically presupposes a sentence S_2 just in case, if S_2 is false, then necessarily S_1 lacks truth-value.

Semantic referent The individual, if one exists, which a description purports to pick out in virtue of the individual's fitting the description; also called the "semantic denotatum."

Speaker-meaning What a speaker means in uttering a sentence; also called, by Grice, "utterer's meaning."

Speaker-reference The object, if any, to which the speaker who uses a description intends to call to the attention of her/his audience.

Truth condition The condition under which a sentence would be true.

Truth-functional A connective is truth-functional if the truth value of compound sentences containing it is strictly determined by the truth values of the component sentences. For example, "and" is a truth-functional connective because the truth value of sentences of the form "A and B" is strictly determined by the truth values of "A" and "B" respectively.

Bibliography

Note: Dates given in the form "1954/1962" refer first to the date of original publication followed by the more accessible reprinting actually cited.

Achinstein, P. (1965) "The Problem of Theoretical Terms," *American Philosophical Quarterly*, 2: 193–203.

Ackerman, D. (1979) "Proper Names, Propositional Attitudes and Non-Descriptive Connotations," *Philosophical Studies*, 35: 55–69.

Adams, E. (1965) "The Logic of Conditionals," *Inquiry*, 8: 166–89.

Almog, J., Perry, J. and Wettstein, H. (eds) (1989) *Themes from Kaplan*, New York: Oxford University Press.

Alston, W. (1963) "Meaning and Use," *Philosophical Quarterly*, 51: 107–24.

Austin, J.L. (1961) "Performative Utterances," in J.L. Austin, *Philosophical Papers*, Oxford: Oxford University Press.

—— (1962) *How To Do Things With Words*, Oxford: Clarendon Press.

Avramides, A. (1989) *Meaning and Mind*, Cambridge, MA: MIT Press.

Ayer, A.J. (1946) *Language, Truth and Logic*, 2nd edn, London: Victor Gollancz.

Bach, K. (1994) "Conversational Impliciture," *Mind and Language*, 9: 124–61.

—— (1999) "The Myth of Conventional Implicature," *Linguistics and Philosophy*, 22: 327–66.

Bach, K. and Harnish, R.M. (1979) *Linguistic Communication and Speech Acts*, Cambridge, MA: MIT Press.

Baker, C.L. (1995) *English Syntax*, 2nd edn, Cambridge, MA: MIT Press.

Barker, S. (1995) "Towards a Pragmatic Theory of 'If'," *Philosophical Studies*, 78: 185–211.

Bar-On, D. (1992) "Semantic Verificationism, Linguistic Behaviorism, and Translation," *Philosophical Studies*, 66: 235–59.

Beardsley, M. (1962) "The Metaphorical Twist," *Philosophy and Phenomenological Research*, 22: 293–307.

—— (1967) "Metaphor," in P. Edwards (ed.), *The Encyclopedia of Philosophy*, vol. 5, New York: Macmillan.

Bennett, J. (1971) *Locke, Berkeley, Hume: Central Themes*, Oxford: Clarendon Press.

—— (1976) *Linguistic Behaviour*, Cambridge: Cambridge University Press.

Bertolet, R. (1980) "The Semantic Significance of Donnellan's Distinction," *Philosophical Studies*, 37: 281–8.

Biro, J. (1979) "Intentionalism in the Theory of Meaning," *Monist*, 62: 238–58.

Black, M. (1954/1962) "Metaphor," in M. Black, *Models and Metaphors*, Ithaca, NY: Cornell University Press.

—— (1973) "Meaning and Intention: An Examination of Grice's Views," *New Literary History*, 4: 257–79.

Black, M. and Geach, P. (eds) (1952) *Translations from the Philosophical Writings of Gottlob Frege*, Oxford: Basil Blackwell.

Blackburn, S. (1984) *Spreading The Word*, Oxford: Clarendon Press.

—— (1993) *Essays in Quasi-Realism*, Oxford: Clarendon Press.

Blakemore, D. (1987) *Semantic Constraints on Relevance*, Oxford: Basil Blackwell.
—— (1992) *Understanding Utterances*, Oxford: Basil Blackwell.
Boër, S. (1978) "Attributive Names," *Notre Dame Journal of Formal Logic*, 19: 177–85.
—— (1985) "Substance and Kind: Reflections on The New Theory of Reference," in B.K. Matilal and J.L. Shaw (eds), *Analytical Philosophy in Comparative Perspective*, Dordrecht: D. Reidel.
Bradley, F.H. (1930) *Appearance and Reality*, Oxford: Clarendon Press.
Brandom, R. (1994) *Making It Explicit*, Cambridge, MA: Harvard University Press.
Burge, T. (1973) "Reference and Proper Names," *Journal of Philosophy*, 70: 425–39; reprinted in Davidson, D. and Harman, G. (1975) (eds) *Semantics of Natural Language*, Dordrecht: D. Reidel.
—— (1974) "Demonstrative Constructions, Reference and Truth," *Journal of Philosophy*, 71: 205–23.
Carnap, R. (1947/1956) *Meaning and Necessity*, 2nd edn, Chicago: University of Chicago Press.
Carston, R. (1988) "Implicature, Explicature, and Truth-Theoretic Semantics," in R. Kempson (ed.) (1988) *Mental Representation*, Cambridge: Cambridge University Press; reprinted in Davis, S. (1991) *Pragmatics: A Reader*, Oxford: Oxford University Press.
—— (2002) *Thoughts and Utterances: The Pragmatics of Explicit Communication*, Oxford: Basil Blackwell.
Cartwright, R. (1962) "Propositions", in R.J. Butler (ed.), *Analytic Philosophy*, vol. 1, Oxford: Basil Blackwell.
—— (1987) "On the Origins of Russell's Theory of Descriptions," in R. Cartwright, *Philosophical Essays*, Cambridge, MA: MIT Press.
Chierchia, G. and McConnell-Ginet, S. (1990) *Meaning and Grammar: An Introduction to Semantics*, Cambridge, MA: MIT Press.
Chomsky, N. (1957) *Syntactic Structures*, The Hague: Mouton & Co.
—— (1965) *Aspects of the Theory of Syntax*, Cambridge, MA: MIT Press.
Churchland, P.M. (1988) "Perceptual Plasticity and Theoretical Neutrality," *Philosophy of Science*, 55: 167–87.
Cohen, L.J. (1964) "Do Illocutionary Forces Exist?" *Philosophical Quarterly*, 14: 118–37.
—— (1971) "Some Remarks about Grice's Views about the Logical Particles of Natural Language," in Y. Bar-Hillel (ed.), *Pragmatics of Natural Languages*, Dordrecht: D. Reidel.
—— (1985) "A Problem about Ambiguity in Truth-Theoretic Semantics," *Analysis*, 45: 129–34.
Cohen, T. (1975) "Figurative Speech and Figurative Acts," *Journal of Philosophy*, 71: 669–84.
Cole, P. (ed.) (1978) *Syntax and Semantics, Vol. 9: Pragmatics*, New York: Academic Press.
Cole, P. and Morgan, J.L. (eds) (1975) *Syntax and Semantics, Vol. 3: Speech Acts*, New York: Academic Press.
Cooper, D.E. (1986) *Metaphor*, Oxford: Basil Blackwell.
Cresswell, M.J. (1973) *Logics and Languages*, London: Methuen.
Davidson, D. (1967a) "The Logical Form of Action Sentences," in N. Rescher (ed.), *The Logic of Decision and Action*, Pittsburgh: University of Pittsburgh Press.
—— (1967b) "Truth and Meaning," *Synthese*, 17: 304–23; reprinted in D. Davidson (1984) *Inquiries into Truth and Interpretation*, Oxford: Clarendon Press.
—— (1968) "On Saying That," *Synthese*, 19: 130–46; reprinted in D. Davidson and G. Harman (1975) *The Logic of Grammar*, Encino, CA: Dickenson, and D. Davidson (1984) *Inquiries into Truth and Interpretation*, Oxford: Clarendon Press.

—— (1970/1975) "Semantics for Natural Languages," in D. Davidson and G. Harman (eds) (1975) *The Logic of Grammar*, Encino, CA: Dickenson, and D. Davidson (1984) *Inquiries into Truth and Interpretation*, Oxford: Clarendon Press.

—— (1978) "What Metaphors Mean" in S. Sacks (ed) *On Metaphor*, Chicago: University of Chicago Press; reprinted in D. Davidson (1984) *Inquiries into Truth and Interpretation*, Oxford: Clarendon Press.

—— (1984) *Inquiries into Truth and Interpretation*, Oxford: Clarendon Press.

—— (1986) "A Nice Derangement of Epitaphs," in E. LePore, *Truth and Interpretation: Perspectives of The Philosophy of Donald Davidson*, Oxford: Basil Blackwell.

Davidson, D. and Harman, G. (eds) (1972) *Semantics of Natural Language*, Dordrecht: D. Reidel.

—— (eds) (1975) *The Logic of Grammar*, Encino, CA: Dickenson.

Davis, S. (1991) *Pragmatics: A Reader*, Oxford: Oxford University Press.

Davis, W. (1998) *Implicature*, Cambridge: Cambridge University Press.

Devitt, M. (1981a) *Designation*, New York: Columbia University Press.

—— (1981b) "Donnellan's Distinction," in P. French, T. Uehling, and H. Wettstein (eds), *Midwest Studies in Philosophy VI: The Foundations of Analytic Philosophy*, Minneapolis: University of Minnesota Press.

—— (1983) "Dummett's Anti-Realism," *Journal of Philosophy*, 80: 73–99.

—— (1989) "Against Direct Reference," *Midwest Studies in Philosophy*, 14: 206–40.

—— (1996) *Coming to Our Senses*, Cambridge: Cambridge University Press.

Devitt, M. and Sterelny, K. (1987) *Language and Reality: An Introduction to the Philosophy of Language*, Cambridge: MIT Press.

Donnellan, K. (1966) "Reference and Definite Descriptions," *Philosophical Review*, 75: 281–304.

—— (1968) "Putting Humpty Dumpty Together Again," *Philosophical Review*, 77: 203–15.

—— (1970) "Proper Names and Identifying Descriptions," *Synthese*, 21: 335–58; reprinted in D. Davidson and G. Harman (eds) (1972) *Semantics of Natural Language*, Dordrecht: D. Reidel.

—— (1974) "Speaking of Nothing," *Philosophical Review*, 83: 3–31.

—— (1979) "Speaker Reference, Descriptions, and Anaphora" in P. French, T. Uehling and H. Wettstein (eds) (1979) *Contemporary Perspectives in the Philosophy of Language*, Minneapolis: University of Minnesota Press.

Duhem, P. (1906/1954) *The Aim and Structure of Physical Theory*, trans. P. Wiener, Princeton, NJ: Princeton University Press.

Dummett, M. (1973) *Frege: Philosophy of Language*, New York: Harper & Row.

—— (1975) "What Is a Theory of Meaning?" in S. Guttenplan (ed.), *Mind and Language*, Oxford: Oxford University Press.

—— (1978) *Truth and Other Enigmas*, Cambridge, MA: Harvard University Press.

Dupré, J. (1981) "Natural Kinds and Biological Taxa," *Philosophical Review*, 90: 66–90.

Edelberg, W. (1995) "A Perspectivalist Semantics for the Attitudes," *Noûs*, 29: 316–42.

Elgin, C. and Scheffler, I. (1987) "Mainsprings of Metaphor," *Journal of Philosophy*, 84: 331–5.

Erwin, E. (1970) *The Concept of Meaninglessness*, Baltimore, MD: Johns Hopkins University Press.

Erwin, E., Kleiman, L., and Zemach, E. (1976) "The Historical Theory of Reference," *Australasian Journal of Philosophy*, 54: 50–7.

Evans, G. (1973) "The Causal Theory of Names," *Aristotelian Society Supplementary Volume*, 47: 187–208.

—— (1977) "Pronouns, Quantifiers, and Relative Clauses (I)," *Canadian Journal of Philosophy*, 7: 467–536.

—— (1982) *The Varieties of Reference*, Oxford: Oxford University Press.

Evans, G. and McDowell, J. (eds) (1976) *Truth and Meaning*, Oxford: Oxford University Press.

Fillmore, C. (1975) *The Santa Cruz Lectures on Deixis*, Bloomington, IN: Indiana University Linguistics Club Publications.

Fine, A. (1975) "How To Compare Theories: Reference and Change," *Noûs*, 9: 17–32.

Fogelin, R. (1988) *Figuratively Speaking*, New Haven, CT: Yale University Press.

Frege, G. (1892/1952a) "On Concept and Object" in M. Black and P. Geach (eds) (1952) *Translations from the Philosophical Writings of Gottlob Frege*, Oxford: Basil Blackwell.

—— (1892/1952b) "On Sense and Reference" in M. Black and P. Geach (eds) (1952) *Translations from the Philosophical Writings of Gottlob Frege*, Oxford: Basil Blackwell; reprinted in D. Davidson and G. Harman (eds) (1975) *The Logic of Grammar*, Encino, CA: Dickenson.

—— (1918/1956) "The Thought," *Mind*, 65: 289–311.

French, P., Uehling, T., and Wettstein, H. (eds) (1979) *Contemporary Perspectives in the Philosophy of Language*, Minneapolis: University of Minnesota Press.

Gazdar, G. (1979) *Pragmatics: Implicature, Presupposition, and Logical Form*, New York: Academic Press.

Geach, P. (1962) *Reference and Generality*, Ithaca, NY: Cornell University Press.

Geis, M. and Zwicky, A. (1971) "On Invited Inferences," *Linguistic Inquiry*, 2: 561–6.

Gibbard, A. (1990) *Wise Choices, Apt Feelings*, Cambridge, MA: Harvard University Press.

Ginet, C. (1979) "Performativity," *Linguistics and Philosophy*, 3: 245–65.

Goodman, N. (1970) "Seven Strictures on Similarity," in L. Foster and J.W. Swanson (eds) *Experience and Theory*, Amherst, MA: University of Massachusetts Press.

—— (1981) "Twisted Tales; or Story, Study, and Symphony," *Synthese*, 46: 331–50.

Gordon, D. and Lakoff, G. (1975) "Conversational Postulates," in P. Cole and J.L. Morgan (eds) (1975) *Syntax and Semantics, Vol. 3: Speech Acts*, New York: Academic Press.

Green, G.M. (1989) *Pragmatics and Natural Language Understanding*, Hillsdale, NJ: Lawrence Erlbaum.

Grice, H.P. (1957) "Meaning," *Philosophical Review*, 66: 377–88; reprinted in H.P. Grice (1989) *Studies in the Way of Words*, Cambridge, MA: Harvard University Press.

—— (1968) "Utterer's Meaning, Sentence-Meaning, and Word-Meaning," *Foundations of Language*, 4: 225–42; reprinted in H.P. Grice (1989) *Studies in the Way of Words*, Cambridge, MA: Harvard University Press.

—— (1969) "Utterer's Meaning and Intentions," *Philosophical Review*, 78: 147–77; reprinted in H.P. Grice (1989) *Studies in the Way of Words*, Cambridge: MA: Harvard University Press.

—— (1975) "Logic and Conversation" in D. Davidson and G. Harman (eds) (1975) *The Logic of Grammar*, Encino, CA: Dickenson, and P. Cole and J.L. Morgan (eds) (1975) *Syntax and Semantics, Vol. 3: Speech Acts*, New York: Academic Press (page references are to the latter); reprinted in H.P. Grice (1989) *Studies in the Way of Words*, Cambridge, MA: Harvard University Press.

—— (1978) "Further Notes on Logic and Conversation" in P. Cole and J.L. Morgan (eds) (1975) *Syntax and Semantics, Vol. 3: Speech Acts*, New York: Academic Press; reprinted in H.P. Grice (1989) *Studies in the Way of Words*, Cambridge, MA: Harvard University Press.

—— (1989) *Studies in the Way of Words*, Cambridge, MA: Harvard University Press.

Grover, D., Camp, J., and Belnap, N. (1975) "A Prosentential Theory of Truth," *Philosophical Studies*, 27: 73–125.

Gunderson, K. (ed.) (1975) *Minnesota Studies in the Philosophy of Science, Vol. 8: Language, Mind, and Knowledge*, Minneapolis: University of Minnesota Press.

Hallett, G. (1967) *Wittgenstein's Definition of Meaning as Use*, New York: Fordham University Press.

Harman, G. (1967–8) "Quine on Meaning and Existence, I," *Review of Metaphysics*, 31: 124–51.

—— (1972) "Logical Form," *Foundations of Language*, 9: 38–65; reprinted in D. Davidson and G. Harman (eds) (1975) *The Logic of Grammar*, Encino, CA: Dickenson.

—— (1974a) "Review of Stephen Schiffer's *Meaning*," *Journal of Philosophy*, 71: 224–9.

—— (1974b) "Meaning and Semantics," in M. Munitz and P. Unger (eds), *Semantics and Philosophy*, New York: New York University Press.

—— (1975) "Language, Thought, and Communication," in K. Gunderson (ed.) (1975) *Minnesota Studies in the Philosophy of Science, Vol. 8: Language, Mind, and Knowledge*, Minneapolis: University of Minnesota Press.

—— (1982) "Conceptual Role Semantics," *Notre Dame Journal of Formal Logic*, 23: 242–56.

Harnish, R.M. (1976) "Logical Form and Implicature," in T. Bever, J. Katz, and T. Langendoen (eds), *An Integrated Theory of Linguistic Ability*, New York: Crowell; reprinted in S. Davis (1991) *Pragmatics: A Reader*, Oxford: Oxford University Press.

Heil, J. (1998) *The Philosophy of Mind: A Contemporary Introduction*, London: Routledge.

Heil, J. and Mele, A. (eds) (1993) *Mental Causation*, New York: Clarendon Press.

Heim, I. (1990) "E-Type Pronouns and Donkey Anaphora," *Linguistics and Philosophy*, 13: 137–77.

Hempel, C.G. (1950) "Problems and Changes in The Empiricist Criterion of Meaning," *Revue Internationale de Philosophie*, 4: 41–63.

Hintikka, K.J.J. (1961) "Modality and Quantification," *Theoria*, 27: 119–28.

—— (1976) "Quantifiers in Logic and Quantifiers in Natural Languages," in S. Körner (ed.), *Philosophy of Logic*, Oxford: Basil Blackwell; reprinted in E. Saarinen (ed.) (1979) *Game-Theoretical Semantics*, Dordrecht: D. Reidel.

—— (1979) "Quantifiers in Natural Languages: Some Logical Problems," in E. Saarinen (ed.) (1979) *Game-Theoretical Semantics*, Dordrecht: D. Reidel.

Holdcroft, D. (1978) *Words and Deeds*, Oxford: Oxford University Press.

Hornstein, N. (1995) *Logical Form: From GB to Minimalism*, Oxford: Basil Blackwell.

Johnson, M. (ed) (1981) *Philosophical Perspectives on Metaphor*, Minneapolis: University of Minnesota Press.

Kamp, H. and Reyle, U. (1993) *From Discourse to Logic*, Dordrecht: Kluwer Academic.

Kaplan, D. (1972) "What is Russell's Theory of Descriptions?" in D.F. Pears (ed.), *Bertrand Russell*, Garden City, NY: Anchor Books; reprinted in D. Davidson and G. Harman (eds) (1975) *The Logic of Grammar*, Encino, CA: Dickenson.

—— (1975) "How to Russell a Frege–Church," *Journal of Philosophy*, 72: 716–29.

—— (1978) "Dthat," in P. Cole (ed.), *Syntax and Semantics, Vol. 9: Pragmatics*, New York: Academic Press; reprinted in P. French, T. Uehling, and H. Wettstein (eds) (1979) *Contemporary Perspectives in the Philosophy of Language*, Minneapolis: University of Minnesota Press.

—— (1989) "Afterthoughts," in J. Almog, J. Perry, and H. Wettstein (eds) *Themes from Kaplan*, New York: Oxford University Press.

Karttunen, L. (1973) "Presuppositions of Compound Sentences," *Linguistic Inquiry*, 4: 169–93.

Karttunen, L. and Peters, S. (1979) "Conventional Implicature," in C. Oh and D.A. Dineen (eds) *Syntax and Semantics, Vol. 11: Presupposition*, New York: Academic Press.

Kempson, R. (1975) *Presupposition and the Delimitation of Semantics*, Cambridge: Cambridge University Press.

Kenny, A. (1973) *Wittgenstein*, Cambridge, MA: Harvard University Press.

Kittay, E. (1987) *Metaphor*, Oxford: Clarendon Press.

Kripke, S. (1972/1980) *Naming and Necessity*, Cambridge, MA: Harvard University Press; an earlier version appeared in D. Davidson and G. Harman (eds)(1972) *Semantics of Natural Language*, Dordrecht: D. Reidel.

—— (1979a) "Speaker's Reference and Semantic Reference," in P. French, T. Uehling, and H. Wettstein (eds) (1979) *Contemporary Perspectives in the Philosophy of Language*, Minneapolis: University of Minnesota Press.

—— (1979b) "A Puzzle about Belief," in A. Margalit (ed.), *Meaning and Use*, Dordrecht: D. Reidel.

—— (1982) *Wittgenstein on Rules and Private Language*, Cambridge, MA: Harvard University Press.

Kvart, I. (1993) "Mediated Reference and Proper Names," *Mind*, 102: 611–28.

Lakoff, G. (1975) "Pragmatics in Natural Language," in E.L. Keenan (ed.), *Formal Semantics of Natural Language*, Cambridge: Cambridge University Press.

Lakoff, G. and Johnson, M. (1980) *Metaphors We Live By*, Chicago: University of Chicago Press.

Larson, R. and Segal G. (1995) *Knowledge of Meaning*, Cambridge, MA: Bradford Books/ MIT Press.

Lemmon, E.J. (1966) "Sentences, Statements, and Propositions," in B. Williams and A. Montefiore (eds) *British Analytical Philosophy*, London: Routledge & Kegan Paul.

Levinson, S. (1983) *Pragmatics*, Cambridge: Cambridge University Press.

Lewis, D. (1969) *Convention: A Philosophical Study*, Cambridge, MA: Harvard University Press.

—— (1970) "General Semantics," *Synthese*, 22: 18–67; reprinted in D. Davidson and G. Harman (eds) (1972) *Semantics of Natural Language*, Dordrecht: D. Reidel.

—— (1986) *On the Plurality of Worlds*, Oxford: Blackwell.

Linsky, L. (1963) "Reference and Referents," in C. Caton (ed.), *Philosophy and Ordinary Language*, Urbana, IL: University of Illinois Press.

—— (1967) *Referring*, London: Routledge & Kegan Paul.

—— (1977) *Names and Descriptions*, Chicago: University of Chicago Press.

Loar, B. (1976) "The Semantics of Singular Terms," *Philosophical Studies*, 30: 353–77.

Locke, J. (1690/1955) *Essay Concerning Human Understanding*, Chicago: Encyclopaedia Britannica.

Loux, M. (1998) *Metaphysics: A Contemporary Introduction*, London: Routledge.

Lycan, W.G. (1974) "Could Propositions Explain Anything?" *Canadian Journal of Philosophy*, 3: 427–34.

—— (1984) *Logical Form in Natural Language*, Cambridge, MA: Bradford Books/MIT Press.

—— (1994) *Modality and Meaning*, Dordrecht and Boston, MA: Kluwer Academic Press.

Lyons, J. (1977) *Semantics*, vol. I, Cambridge: Cambridge University Press.

MacKay, A.F. (1968) "Mr. Donnellan and Humpty Dumpty on Referring," *Philosophical Review*, 77: 197–202.

—— (1972) "Professor Grice's Theory of Meaning," *Mind*, 81: 57–66.

McKinsey, M. (1976) "Divided Reference in Causal Theories of Names," *Philosophical Studies*, 30: 235–42.

—— (1978) "Names and Intentionality," *Philosophical Review* 87: 171–200.

Malcolm, N. (1958) *Ludwig Wittgenstein: A Memoir*, Oxford: Oxford University Press.

Marcus, R.B. (1960) "Extensionality," *Mind*, 69: 55–62.

—— (1961) "Modalities and Intensional Languages," *Synthese*, 13: 303–22.

—— (1981) "A Proposed Solution to a Puzzle About Belief," *Midwest Studies in Philosophy*, 6: 501–10.

Marsh, R. (ed.) (1956) *Logic and Knowledge*, London: Allen & Unwin.

Meinong, A. (1904/1960) "The Theory of Objects," in R.M. Chisholm (ed.), *Realism and the Background of Phenomenology*, Glencoe, IL: Free Press.

Mill, J.S. (1843/1973) *A System of Logic*, London: Longmans.

Montague, R. (1960) "Logical Necessity, Physical Necessity, Ethics and Quanitifiers," *Inquiry*, 3: 259–69.

—— (1968/1974) "Pragmatics," in R. Montague (1974) *Formal Philosophy*, New Haven, CT: Yale University Press.

—— (1970) "English as a Formal Language," in B. Visentini *et al.* (eds) *Linguaggi nella Società e nella Tecnica*, Milan: Edizioni di Comunità.

—— (1974) *Formal Philosophy*, New Haven, CT: Yale University Press.

Moore, G.E. (1953/1962) *Some Main Problems of Philosophy*, New York: Collier Books.

Moran, R. (1997) "Metaphor," in C. Wright and R. Hale (eds), *A Companion to the Philosophy of Language*, Oxford: Basil Blackwell.

Morgan, J.L. (1978) "Two Types of Convention in Indirect Speech Acts," in P. Cole (ed.), *Syntax and Semantics, Vol. 9: Pragmatics*, New York: Academic Press.

Morris, C. (1938) *Foundations of the Theory of Signs*, Chicago: University of Chicago Press.

Neale, S. (1990) *Descriptions*, Cambridge, MA: MIT Press.

Nunberg, G. (1993) "Indexicality and Deixis," *Linguistics and Philosophy*, 16: 1–43.

Ostertag, G. (1998) *Definite Descriptions: A Reader*, Cambridge, MA: Bradford Books/MIT Press.

Parsons, K. (1973) "Ambiguity and the Truth-Definition," *Noûs*, 7: 379–93.

Parsons, T. (1980) *Nonexistent Objects*, New Haven, CT: Yale University Press.

Peirce, C.S. (1878/1934) "How To Make Our Ideas Clear," in C. Hartshorne and P. Weiss (eds), *Collected Papers of Charles Sanders Peirce*, vol. 5, Cambridge, MA: Harvard University Press.

Pitcher, G. (1964) *The Philosophy of Wittgenstein*, Englewood Cliffs, NJ: Prentice-Hall.

Plantinga, A. (1978) "The Boethian Compromise," *American Philosophical Quarterly*, 15: 129–38.

Platts, M. (1979) *Ways of Meaning*, London: Routledge & Kegan Paul.

—— (ed.) (1980) *Reference, Truth and Reality*, London: Routledge & Kegan Paul.

Putnam, H. (1975a) "The Meaning of 'Meaning'," in K. Gunderson (ed.) (1975) *Minnesota Studies in the Philosophy of Science, Vol. 8: Language, Mind, and Knowledge*, Minneapolis: University of Minnesota Press.

—— (1975b) *Mind, Language and Reality: Philosophical Papers*, vol. 2, Cambridge: Cambridge University Press.

—— (1978) *Meaning and the Moral Sciences*, London: Routledge & Kegan Paul.

Quine, W.V. (1951) "Two Dogmas of Empiricism," *Philosophical Review*, 60: 20–43.

—— (1953) *From A Logical Point of View*, Cambridge, MA: Harvard University Press.

—— (1960) *Word and Object*, Cambridge, MA: MIT Press.

—— (1969) *Ontological Relativity and Other Essays*, New York: Columbia University Press.

Radford, A. (1997) *Syntactic Theory and the Structure of English: A Minimalist Approach*, Cambridge: Cambridge University Press.

Recanati, F. (1989) "The Pragmatics of What is Said," *Mind and Language*, 4: 295–329.

—— (1993) *Direct Reference*, Oxford: Blackwell.

Reeves, A. (1974) "On Truth and Meaning," *Noûs*, 8: 343–59.

Reimer, M. (1992) "Incomplete Descriptions," *Erkenntnis*, 37: 347–63.

Rhees, R. (1959–60) "Wittgenstein's Builders," *Proceedings of the Aristotelian Society*, 60: 171–86.

Rosenberg, J.F. (1974) *Linguistic Representation*, Dordrecht: D. Reidel.

—— (1994) *Beyond Formalism*, Philadelphia: Temple University Press.

Ross, J.F. (1981) *Portraying Analogy*, New York: Cambridge University Press.

Routley, R. *et al.* (1980) *Exploring Meinong's Jungle and Beyond*, Canberra: Departmental Monograph #3, Philosophy Department, Research School of Social Sciences, Australian National University.

Russell, B. (1905/1956) "On Denoting," *Mind*, 14: 479–93; reprinted in R. Marsh (ed.) (1956) *Logic and Knowledge*, London: Allen & Unwin, and D. Davidson and G. Harman (eds) (1975) *The Logic of grammar*, Encino, CA: Dickenson.

—— (1918/1956) "The Philosophy of Logical Atomism," in R. Marsh (ed.) (1956) *Logic and Knowledge*, London: Allen & Unwin.

—— (1919/1971) *Introduction to Mathematical Philosophy*, New York: Clarion Books/Simon & Schuster.

—— (1919/1956) "On Propositions: What They Are and How They Mean," in R. Marsh (ed.) (1956) *Logic and Knowledge*, London: Allen & Unwin.

—— (1957) "Mr. Strawson on Referring," *Mind*, 66: 385–9.

Saarinen, E. (ed.) (1979) *Game-Theoretical Semantics*, Dordrecht: D. Reidel.

Sadock, J. (1975) "The Soft, Interpretive Underbelly of Generative Semantics," in P. Cole and J.L. Morgan (eds), *Syntax and Semantics, Vol. 3: Speech Acts*, New York: Academic Press.

Sag, I.A. and Wasow, T. (1999) *Syntactic Theory: A Formal Introduction*, Stanford, CA: CSLI Publications.

Salmon, N. (1981) *Reference and Essence*, Princeton, NJ: Princeton University Press.

—— (1986) *Frege's Puzzle*, Cambridge, MA: Bradford Books/MIT Press.

—— (1998) "Nonexistence," *Noûs*, 32: 277–319.

Schiffer, S. (1972) *Meaning*, Oxford: Clarendon Press.

—— (1979) "Naming and Knowing," in P. French, T. Uehling, and H. Wettstein (eds), *Contemporary Perspectives in the Philosophy of Language*, Minneapolis: University of Minnesota Press.

Schwartz, S. (ed.) (1977) *Naming, Necessity, and Natural Kinds*, Ithaca, NY: Cornell University Press.

Scott, D. (1970) "Advice on Modal Logic," in K. Lambert (ed.), *Philosophical Problems in Logic*, Dordrecht: D. Reidel.

Searle, J.R. (1958) "Proper Names," *Mind*, 67: 166–73.

—— (1965) "What Is A Speech Act?" in Black, M. (ed.), *Philosophy in America*, Ithaca, NY: Cornell University Press.

—— (1969) *Speech Acts*, London: Cambridge University Press.

—— (1975) "Indirect Speech Acts," in P. Cole and J.L. Morgan (eds) (1975) *Syntax and Semantics, Vol. 3: Speech Acts*, New York: Academic Press; reprinted in J.R. Searle (1979a) *Expression and Meaning*, Cambridge: Cambridge University Press.

—— (1979a) *Expression and Meaning*, Cambridge: Cambridge University Press.

—— (1979b) "Metaphor," in A. Ortony (ed.), *Metaphor and Thought*, Cambridge: Cambridge University Press; reprinted in J.R. Searle (1979a) *Expression and Meaning*, Cambridge; Cambridge University Press.

—— (1979c) "Referential and Attributive," *Monist*, 62: 190–208.

—— (1983) *Intentionality: An Essay in the Philosophy of Mind*, New York: Cambridge University Press.

Sellars, W. (1963) "Some Reflections on Language Games," in N. Sellars, *Science, Perception, and Reality*, London: Routledge & Kegan Paul.

—— (1974) "Meaning as Functional Classification (A Perspective on the Relation of Syntax to Semantics)," *Synthese*, 27: 417–37.

Soames, S. (1987) "Direct Reference, Propositional Attitudes, and Semantic Content," *Philosophical Topics*, 15: 47–87.

Sosa, E. (1970) "Propositional Attitudes *De Dicto* and *De Re*," *Journal of Philosophy*, 67: 883–96.

Sperber, D. and Wilson, D. (1986) *Relevance: Communication and Cognition*, Cambridge, MA: Harvard University Press.

Stalnaker, R. (1970) "Pragmatics," *Synthese*, 22: 272–89; reprinted in D. Davidson and G. Harman (eds) (1972) *Semantics of Natural Language*, Dordrecht: D. Reidel.

—— (1978) "Assertion," in P. Cole (ed.), *Syntax and Semantics, Vol. 9: Pragmatics*, New York: Academic Press.

Stern, J. (1985) "Metaphor as Demonstrative," *Journal of Philosophy*, 82: 677–710.

Stich, S. (1976) "Davidson's Semantic Program," *Canadian Journal of Philosophy*, 4: 201–27.

Stove, D. (1991) *The Plato Cult and Other Philosophical Follies*, Oxford: Basil Blackwell.

Strawson, P.F. (1950) "On Referring," *Mind*, 59: 320–44.

—— (1964) "Intention and Convention in Speech Acts," *Philosophical Review*, 73: 439–60.

—— (1970) *Meaning and Truth*, Oxford: Clarendon Press.

Tarski, A. (1956) "The Concept of Truth in Formalized Languages," in J.H. Woodger (ed. and trans.), *Logic, Semantics, Metamathematics*, Oxford: Clarendon Press.

Taylor, K.A. (1988) "We've Got You Coming and Going," *Linguistics and Philosophy*, 11: 493–513.

—— (1998) *Truth and Meaning*, Oxford: Basil Blackwell.

Tirrell, L. (1989) "Extending: The Structure of Metaphor," *Noûs*, 23: 17–34.

Travis, C. (1975) *Saying and Understanding*, New York: New York University Press.

Tversky, A. (1977) "Features of Similarity," *Psychological Review*, 84: 327–52.

Unger, P. (1983) "The Causal Theory of Reference," *Philosophical Studies*, 43: 1–45.

Waismann, F. (1965a) *The Principles of Linguistic Philosophy*, ed. R. Harré, New York: St. Martin's Press.

—— (1965b) "Verifiability," *Aristotelian Society Supplementary Volume*, 19: 119–50.

Warner, R. (1982) "Discourse Logic and Conventional Implicature," *Studia Anglica Posnaniensia*, 14: 91–102.

Weinreich, U. (1966) "Explorations in Semantic Theory," in T.A. Sebeok (ed.), *Theoretical Foundations*, The Hague: Mouton.

Weinstein, S. (1974) "Truth and Demonstratives," *Noûs*, 8: 179–84; reprinted in D. Davidson and G. Harman (eds) (1975) *The Logic of Grammar*, Enico, CA: Dickenson.

Weisler, S. (1991) "An Overview of Montague Semantics," in J. Garfield and M. Kiteley (eds), *Meaning and Truth*, New York: Paragon.

Wettstein, H. (1991) *Has Semantics Rested on a Mistake?* Stanford: Stanford University Press.

Wilson, D. (1975) *Presuppositions and Non-Truth-Conditional Semantics*, New York: Academic Press.

Wittgenstein, L. (1953) *Philosophical Investigations*, trans. G.E.M. Anscombe, Oxford: Basil Blackwell.

Wolterstorff, N. (1970) *On Universals: An Essay in Ontology*, Chicago: Chicago University Press.

Yourgrau, P. (ed.) (1990) *Demonstratives*, Oxford: Oxford University Press.

Ziff, P. (1960) *Semantic Analysis*, Ithaca, NY: Cornell University Press.

—— (1967) "On H.P. Grice's Account of Meaning," *Analysis*, 28: 1–8.

Index